The Grand Duchy of Luxembourg

The Evolution of Nationhood 963 A.D. to 1983

By James Newcomer

105088

UNIVERSITY
PRESS OF
AMERICA

LANHAM • NEW YORK • LONDON

TEXAS CHRISTIAN
UNIVERSITY

Library of Congress Cataloging in Publication Data

Newcomer, James.
  The Grand Duchy of Luxembourg.

  Bibliography: p.
  Includes index.
  1. Luxembourg—History.   I. Title.
DH908.N48   1984   949.3'5   84-2236
ISBN 0-8191-3845-2 (alk. paper)
ISBN 0-8191-3846-0 (pbk. : alk. paper)

Dedicated to
RUTH SALISBURY NEWCOMER
and to
the citizens of the Grand Duchy of
Luxembourg who gave inspiration and
help in the writing of this book.

THE GRAND DUCHY OF LUXEMBOURG is published with
the assistance and encouragement of A. M. Pate, Jr., Honorary
Consul of Luxembourg for Texas, New Mexico, and Arizona.

Contents

Maps

Chapter I

The Grand Duchy: A Summary Essay

AMID THE WESTERN EUROPEAN nations, generous in extent and population, stands the Grand Duchy of Luxembourg, upright, proud, and independent. It lived an infancy of nine hundred years. Its adolescence endured a hundred. It came of age with the celebration of its thousandth birthday something like two decades ago. Its culture, economy, and government define a physiognomy, give it a stature that ranges it self-confidently alongside nations ten times, a hundred times, five hundred times its size.[1]

A distant goal in this history is a perception of the national character of the Grand Duchy of Luxembourg. Such a goal accepts the hypothesis that such a phenomenon as a national character exists.

We shall be 2000 years, historically speaking, in arriving at our destination. Along the millenial route we shall be interested in the circumstances of the nation at any given moment as they relate to the Luxembourg of the late 20th century. A major question is this: How did Luxembourg come to be the country that it is?

A state presupposes geographical limits.[2] Present to the mind's eye is the Grand Duchy of the 1980s: 999 square miles niched into Western Europe, with Germany on the east and France on the south and Belgium on the west and north. A single county,

Brewster, in Texas is more than seven times the size of Luxembourg. We can imagine a geological cataclysm in which the entire physical state could be folded into its neighbors without a trace. Political cataclysms accomplished what no geographical upheaval ever brought about. In the 1980s it has the smallest dimensions of its entire history. In times past it comprehended lands four times the extent of the Grand Duchy.

Luxembourg's three great neighbors, by appropriation or decree, made three-quarters of the old Duchy's extent their own lands. By no stretch of the imagination could we suppose that those lands will ever again be Luxembourgian. Nor could we entertain the idea that Luxembourg could ever be incorporated in another state except as a Napoleon or a Hitler or a Stalin seized it and crushed it. The temper of today's citizens is that they will gladly become a part of a united Europe, but of no sovereignty less comprehensive than that.[3]

The inherited nature of Luxembourg is rural and agricultural. The rich and sophisticated state of the 1980s is a contradiction of 1900 years of its history. Its only city, even now, is not so large even as such a big town in America as Waco, say, in Texas, or Bath in England — small cities of little national and of no international dimensions. The agricultural lands are a joy to the eye because nature made them beautiful and the husbandry of Luxembourg farmers makes them neat and respectable. Nature, though, did not endow them with fertility; the farmer's industry and modern technology gave them something better than a minimal productivity. But in the early 1980s fewer than six percent of the employed population are engaged in agriculture.[4]

The Lorraine plateau, sweeping up from France, meets the Ardennes Forest, of vast extent across Belgium, northern Luxembourg, and Germany, where the mountains are called the Eifel. The Ardennes are fancifully rugged, the forests are thick, the soil is recalcitrant, the winters are bitter. The forbidding difficulties have helped determine Luxembourg's circumstances and even her fate from earliest times to this very day. That northern area is called the Oesling; in contrast, the southern two-thirds of the country is called the Gutland or Bon Pays — the Good Land.

Nature endowed Luxembourg badly to be a crossroads of Europe. One might box the compass for all Europe most conveniently from Luxembourg. From south to north, from east to west, and diagonally one might plot one's progress easily. But there are reasons that the old maps show Luxembourg to be almost empty compared with contiguous lands. There are reasons that Luxembourg has never possessed a real city—large in extent and population; reasons that, until modern times, highways were few and in some locales interconnecting roads were almost nonexistent. The Ardennes imposed an all but insuperable obstacle to penetration from any direction. They impose an obstacle even today. Since the greatest part of Luxembourg's history is, in a way, a foreign history, it may seem almost illogical to say that foreigners found it difficult to get into Luxembourg, and for the same reasons citizens found difficulty in getting out. But the geographical Grand Duchy was never thought of as an entity until the late modern era. When foreign powers owned or possessed Luxembourg, they gathered up the little sparsely populated extent of the Grand Duchy along with all the rest. Spiritually the entity continued to exist even as great pieces of the land known as Luxembourg fell away into the political fold of the acquisitive neighbors.

Agricultural though it may be, Luxembourg's agriculture could never have brought the nation into the international world of the twentieth century. The economy could not have sustained the state. Probably nothing beyond a folk or rural culture would have evolved. Without sufficient money and goods, without a self-conscious culture to be protected and served it is doubtful that there would have been a national self-consciousness distinct enough and assertive enough to keep the nation independent. But in the southwest corner of the country Luxembourg possessed rich deposits of iron ore. The European world needed the raw iron and the steel products that Luxembourg, with foreign help, learned how to produce. It became a world power in the economies of iron and steel. They brought prosperity, prosperity stimulated ambition, ambition fostered education, education led to the expansion of cultural and intellectual horizons, awareness evolved into emulation.[5]

It has been only within a little more than a hundred years that the nation that had been unable to keep all its lands together in a unit comparable in size to the modern Belgium or Netherlands began to assert its own separateness. *Mir wëlle bleiwe wat mir sin* (We want to remain what we are) is not an idea as old as time in Luxembourg. It has not been a motto in the mouths of Luxembourgians for much more than a century, and *Letzeburg de Letzeburger* dates only to 1915.

What is characteristically Luxembourgian, then, is not spread out like a carpet for a historian to walk on for hundreds and hundreds of years through time. Rather, it is there like the warp beneath the nap, to be felt for and found by searching fingers. Or it is like an undergrowth, unperceived beneath the obvious trees, but as rooted as the trees themselves.

*   *   *   *   *   *   *

The population of Luxembourg in 1980 was close to 365,100.[6] But only 271,100 of those people were citizens. The rest — 94,000 people — were Portuguese (almost one-third), Italians, Frenchmen, Germans, Belgians, Dutch, and Spanish, in that order. The steel mills brought them there. The iron mines, the steel mills, the construction trades, the railroads — any kind of hand labor that Luxembourgers did not want to do — or of whom there were too few to do it — brought foreigners who could earn a better living and lead a better life there than at home. Obviously, the make-up of today's population is one of the most important factors in the equation of Luxembourg. We shall consider it in the last chapter of this book.

We shall learn that the Luxembourger is wonderfully adaptable to twentieth century life. In all the amenities and securities of that life he has kept pace with the world. What we know of him before World War I would hardly justify the expectation of such a state of affairs. His rural existence had persisted for centuries, and he resisted absorption into industrial life. His daily life did not militate against intelligence, however, and education was extended to more and more of the citizenry as fast as the government could facilitate. The farmer's practicality persisted into the sophisticated modes of making a living in the late twentieth century. That practicality is like a steam roller, set going in the distant past, that continues to move ahead through the political and economic international landscape of the present.

Perhaps we should not be so fanciful. More likely, a character and an intellect were formed through the centuries that prove adequate to the challenges of today. Endurance surely must be one factor. The character is not so much that of the eager young Luxembourgers who seized swords and went off to battle; they were likely killed and left few offspring to perpetuate their romantic boldness. It is not that of the dreamers and the rebellious who sought their future in foreign lands; they left their homes and took their progeny with them. It is not that of the women whom invading soldiers raped or seized and carried off; the women who stayed and survived to people the next generations were those who could plow and haul and endure all the burdens that a hard life imposed on them. The citizens who stayed and survived did not write poetry or compose music or propound theories; the best that they could do was to keep flesh and blood alive. Modern Luxembourgers spring from forbears like those. Affluence has put a gloss on them now. Opportunity has stimulated opportunism and imagination. But the old physical characteristic of solidity and the spiritual characteristic of adaptability remain. If circumstances were to reduce these people to life in a rough farmhouse, heat from a hearth, meals of milk and potatoes, the drudgery of following a hand plough, they would know how to survive. If the enemy one day comes again and stays, they will find ways to endure; and when the enemy grows lax and effete, they will come out of the undergrowth and the cellars to start making a better life all over again as their ancestors of a thousand years have repeatedly done.

Some aspects of their nature tempt the expression of a mean judgment. Of those German citizens on the east side of the Moselle on farms and in villages once Luxembourgian the comment is made that "all they do is work, pray, and drink." Napoleon called Luxembourgers "square heads." Illiteracy and dull subjection to the daily, yearly life-time drudgery of farm labor did not liberate the imagination; art did not flourish. The church service was the one sure interruption of hard routine; the Catholic religion, never reexamined in the way of reformation, provided the one sure hope for better things. Pilgrimages now and then eased the daily suppression of mystery and wonder; adoration of the virgin periodically brought gleaming light into the dull routine of existence. Customs centuries old, like the spring Octave in the cathedral of Luxembourg City, and the dancing procession at Echternach, attract not only the citizens but the offspring of ancient Luxembourgers living on the French, Belgian, and German fringes of the Grand Duchy. Something primordial and chauvinistic stirs on the rhythm of the calendar in blood once Luxembourgian, now foreign.

Of no less importance than work and religion in the Luxembourg character is drink. Cafes are not much less numerous than pubs in Ireland. Most often they are rather bare and stark with clear wooden table tops, straight chairs, and unadorned floors and walls. The cocktail lounge is foreign to Luxembourg. When a guest arrives in a private home, the first action is the offering of a drink — strong spirits like quetsch or mirabelle, perhaps, or the good Moselle white wine. These and beer are local products. The work day as often as not ends with a visit to the cafe. Patrons have their favorite cafe, which they visit loyally and regularly. The tone is quiet; conversation is spare and low. Luxembourg pays a penalty for its pleasure in alcohol. Of 28 countries, it ranks eighth in consumption of pure alcohol; it ranks fourth in alcoholism.[7]

It is almost without question, then, that art and architecture have been through the centuries a folk expression; and without any tradition of artistic expression, it would be difficult to label any present production as typically Luxembourgian. Conventional carved wooden furniture and paneling remain from sturdy farmhouses of the past two centuries. There was a tradition of decorative wrought iron work from small foundries. The more affluent people brought furniture and pictures from France and Germany. The farmhouse with connecting barns evolved toward solidity and comfort, without eaves, sometimes painted in pretty colors, the dung heap a sign of comparative worth on the cobbled court. The memory of repeated destruction through the centuries and a continuing poverty are explanation enough for infrequent architectural remains older than the 18th century.

With the exception of castles and churches. As for the castles, that is no mean exception. They bristle and bridle, the 76 that remain either whole or in ruins, more thickly within the Grand Duchy than in any other landscape of similar size in Europe. How thickly we may judge from the fact that the old Duchy held almost 150 of them, while in the area of the Grand Duchy alone there were 100.[8] The remains of some take the pondering viewers' thoughts back to the tenth century. Such is the case of the rough remains of the castle on the Bock in Luxembourg City. The castle at Vianden — magnificent, defiant, beautiful on the top of its own small peak — has pieces of wall much older than a thousand years; while higher up, knights' hall and chapel reveal their kinship with the great Gothic building of the Middle Ages.[9] It was of this castle that Victor Hugo said, "The past is beautiful only thus. In ruins." Some castles have continued to exist as residences settled in the midst of decay. Some are only picturesque, warlike ruins, as at Esch-sur-Sure; or round towers and rough stone square donjons such as that of Hollenfels, showing attempts at beauty in fireplace and door surrounds and ceiling. Some, as at Bourglinster, have their architectural roots in the Luxembourg farmhouse. Generally now they take on the fanciful aura of romance, as if the business of war in which they once functioned had the character of colored illustrations in a children's book. Since the Luxembourg peasant has probably never been a warlike person, the influence of the castles on the national character is open to speculation. That influence is more likely that of the sturdy workmanship in stone than the chivalric exploits of mailed knights who issued from those castles to do battle.

Comparison of the fortress castle at Luxembourg City with castles in neighboring countries stimulates speculation that has some bearing on the national character. Consider the castle at Montmédy in France, designed by Vauban like the Luxembourg fortress, not many miles beyond the Luxembourg border, once a part of old Luxembourg. It stands in its decay on a peak from which the ground falls away sharply to the valley. The walls are intact, and the buildings on the inside, dating from the 18th century and 19th century, stand in their entirety, but decrepit and decayed. In its completeness the 20th century has forgotten it entirely.

Of the medieval castle in Luxembourg City practically nothing remains — ruins, but nothing remotely useful. With the need to expand came the demolishing of walls, the razing of buildings, the spread of working and living space. Hampered by ravines, the city threw great bridges across them, repeating the process as late as our own time. In Montmédy the surviving past has been the agent of failure. In Luxembourg the disrespect for it has been the good angel of its perpetuity. Even today, the city destroys the pretty, imitative, romantic buildings of the 19th century to build faceless concrete bank buildings that might be in Lubbock, Texas, or Windsor, Ontario. The unromantic process of being up to date carries in it the vitality of the healthy balance sheet. For the Luxembourg peasant who built the castle, the castle was a matter of sweat and fatigue and subsistence. For the peasant who carted stones from the abandoned castle to build his barn, there was no romance in the castle; for the Luxembourg citizen of the 1980s romance takes second place to income and security. The citizen of today is not unmindful of the past or insensitive to considerations of beauty and the picturesque; he protects his heritage within his economic dimensions. But that heritage does not take precedence over the considerations by which he gets his daily bread or plots his future in an uncertain world.

If the castles are important in Luxembourg's artistic heritage, so too are its churches, ubiquitous, infringing on the stranger's attention, just as churches in England make their assertion everywhere he looks. There is no village without its church. But there is an important difference. In England the churches from the past everywhere delight. The small ones stimulate soft adjectives like charming, lovely, pretty; the great churches are stunning in their majesty and beauty. There is nothing similar in Luxembourg. For the most part the Luxembourg churches sit firmly, matter-of-factly (to our eyes) on their sites, having so sat for centuries. There are few thin spires to send into the sky, no soaring towers in perpendicular gothic. In contrast to the village church in Germany, the Luxembourg church seldom has anything fanciful about it. In terms of the English or French or German cathedral, Luxembourg has nothing comparable in size or splendor or spirituality. It possesses only two large church structures — the cathedral at Luxembourg City and the basilica at Echternach. Both are worth a visitor's viewing, and both are part of the Luxembourger's pride, but as architecture they do not find a place in an account of Europe's ecclesiastical possessions. When we call to mind the churches of Ghent or Bruges or Antwerp — or even Huy, Liège, or Tirlemont—we are impressed by the small dimensions of Lux-embourg in every way, from the overall extent to the individual units that make up its smallness.

The churches, many of them, have the same character as that of the people. The Romans built something into their crypts and foundations; a Roman fortress underlies the Church of Sts. Peter and Paul at Echternach, for example. The Franks and their descendants built structures out of which some standing churches evolved; in the days of Romanesque architecture most of the churches got their main fabric of wall, window, pillar, and deco-ration; the Gothic found expression in modifications of the old and in the construction of new; striking baroque decorations and furnishings appear in some churches, as at Koerich — and so through the centuries the spirit of the varying times made itself felt. The quality that tells, however, is the quality of enduring.

The same characteristics show themselves in the sculpture, which often is moving and spiritual in its sincerity, but seldom aquiver with genius.[10] The Virgin is everywhere.[11] The pietà is the most frequent of all subjects, apart from Mother and Child, and the most affecting. In a land that has always known trouble, the sorrows of the Mother and the dead Christ seem to make their appeal more powerfully than triumph and resurrection. It has something to do, perhaps, with the habit of enduring.

On the whole, religion as it finds itself expressed in art and architecture in Luxembourg is dour.

But we must look at an exception. In the 8th century and again in the 11th the scriptoriums of the abbey at Echternach produced some of the most beautiful illuminated manuscripts known to man.[12] They were heirs to the Celtic art of Ireland, brought to Luxembourg in 698 by the monk, Willibrord, who founded the abbey. Oddly, the Celtic heritage of Luxembourg reveals itself more clearly by way of Ireland than by its own native ground. In design, color, strength, and spirituality the illuminations mark a height of artistic achievement within the limits of the Grand Duchy never matched in the next thousand years. Their influ-ence spread throughout the continent. The effect of them—the pride of them—is bred into the subconsciousness of today's Lux-embourger, though their ownership is spread far and wide. And because Echternach is still a part of Luxembourg, it is proper for us to make particular note of the illuminations as a Luxembourg accomplishment.

Luxembourg makes no claims to an artistic achievement — be it architecture, painting, music, or literature — that lifts it above its neighbors, or even that puts it on an even plane with its neighbors. It does have one cultural claim, however, that distinguishes it from any other nationality. It has to do with language, which is symptomatic of its individuality and peculiar to its identity.

* * * * * * *

The languages that Luxembourgers speak account in part for the economic and political well-being of the nation. To speak generally and with some exaggeration, Luxembourgers have command of three languages — their native Letzeburgesch, German, and French. When the oldest generation dies out, there will be no exceptions.

Something like 350,000 people including neighbors across the Belgian and German borders speak Letzeburgesch in the familial and daily living.[13] Variations of diction and pronunciation occur even among so few. Only in the last 30 years, with the publication of a dictionary, has there been some agreement as to spelling and grammar. There is little tradition of literature, even of written folk tales and verse. When, during World War II, the Germans interdicted the use of French in publications and the Luxembourgers refused to use German, their rebellious recourse was publication of newspapers in Letzeburgesch, which proved to be inadequate for full and clear communication. Their inner drive to use French or German, and the pressures from the outside to use French and German, have brought about a trilingual nation.

The word "patois" is inadequate or misrepresentative as a designation for Letzeburgesch. The language is Germanic; at one time the citizens called their language *Lëtzeburger Däitsch*. But it did not derive from German. Its roots are in the language of the Moselle Franks so that it can rightly be called a Frankish dialect. Early on it took into itself some Latin. Both French and German left their marks century after century and continue to do so on the eve of the 21st century, since Letzeburgesch apparently lacks the genius to replenish itself. Until required education became universal, the Luxembourg neighbors of France knew and used French, the neighbors of Germany knew and used German; many more knew German than knew French. As a rule only the well educated knew both languages. As late as World War II the division was marked.

The public schools after 1912 began changing that situation. Whatever the language that a child has been comfortable with in his first five years, when he goes to school all his instruction is in German. In his second year of school he begins formal instruction in French. By the time that he is in high school practically all his instruction is in French, while he studies German literature and continues formal study in the English language. When he finishes his schooling below the college level, he is easy with French and German and can communicate fairly well in English. The economic advantage to a nation in which 80 percent of the gross national product derives from foreign trade, where international banking gives it a leading place along with Switzerland and England, where the tourist industry enjoys popularity — that advantage is obvious.

On the practical level the active possession of three languages creates no real problem. The practical purposes to which language is put divide themselves up rather easily. Though French and German are not designated by the Constitution as official languages of the government, government publications appear chiefly in French. When we observe that in order to reach absolutely every citizen the government prints certain publications in German, we are aware of a subtlety worth noting. Associated with that subtlety is the fact that the Luxembourg newspapers appear in German, a language more nearly akin to Letzeburgesch than French. The offices of the church will probably be read in German, but the prayers may be in French or German, and the sermon will be in Letzeburgesch if it is not in French.

However comfortable the Luxembourger may find himself in the use of German, there is hardly any possibility that it will drive French quite out of use.[14] The Luxembourger would never allow himself to be thought to be a German or to feel himself to be German. Many a Luxembourger is still stirred by a feeling of hatred toward anything that is German. A Luxembourg woman is never addressed as *Frau*, a polite Luxembourger will never say *bitte* or *danke*, but *s'il vous plait* and *merci*; in other words, he feels impelled to indicate, even as he speaks German and finds it comfortable, that he is not a German. Subconsciously there must be a conviction that the German language is as much his possession as it is the German's.

As obvious as the economic advantage of three languages is a certain cultural advantage. There is no mystery to the fact that the music and art of all western nations are the possession of any one of them. But literature, philosophy, theater, the productions of the news media are the authentic possession of only the person who possesses the language. For the Luxembourger the cultural productions of the French and German worlds can be his possession too. The great bulk of his reading matter comes from Germany and France and Belgium. Luxembourgers write — as we shall see shortly — but few make a mark for themselves in French and German, and few have written well enough in Letzeburgesch to find a place in the literary history of their nation. If being trilingual is a blessing, it is not an unmitigated blessing.

The subtleties of the situation as regards languages can mislead the Luxembourger as well as the foreigner. A Luxembourg philologist has said that "the Luxembourg writer, whatever he writes, uses a foreign language"[15] — a position that would seem to be untenable. Still, the fact remains that in neither French nor German has Luxembourg produced a literature that the natives feel to be their own with any pride, nor has that writing found an audience in neighboring countries.[16] Perhaps the Luxembourg critic should be less self-conscious in his indictment of the literary situation. What single city of moderate size in America, dating its beginnings from the days when Luxembourg initiated its independence, and using one language, English, exclusively, has produced a literature larger in volume or more extensive in distribution?

That same critic has said that "wherever arms reign, Letters have only to hold their tongue." War, illiteracy for the generality of citizens, and distracting national loyalties were the milieu up from the depths of which the Luxembourg writer had to find his way to the surface.

As outsiders we recognize three writers that Luxembourgers themselves hold dear as writers in their native tongue.

"Edmond de la Fontaine [popularly called Dicks] became the father of that dialectical literature, and the child would carry within himself, forever, the genes of the father."[17] The Letzeburgesch poetry of several writers had appeared before Dicks came on the scene, but the songs that he wrote for his plays have remained a Luxembourg possession.

In 1859 Michel Lentz wrote the poem that became the national anthem, "De Feierwon." It celebrates the national pride that the Luxembourgers felt when the country opened its first railroad. What better example of the language can we look at, with an English translation alongside?

I. De Feieriwon dén as berêt
   E pêift durch d'Loft a fort et gêt
   Am Dâuschen iwer d'Strosz fun
     Eisen,
   An hiê gêt stolz den Noper
     weisen,
   Dat mîr nun och de Wé hun font,
   Zum éwég grôsse Felkerbond.

The locomotive [fire wagon] stands
     ready,
The whistle rends the air and away
     it goes
In a roar, over the road of iron,
And it will proudly show
     our neighbors
That now we too have found
     the way,
To the great eternal league
     of peoples.

Chorus:
Kommt hiêr âus Frankreich,
   Belgie, Preisen,
Mîr wellen iêch ons Hémécht
   weisen:
:,:Frot dîr no alle Sêiten hin,
Wê mir eso zefride sin.:,:

Come here from France, from
   Belgium, and from Prussia,
We want to show you our Homeland;
Ask on every side
How contented we are.

II. Mîr hu kèng schwéer Lèscht ze
     dro'n
   Fir onse Statswon dun ze go'n:
   Keng Steire kommen ons
     erdrécken,
   Kên Zwank de frêie Gêscht
     erstécken;
   Mir mâche spuorsam onse Stot,
   Kê Birger a kê Bauer klot

We have no heavy load to bear
To keep our wagon of state going:
No taxes oppress us,
No force stifles the free spirit;
We run a frugal household,
No townsman and no farmer
   complains.

Another poem by Lentz, "Our Homeland," replaced "The Fire Wagon" as the national anthem in 1895. It speaks of the Alzette, the Sure, the Moselle, of the dark forest and liberty and home; but it lacks the rugged particularity and the stubborn zest of the first song, which in its character and in its sound catches the Luxembourg nature. On the other hand, it invests the words "Ons Hémecht" (Our Homeland) with all the love and patriotism that a Luxembourger can find in his soul.

The Luxembourg language would not come under an international aesthetic of the pretty. It is prolonged in rhythm, though staccato, rough, raised above a relaxed tone, assertive. It does not seem to be conditioned to soothe or placate. To the foreign ear it lacks niceties. The articulation is bold rather than refined. A Luxembourg scholar would make of it the epitome of the Luxembourg character: "And the pattern of our peasants, in the Ardennes above all, but in the Bon Pays also, does it not correspond absolutely to these exterior signs of the race? We find them to be uncommunicative, difficult to stir up, their body formed by hard work. . . . But we know also that they do not shirk the effort, that they are tenacious in everything, and that a wide awake cleverness enables them to adapt themselves to the most varied conditions. Along with that a heart of gold and an ironic spirit always on the ready, when the ice of a first acquaintance is broken."[18]

The third of Luxembourg's writers to find a place in their pantheon was Michel Rodange, "the epic teacher of the nation."[19] His *Renert* is long — 1513 stanzas of 6052 verses on an ancient pattern.[20] It appeared in 1872 following one more of the troubled periods in Luxembourg history. Its protagonist is the Fox, Reynard, that satiric animal hero of European folklore. Renert's observations and shenanigans lay bare — satirically and humorously, but not attractively — the soul of the Luxembourgers.

The Luxembourg society that Rodange portrays is crippled by all the warts and scabs of faulty human nature. He attacks the high and the low. His scalpel is sharp, his satire keen; perceptive criticism and wry laughter make a happy mix. No doubt even the victim of his cut could sometimes laugh. His darts pierce the country's leaders, the Chamber, elections, political parties (rudimentary then), the newspapers, justice, the church, the economy, folklore, the army, the police, the railroad, corruption, scandals, and the tag end of efforts to annex the country to one of its neighbors. The Luxembourger of today can still see his reflection there. In the schools *Renert* takes first place in the study of native-language literature.

> It's a shame: were I a rich man,
> one of the country's upper crust,
> there would be other witnesses
> and judges at my disposal.
> . . . . (P. 120)

> We've already got enough Communists
> without him;
> they're a curse for the rich, the poor
> and the whole world.
> . . . . (P. 233)

> No matter what freedom's brooding hens hatch out,
> even with the best of intentions
> what grows out of it is nothing but roosters,
> and not one ordinary chicken
> . . . . (P. 234)

> One day the wolf went out,
> decked out in his red scarf,
> in order to bribe the voters
> before the parliamentary election. . . .

> No village is too dirty for him,
> no peasant too stupid,
> no cafe too vulgar and low: . . .

> and though their trouser belts are bursting
> he cannot quench their thirst . . . .

> There the ox votes for the tiger,
> the ram for the wolf:
> first they get fed,
> and then clubbed with a rifle butt.
> . . . . (Pp. 244-248)

> On grabbing and stealing
> they always set their sights:
> just make one a verger
> and he'll steal the church's lights
> . . . . (P. 251)

15

> What doesn't bring you a profit,
> you toss overboard
> even if it means your neighbor
> is thereby completely ruined. . . .
>
> What do I care about morals,
> I have my stocks and bonds!
> The most beautiful "Credo" is sung
> by my Talers at the exchange.
> . . . . (P. 252)

There has not been another Rodange. "Of such honest moments," says a Luxemburg critic, "there were . . . no more of them . . . of denunciation, nothing: of a new message, nothing; no literature at all. . . . Therefore: the wound, the half-shame, the almost-nothing, the dead body."[21]

If a learned citizen cannot clearly discern a body of Letzeburgesch literature, it is doubtful that the American or the Englishman can.

* * * * * * *

Luxembourg, in its thousand years and more of continuous history, has been a county, a duchy, and finally a grand duchy (as of 1815). Its sovereigns have borne the appropriate titles successively up to this very day. Its parliament, unicameral, has been the Chamber of Deputies since 1848. It has had universal suffrage, men and women, as a true democracy since 1919. Its courts are quite free from the control of any other agency of government.

The Grand Duchy is unique. Before Napoleon there was one grand duchy, Tuscany. At Napoleon's defeat there were seven, including Luxembourg, which is the only one that survives. The Grand Duke is Jean, the admired son of a beloved Grand Duchess, Charlotte, who abdicated in his favor in 1964. The Grand Duchess is Josephine-Charlotte, sister of the King of Belgium. The heir is Henri, and there are four other children. Their family is the house of Nassau. Jean declares himself Grand Duke of Luxembourg and Duke of Nassau, Prince of Bourbon-Parma. The setting for the official activities of the royal family is the Spanish Renaissance palace in the center of the city.

The Grand Duke is not a mere figurehead, though much of the formality of the government, internal and foreign, centers in him.[22] He has the right to initiate legislation and the duty to assent or withhold assent to bills passed by the legislature. He appoints the ministers under the requirement that they have the support of a majority of the Deputies. He may adjourn or dissolve the Chamber.

Voting for representatives in the Chamber of Deputies is direct and secret. There are now 59 Deputies from four electoral districts. Ordinary elections occur every five years. The President of the Government carries the title of Minister of State, under whom the Deputies serving as ministers function. A bill makes its way into law by the advice and recommendation of another body, the Council of State, the consent of the Grand Duke, and a series of repeated votes, the last after an interval of three months. Protection of initiative, the rights of the people, and the democratic process is stringent.

The Council of State is not a legislative body, but it functions to some extent as a second chamber. It consists of 21 members, appointed in one category or another by the Grand Duke. Its main function is to analyze legislation and to recommend or withhold recommendation for action. Its Disputes Committee renders judgment on all administrative disputes.

The judiciary is organized from the Justice of the Peace through the intermediary and district courts to the Superior Court of Justice or Supreme Court. It is completely separated from the legislative and executive branches and protected by careful means from control or influence.

All other agencies of government, however small, are carefully controlled by constitutional and legal means and conform in a general way to the practice of all truly functioning democracies.

*　*　*　*　*　*　*

Thus a sketch of the Grand Duchy of Luxembourg—beautiful, industrious, affluent, and up-to-date in a modern world.

It means to play its part with other nations, take its share of responsibility, and make its contribution. That contribution includes, for the protection of the Western World, its armed forces. The Grand Duke is their commander. The entire army can be seen, on occasion, at dress parade in the Place Guillaume in front of the Town Hall. Altogether the army numbers 630. And now for the Palace Guard. Ordinarily one soldier is on duty at the front door. When a chief of state visits Luxembourg, two soldiers stand guard. We have no truer measure of the smallness of the Grand Duchy of Luxembourg.

NOTES: Chapter I

[1]Georges Als, *Luxembourg: Historical, Geographical and Economic Profile* (Luxembourg, Ministry of State, Information and Press Service, 1980). The reader will do well to acquire a copy of the Als book (in French or English) and use it as a handbook. In small space it collects a great many facts, often in the form of charts, for which there is no room in this book. The Als figures are updated by "Le Grand-Duché de Luxembourg en Chiffres 1981" (Ministère de l'Economie, Service Central de la Statistique et des Etudes Economiques).

[2]Ibid., pp. 23-26.

[3]". . . This dear Grand Duchy of Luxembourg, cradle of the new Europe, which pursues without let-up its historic destiny of tireless proponent of reconciliation and union at the very heart of the old continent." Monsignor Eugène Cardinale, Papal Nuncio, in *Bulletin documentation* (Luxembourg, Service Information et Presse, April, 1982), p. 5.

[4]Als, p. 49.

[5]Ibid, pp. 55-63.

[6]Ibid., pp. 23, 43.

[7]The figure is from the Ministry of Public Health. Published in a "Note Documentaire," Information and Press Service, May, 1978.

[8]See J. P. Koltz, *Les châteaux historiques du Luxembourg* (Luxembourg, L'Imprimerie Saint-Paul, 1975). Also, *L'Art au Luxembourg* (Luxembourg, Publications Nationales du Ministère des Arts et des Sciences, 1966). See chapters as follows: Richard-M. Staud, "L'Architecture religieuse préromane et romane"; Albert Nothumb, "L'Architecture religieuse aux temps gothiques."

[9]Jean Milmeister, *Vianden et la vallée romantique de l'Our* (Luxembourg, Edi-Centre, 1971). Individual texts deal with other municipalities — Esch-sur-Sure, Differdange, Echternach for example.

[10]*L'Art au Luxembourg.* See chapter by Georges Schmitt, "La sculpture romane et la sculpture gothique."

[11]Joseph Hirsch, *Vierges de pitié luxembourgeoises* (Luxembourg, Hémecht, 1967 and 1968) in two volumes.

[12]*L'Art au Luxembourg.* See chapter by Joseph-Emile Muller, "Les miniatures d'Echternach."

[13]Luxembourger Wörterbuch, 4 t., 1950-1975. There will be further treatment of the language later on. See the Bibliographic Essay.

[14]". . . the German language has become envenomed by the history of its people." Michel Raus, "La littérature d'expression allemande," in *Littérature du Grand-Duché de Luxembourg* (Luxembourg, from the collection *Petite Dryade*, 1976), p. 10.

[15]Ibid., p. 9.

[16]"Luxembourg literature written in German, when it really exists, sounds false." Ibid, p. 14. Consider the whole essay.

[17]Cornel Meder, "Notre littérature dialectale," in *Littérature du Grand-Duché de Luxembourg*, p. 5.

[18]N. Braunshausen, "Les langues et l'enseignement," in *Le Luxembourg: Livre du Centenaire* (Luxembourg, l'Imprimerie Saint-Paul, 1948), p. 263. Mr. Braunshausen speaks of the "negligent articulation and the heavy rhythm of our national language."

[19]Meder, p. 6.

[20]*Renert: oder de Fuuss am Frack an a Maansgre'sst* appears in an easily accessible edition, ed. Joseph Tockert (Luxembourg, Edi-Centre, 1968). William E. Pohl gave help in the translations from the Letzeburgesch.

[21]Meder, p. 8.

[22]The summary statement that follows appears in some detail, in English, in Pierre Majerus, *The Institutions of the Grand Duchy of Luxembourg* (Luxembourg, Ministry of State, Information and Press Service, 1973).

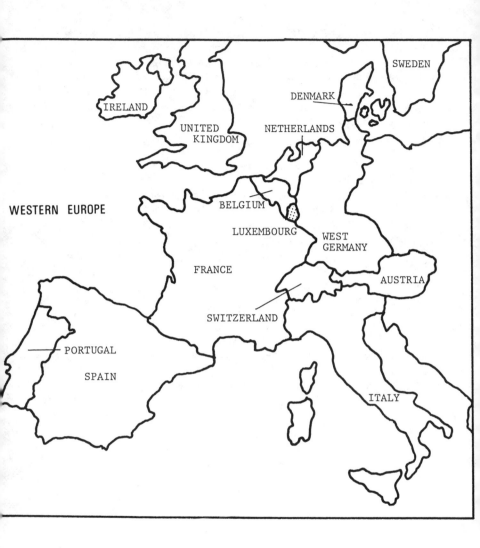

WESTERN EUROPE

IRELAND

UNITED KINGDOM

SWEDEN

DENMARK

NETHERLANDS

BELGIUM

LUXEMBOURG

WEST GERMANY

AUSTRIA

FRANCE

SWITZERLAND

PORTUGAL

SPAIN

ITALY

Chapter II

A Thousand Years of Prologue

The Year One to 963 A.D.

Luxembourg CONSIDERS ITSELF to have been founded in 963 A.D. Before that date it cannot be thought of as an entity. Of course it was a part of something. Of course everything of which it was a part, beginning historically with the Romans, went into its making. Whatever it was in 963 derived in some way or other from the identities of which it had been a part. Our purpose now is to establish those identities and to draw conclusions, however tentative, concerning their contribution to the identity that is Luxembourg.

To cover a thousand years in a single chapter we must reduce the confusion of places, people, and dates to the simplest terms. As many as we can do without we shall let slip through our fingers. Still, too many remain from which to make a coherent whole of those centuries preceding the birth of Luxembourg. The birthing was long and difficult.

We focus first on one small rocky promontory of some 150 acres surrounded by three valleys, the route of two watercourses. This is the Bock (the Celtic word was "Büück," denoting the promontory on which a little castle was reared). Because the Bock provided an admirable offensive and defensive position, the founder of Luxembourg built a little castle there called simply "Lucilinburhuc" — little castle or fortified place — from which the name of Luxembourg derives. The name at that time did not apply to any territory that took in the entire area of which the country now consists.

This little piece of rugged land, which would become Luxembourg City, was located in High Lotharingia or High Lorraine. High Lorraine was divided from Low Lorraine along a line stretching from Coblenz in the east to the Meuse beyond Bouillon in present-day Belgium, some 25 miles above Luxembourg City. If one identifies the little Sure River clearly on the map and sees where, in the west, it takes its rise in Belgium and where, in the east, it joins the Moselle River, which 62 miles beyond that confluence joins the Rhine — if one sees all this clearly on the map, one gets an idea of what the terms Low Lorraine and High Lorraine refer to.

But let us leave High and Low Lotharingia and the Lucilinburhuc of 963 for the moment and place Luxembourg geographically, before considering what is known about the history of that area from the time of the Romans.

Another of the rivers that helped determine the geographical limits of the early Luxembourg was the Meuse. The Meuse takes its rise in France south of the point where Luxembourg, France, and Belgium come together. In that general area where the three nations meet the little river Chiers flows through France in a westerly direction to join the Meuse.

The Meuse travels northward in Belgium something over 20 miles, travels then east by northeast to Liège, before it turns north again on its way to the North Sea. It is about at the Meuse that the Ardennes Mountains begin their rise eastward, growing higher and more rugged as they make their way toward Luxembourg and into it. A relief map that is large scale and not too refined shows plainly that the easiest routes of travel that would span present-day Belgium and Luxembourg through the Ardennes would be in an east-west direction. There is no natural feature that could determine the western boundary of today's Grand Duchy. The Meuse appears to make a natural confinement of the Belgian province of Luxembourg and the Grand Duchy of Luxembourg, which formerly were one political unit, in a homogeneity of physical landscape.

Moving eastward, the Ardennes lose their west-east orientation within the Grand Duchy, about halfway in the southern section, well to the east farther north. The ninety degree change in the direction of the ridges provides for the Our River to flow through rugged terrain down from the northmost peak of Luxembourg and thus to offer itself naturally as a border. The Our joins the Sure, which begins to flow from north to south at the point of confluence, and the Sure joins the Moselle as the Moselle turns roughly northeast to join the Rhine some 70 miles away. In the other direction, from the point where Luxembourg, France, and Germany come together at the southeastmost point of the Grand Duchy, the Moselle is flowing north, offering itself as a border between Luxembourg and Germany, to the point where the Sure joins it at Wasserbillig, where it starts its Rhineward journey. On the east side of the Our and the Sure Rivers, in Germany, are the mountains called the Eifel but which are a continuation of the Ardennes.

But note: on the east side of those rivers the Eifel mountains have a north-south orientation. The river valleys are flowing from north to south to join the Moselle. Even more interestingly westward from the Our in the Grand Duchy the mountains parallel the mountains in the German Eifel. The River Sure, which enters the Grand Duchy from Belgium at a point directly west of Diekirch, crosses Luxembourg from west to east, providing a natural division between two differing landscapes and differing orientations for communication.

One more point. The Lorraine plateau of France, which differs markedly in character from the Ardennes, extends up into the southern part of the Grand Duchy to provide a form of sustenance for a self-sustaining people quite different from that to the north, that to the east, and that to the west. Of the three escarpments that traverse the area from the west to the east, the southern one called the *Côte Calcaire de Longwy* helps determine the political frontier.

The Meuse, the Rhine, and the Moselle, then, provide a natural containment for people that might be identified as having some kind of unification. But within the unit defined by the rivers there are three distinct areas that might well have provided for three separate tribal identifications. One might have been Belgian; one might have been French; both were Gallic. The third might have been German. Within the river boundaries apparently an amalgamation of the three disparate groups took place that over 2000 years proved stronger than the inner tensions that tended to split the area up.

The Ardennes Forest was the largest forest in all Gaul. The Romans took the Celtic name for the high forests of that area and called it Arduenna. The Celtic tribes here perhaps had ruder manners, reflecting their ruder circumstances, than the other Gauls; they more nearly resembled the Germans, with whom they were contiguous. In fact, the Treveri, who rather thickly occupied the Bon Pays (the gentler southern part of the Grand Duchy), may have been of German origin. The Paemani (the Poemanni) of the Famenne (an identifiable Belgian area well to the west of Luxembourg), the Caeroesi along the Kyll and Prüm Rivers (in German territory beyond the northeast border of the Grand Duchy), and the Mediomatrici toward the south — all these, if Belges, were also Germanic. At the same time, if they were Germanic, still, they were Belges. The theory that they all were the last of the Celts to withdraw from Germany may be a fact.

All this, with regard to the Grand Duchy, is to the point. The language of the Grand Duchy, deriving from the Franks, spoken still in the late twentieth century, is also spoken still to the east of the Grand Duchy as far as the Prüm River, to the west of the Grand Duchy in the Arlon area, and to the south as far as Thionville. The official language to the west of the Grand Duchy, as in the Grand Duchy itself, is French; on the east side of the Moselle, the Sure, and the Our it is German. The citizens of Belgian Luxembourg do not speak German; the Germans do not speak French; the Luxembourgers speak both German and French as well as their own Letzeburgesch.[1] Here again is a particularization that sets off the Grand Duchy from its neighbors on all sides.

Why, long ago, did Luxembourg not become absorbed into Belgium and before that the Netherlands? Into France? Into Germany? The Frankish tribal configurations contribute the suggestion of an answer. The circumstances deriving from the Roman domination lasting almost five hundred years make their contribution. The important factor in those circumstances is roads.

We find a clue to the significance of Celtic and Roman roads in the publication, by the Ministry of Arts and Sciences, *L'Art au*

Luxembourg: "Located apart from the great commercial routes, Luxembourg could participate only feebly in the general prosperity that was developing in the epoch."[2] The epoch referred to is that of Gothic times, about the 1200s, a thousand years later than the period that we are now examining.

Was Luxembourg ever on the great commercial routes? Almost every history of Luxembourg carefully places it at the center of Europe, labels it as the great crossroads of Europe, gives it a geographical and commercial significance that one is reluctant to refute. It can hardly be refuted, but that the area of the Grand Duchy was of major importance to the Roman world can be seriously doubted.

In the Roman world Liège and Aachen lay to the north of the Grand Duchy; Brussels, Ghent, and Bruges to the northwest; Reims to the west; Thionville and Metz to the south; Trier and Mainz to the east. The Reims-Trier road crossed the Grand Duchy from Arlon to Wasserbillig by way of the site of Luxembourg City. The Metz-Trier road came up from the south and joined the Reims-Trier road at Widdenberg, midway between Luxembourg City and Wasserbillig. Both carried important traffic, of course, mostly military. The Reims-Cologne road barely touched the Grand Duchy at its topmost point. There is no spot in the Luxembourg area that rates mention with the towns that lay at the ends of the major roads.

In a general sense it is probably safe to say that the Romans were everywhere. The land was theirs. The chief military force was theirs. The higher civilization was theirs. They built on the land, produced on the land, and, in many an instance, amalgamated on the land. But even as the natives were Romanized, the Romans established no permanent camp or fort in the area, and the natives maintained their tripartite division into the Civitas Trevererorum (oriented toward Trier) of the Our country, the Civitas Mediomatricorum (oriented toward Metz) to the south, and the northern people who belonged to *Germania inferior*. The language of the more affluent and powerful became Romanized; Roman arts and crafts developed; Roman agriculture took hold; there was even a school that taught Greek and Latin literature and rhetoric at Trier. As the centuries passed, the center of Roman government shifted, until in 277 the capital of Gaul came to Trier. From Trier went orders and power and laws to the Atlantic, to the Mediterranean.

Beginning in the middle 200s the Franks crossed the Rhine and began their repeated infiltrations. The Germans destroyed Trier in 275. Constantine, who became caesar (subemperor in Western Europe) in 295 and emperor in 305, rebuilt the city and gave it the name Treveris. Later emperors preferred Trier, *urbs opulentissimos*, as their capital; schools, artisaneries, weapons manufactories, a mint flourished there. The civilization that it fostered found its expression in the work of merchants, army officers, landed proprietors. Farming spread and developed. In the 300s the Romans developed viticulture on the Moselle. Wooden farm buildings gave way to brick, tile, and stonework. The Romans used stone from quarries in the southern part of present-day Luxembourg.

The museum at Luxembourg City displays the Roman domestic objects — cinerary urns, clasps, rings, bracelets, and vases — that the soil of the Grand Duchy has yielded to the diggers. New remains of Roman roads are found yearly. One assumes in the 500-year Roman history in Gaul a Roman order founded on Roman law that flourished for two centuries, resisting and recovering from invasions. We infer the threat by the strength of resistance that was needed. The country of the Treveri found itself caught in the crisis and the decadence that afflicted the Byzantine empire. The emperors opposed the German invaders with other Germans whom they transplanted into defense zones (these would have included Luxembourg) with their wives and children. These German men in the military service in the empire were placed among the Treveri as early as the late 200s. These mercenaries, located in the *castra* (there are at least seven Luxembourg sites) and the *castella* and the *burgi*, assured freedom of movement on the Roman highways. A *burgus* was located about 260, probably, on the Bock, which became the site of Luxembourg City. Arlon, Virton, and Bitburg (all outside the present boundaries) were all fortified. The term *castellum* was to pass into the vulgar language, in the first centuries of the Middle Ages, under the forms *castel, chatel, kastel,* and *kascht* (a place name frequently found in Luxembourg); and the Letzeburgish *kiem* comes from *caminus,* "road."

A second line of defense behind the Rhine that depended on Trier and defended it involved Luxembourg. But Trier, too much exposed, lost its importance about 395. When Rome abandoned the frontier of the Rhine, the way was open to the Franks. By 459 the Ripuarian Franks, coming from the Rhine-Cologne area, definitely were occupying Trier. The roads that the Romans built so well and so confidently to serve their own purposes easily conducted the Franks on their routes of invasion. Roman dominion in Luxembourg was at an end.

It may be safe to draw some conclusions about the homogeneity of the Luxembourg that was to become a county, then a duchy, and finally the Grand Duchy from circumstances that were identifiable as early as the first centuries of the first millenium. Already we confront a set of circumstances that helped determine the geographical limits of the Luxembourg of today. The great posts of Rome located in the general area of the Grand Duchy were Trier, Bitburg, Aachen, Arlon, Virton, and Thionville. The Grand Duchy lies within the confines of a rough circle connecting those places. Today's Letzeburgesch language extends to those points beyond the borders. There were identifiable posts on the north-south waterway of the Alzette River. There were farms and settlements thickly located in the south and less thickly in the rougher north, and the length of the Moselle was fortified. Could the inhabitants of this area have found a cohesiveness that was stronger than the attractions of other definable areas to east, north, west, and south? And could its unimportance, other than as a highway, have been one of the anchors that, finally, held its identity through the stresses of fifteen hundred years?

There was no Luxembourg town of sufficient size and importance to be remembered. After 395 both sides of the Moselle lost most of their cultivation as much of their population melted away. The Germans who had come into Luxembourg and been incorporated in the Roman domination probably stayed. The barbarian Huns who came in waves against the Romans and the settled Germans and the natives withdrew without leaving much behind. The invading Franks refilled the spaces that had been emptying, the Ripuarian Franks succeeding the Allemans. Since after 459 Trier was completely a Frankish town, no doubt the

27

Luxembourg corresponding to the Grand Duchy was a Frankish area even as its territory was divided up among four separate cantons, each headed by its own lord (*Gaugraf*). Again the inference seems reasonable that the geographical distance from an urban administrative center encouraged among the country people a cultural cohesiveness — or a cultural inanition — that was greater than the four divided loyalties invited by the administrative arrangements. There may have been so little cultural tension that what was idiosyncratic to the area received almost no dilution for hundreds of years.

* * * * * * *

It appears to be impossible to identify a history of the grand-ducal area in the fifth century — or for hundreds of years thereafter — that is separate from that of hundreds of miles surrounding it. Its history it shared with that of the Franks to whom the Romans gave way. The Franks, both those who had been protégés or partners of the Romans and those who came later, used the Roman roads, occupied the settlements, and took the land. We may believe that in that time of "the universal shipwreck of civilization" those who lived in Luxembourg shared in the general destruction. The shipwrecked, those who survived, merged with those who wrecked the ships, merged with the companions of the Frankish king Merovaeus, and became submerged in their Merovingian descendants. By 500 the wild and barbaric Clovis was master of a vast country, had destroyed the Roman vestiges and driven off the Visigoth, killed his Frankish competitors. The territory was one, was split, was again united under Clothair II and Dagobert I. Kings lost power and underlings gained power. The Merovingian line approached its end, and the Carlovingians, who led off with Pepin (died 714), then Charles Martel (died 741), then Pepin the Short, then Charlemagne, made the vast territory, and more, their own. Of the great divisions of the Franks, the Frisians, and the Saxons, the alien Franks became dominant. Where Luxembourg now exists, Frankish spirit and language and customs dominated all others. And through all the bloody progress toward the Frankish domination, as early as Clovis's conversion in 496 and much, much earlier, Christianity was the warrior's companion, lure, inspiration, strengthener, and temptation. It was a leaven, even as the old tribal barbarism in the Luxembourg area was a lingering superstition and dilution of Christianity. "In this atmosphere of cunning and deceit, treachery and fratricide, crime and sensuality . . . the beautiful flower of Christianity opened" [Petrus Johannes Blok].

Some lights shine within the Dark Ages in Luxembourg. The term here indicates those centuries between the fall of Rome and 963. That first century (the 400s) has been called the century of misfortune. For Luxembourg as a whole that term would probably be apt for each of the five succeeding centuries, though the invader, whether military, governmental, or religious, might from his point of view have found his circumstances to be quite the opposite of misfortune. The native language disappeared. The native culture before 470 had been pretty well absorbed into the Romanic-Germanic-Celtic amalgam, and after 470 all that was absorbed into the Frankish, or one might better say that the Frankish culture, while dominant, was leavened by the civilization that it found there. A romanic population (whatever the term may mean, it does not mean Roman) still existed after Charlemagne along the Moselle and in the south of Luxembourg. If today's Luxembourger is set off from his German, French, and Belgian neighbors, the difference may be owing in part to the fact that enough of the Roman remained, in language, in the peculiar quality of the Christianity, and in some aspects of agriculture, into the high Middle Ages that characteristics were engrafted in the culture out of which present-day Luxembourg identifiably grew. Rhenish, Belgian, and Luxembourg scholars have had the yieldings of Merovingian and Carolingian excavations to study. Place names and known names of persons have yielded convincing results about the history of dwelling places. It is certain that the Franks preferred the grass lands of the Alzette, the Attert, and the middle course of the Sure Rivers. The place name suffixes -ingen, -heim, and -dorf show that in the Oesling they settled generally along the old Roman roads. Later settlements carry the term -weiler, deriving from the Latin villare. In the eighth century, particularly along the line dividing the Oesling from the Bon Pays, names ending in rod, holz, and scheid appeared. Probably the inhabitants of those years preserved the advantages of the Roman villa architecture as an improvement on the Treveran hut.

Preoccupation with the language is always with us. One assumes, partly because of the rugged forests of the Ardennes, that the Gallic population of the grand-ducal area was small. The Franks and Romans must have dominated the Gauls even beyond comparison in numbers, strength, craftsmanship, communication, and culture. With their submission and assimilation their language too succumbed to that of the invaders, so that the Letzeburgesch that now stubbornly flourishes must have derived, not from the Treveri, but from the Franks after 500, along with that of the Romans that the Franks made their own. Between the Chiers River on the southwest, the Ourthe on the north, and the Moselle on the east the new language began its continuous history, retaining to this moment Gallic-Roman words and turns of phrase that the Franks took over.

One must speculate further about the language of the grand-ducal area. If that small physical area was divided among four cantons in the late fifth and sixth centuries — those of the Moselle on the southeast, Bitburg or Bedensis on the northeast, the Arduennensis on the north, and the Wabrensis on the west —was the language divided too among four dialects?[3] The Franks did blot out both the Gallic and the Latin languages, while adopting traces of them of course. The line that split off the Flemish from the Walloon established itself on a north-south axis roughly along the Meuse, which was the westernmost limit of Luxembourg at its most extensive. It is thought that the displaced romanic language did not disappear in the Moselle valley until at least 1100. Some would have it that there were, later, Saxons settled in the Oesling, and they would have contributed to the use of Letzeburgesch too. There are place names like Sassenheim (Sanem), Sassel (near Troisvierges), and Sasselbach. But these would not have occurred until the time of Charlemagne.

Never in the Frankish centuries was Luxembourg really in the center of things. When Clovis (466-511) subdued all the Franks, Salic and Ripuarian alike, to accept his single leadership, his center of operations was at Tournai in west Belgium on the Scheldt. He was baptized at Reims, west of Luxembourg. Metz, south of the eastern border of Luxembourg, was one of the Frankish capitals. Two towns most intimately associated with Charlemagne three centuries later were Thionville and Aachen (to the south and to the north of Luxembourg). Luxembourg with its great forests and its small settlements was only a backwater, the backwoods of an era marked by excursions and alarums, murders and mayhem. It was the cork bobbing on the surface of turbulent waters, never sunk into the mainstream, never cast up permanently on the shores of an alien, though related, people. It continued so through the period labeled Merovingian (until 751) and the period labeled Carlovingian (until 987). It matters little what the names of the kings and queens were except that, when we see them, we should know that Luxembourg, enduring and apart, weathered the fortunes of them all: Clovis, Clothair (I and II), Dagobert, Brunhilda and Louis, Lothaire, Arnulf.

At the end of the period when political Luxembourg was divided, along the east-west course of the Sure River and the Our River coming down from the north, between Low Lotharingia and High Lotharingia, we can speculate that, to the Luxembourgers, the division made little difference.

*   *   *   *   *   *   *

From the sixth to the ninth century the country was covered with rural Frankish villas. They were often, along with their cluster of tenants and serfs and the little church built and administered by the proprietor, the historical origin of the Grand Duchy's rural villages. The lands for revenue in the grand-ducal area, that is to say the royal domains at Mersch, Mamer, Remich, and Mondorf, along with other parts of the patrimonial domains of the Carlovingians, had a privileged situation that they would rarely lose in the process of time. Charlemagne often resided in his palace at Thionville, by preference in winter, like Pepin the Short before; it was at Thionville that his wife Hildegarde died, in April, 783, at the age of 25.

The forest of the Ardennes was, as in the preceding epoch, a vast hunting terrain for the use of the king. Other domains were in the hands of ecclesiastical institutions and of lay potentates with whom the king was surrounded and who constituted the new seigneurial class.

31

The *villa*, called sometimes *curtis*, continued to be the principal seat of the Luxembourg rural habitat. It included the dwelling house of the proprietary lord, the agricultural buildings, the fields, the forests, the mill, often a little church, and was divided into two parts: the one reserved to the proprietor, the principal *manse* developed by himself and his servants, the other divided among leases which free, indebted tenants cultivated with a *servitium* (paid in money or in kind) or peasants in a servile state. The *mansi* consisted of parcels of land in each of the three zones of culture of the domain; because the crop rotation was triennial, that is, the lands were let to lie fallow one year in three. At the head of the villa was found a mayor; a certain number of agents, foresters, hunters, foremen were under his orders. The celebrated *Capitulare de villis*, a kind of rural code, that is dated from Charlemagne or from Louis the Pious, fixed the property organization of the epoque.

* * * * * * *

The Grand Duchy of Luxembourg is a religious country. If 95 percent of its population in the twentieth century is Roman Catholic, without equivocation it is a Catholic country. To the south, in France, there has been a falling away from religion. To the west in contiguous Belgium there is for all practical purposes no religion. To the east in contiguous Germany Catholicism prevails in a thin north-south line, but protestantism encroaches closely on it. In the little Luxembourg geographical territory Catholicism neither decreased nor gave way to replacement.

This religious pertinacity sets it apart from all its neighbors. This fact becomes even more remarkable in view of the fact that, though very early in history there were strong monasteries in Luxembourg, Luxembourg was never a bishopric. Luxembourg was to become a bishopric only in 1870. Again we consider the circumstances of an area divided among bishoprics, with each division located at the far reaches of a bishopric, so that political-religious authority lost its edge there and its directness. Left somewhat apart from the intensity of religious capitals, which surrounded it on all sides, the area tended perhaps to find its own cohesiveness.

The first Christians appeared in Trier before the third century; the first missionaries and the first organization of the church appeared soon afterward. The freedom from persecution that the Christians enjoyed there encouraged the spread of their religion, which tended to follow the lines of trade and defense between the early market places — Arlon, Bitburg, Altrier, Dalheim. It was a slow growth through three centuries, interrupted by invasions, until a Christian Frank, Count Arbogast, established himself in Trier at the head of Francia Rinensis, which included the Moselle area and the Ardennes. Succeeding him was Clovis, who united the various Frankish units in the kingdom of the Franks.

With the unification of the tribes that Clovis imposed came an increase in missionary activity and the number of converts. Irish and Anglo-Saxon, Gallic and Frankish missionaries opposed their teachings to the pagan beliefs, destroyed the old idols, and brought the ministry of Christian charity to both the Bon Pays and the more difficult areas of the Ardennes. So thorough was their work that Christianization of the Luxembourg area was almost complete by the end of the sixth century. In the century following came the establishment of the great monasteries that would complete the triumph over paganism — Saint Maximin at Trier in 633, Stavelot-Malmédy 650, St. Hubert 687, Mettlach 690, Echternach 698, Prüm 721.[4] Note again, as in the case of important towns, all the monasteries except Echternach were located beyond the present grand-ducal boundaries. Here is evidence again that the land that we call Luxembourg lay withdrawn from the centers of the liveliest political and religious activity and may have taken its singularity in centuries termed the Dark Ages from that fact.

We should move through the years between 481 and 771 with some attention to the broad outlines of change at least in the Luxembourg area, for those changes had a bearing on the amorphous evolution toward a Luxembourg state. The period is approximately that of the Merovingians, of whom Clovis is the personality that brought the most influence to bear on the territory that included Luxembourg, and the earliest Carlovingians.

Clovis became leader or king of all the Franks, Salian and Ripuarian alike, in 481, making the seat of his authority in Trier. Apart from his political power, his becoming a Christian is no doubt the event that had the weightiest influence on the developing character of the region. We have already seen how the surge of Christianization then carried on into the vital years of the 600s, and we shall shortly see the continuation of that religious vitality a century and more later. But, for the moment, we should not rush into the years of Charlemagne.

The unification brought about by Clovis did not last beyond his death in 511. Frankish law required the division of his lands among his heirs. All these changes subtly tended toward the homogeneity of a Luxembourg identity in this wise. In the decades before Clovis Luxembourg territory had been split into four political parts, each identified with the tribal or political areas to north, east, south, and west. Without any urban focus whatever, however, life in the four segments was characterized by the sameness of its quiescent and rural character.

Anarchy and civil war succeeded the death of Clovis. Frankish lands were divided into three nations — Neustria to the west, Austrasia to the east, and Burgundy to the south (this last need not concern us now). The dividing line here between east and west was the Meuse River. Luxembourg, now, lay totally within one political and geographical unit, Austrasia, the general boundaries of which were the Rhine, the Moselle, and the Meuse. On the south Austrasia included Reims and Metz. There we have adumbrated the Duchy of Luxembourg that will be centuries in the forming. A nation is in embryo here long before the developed personality of a state appears on the political scene.

When we read about the Merovingians and Carlovingians in the broader history of Europe, we are not aware of the inhabitants of the area we call Luxembourg, changing by only so much as the cultivation of land spread and Christianity displaced paganism. They were left outside the continuing warfare by chiefs and kings and kings' representatives who directed affairs from the large cities that made a ring around the countryside and forests that concern us here.

It was the kings' representatives who gradually took on power — the mayors or intendants of the palace, the majordomos. Arnoul and Pepin who came to the fore in Austrasia were two of the earliest. Then among their heirs the more famous Charles Martel, who, by defeating the Neustrians in 716, brought about a new unification. There was division again in 741, unity again under another Pepin (751), division among his sons, and then the great unification of all the Franks under Charlemagne in 771. When Charlemagne was crowned emperor in 800 he was ruler not only of all the Franks but of all the Christians. The results of the great work that Willibrord and his fellow evangelists had accomplished was now to be organized and formalized under the great emperor. Civilization was to become more pronounced under a more particularized political, judicial, and religious system. Schools were developed and art was encouraged. Inspectors General of Charlemagne included bishops of Metz and abbots of the great abbeys that surrounded the territory that would become Luxembourg. They were instructed to work for the good of all the people. Charlemagne directed the affairs of Europe from Aachen, Trier, and Thionville on the very fringes of that territory. We cannot know exactly what went on there, but it is not to be imagined that it was unaffected by the vitality of that particularly vital period.

Before, during, and after this time farms and parishes and villages were being defined as property grants were made to governmental officials and the services of churchmen were extended and formalized. Affiliations and loyalties were being established upward and downward on the social and economic scale. Smaller geographical entities were finding their associates within larger entities, each with its owner or head official or overseer or lord.

Our target date of 963 is a long way removed from 739, the date of Willibrord's death, and from 814, the date of Charlemagne's death. It is impossible, it seems, to establish a year-to-year—or even a decade-to-decade—history of Luxembourg as an entity. Generalizations then, might serve our purposes at this point as preparation for the chronology that follows this section. The generalizations become the matrix in which territorial Luxembourg lies half hidden, its dimensions below the surface only to be guessed at:

In this period of two and a half centuries feudalism assumes its definitive condition.

The affairs of church and state become inextricably mixed.

The Frankish custom (law) requiring the division of a ruler's property, at his death, among his heirs creates war.

Competition is for property, property is the condition of wealth, wealth is the condition of power, power is the *sine qua non* of lordship and kingship.

All these events and circumstances had a bearing on the founding of Luxembourg as an entity. Let us start with the fact that in 963 Sigefroid was attorney of the St. Maximin Monastery at Trier (15 miles from the present Luxembourg border) and lay abbot of Echternach. These had been and were positions of great power. Thus in Sigefroid we see a direct descendant of Willibrord, though now church and state have come together. In him is personified one of the great characteristics of feudalism.

On almost a continental scale church and state had come together in Charlemagne, beginning in 800. We shall do well to trace some developments between Charlemagne as a great ruler and Sigefroid, the noble adventurer who established a mere county.

Disintegration followed on the death of Charlemagne, who had maintained a kind of political and religious equilibrium by the force of his personality. Violence, insecurity, conspiracy, and tendencies toward disintegration were constants of the Carolingian situation. He himself did not plan to perpetuate his empire, and perhaps, even, he could not have done so. The whole empire went to his feeble son, Louis the Pious, only because other sons had died. As early as 817 Louis named his son Lothaire sole heir. But when Charles (who would be called the Bald) was born to a second marriage in 829, Charles was named heir of all the Moselle country (including Luxembourg) and the country of the Woëvre to the south. This heritage was never received. The older sons conspired, and in 839 Lothaire had himself acclaimed duke of the Moselle country, including Trier and Metz and the Ardennes. The fratricidal troubles that continued after the death of Louis resulted in the threeway division of the Frankish kingdom at Verdun in 843.

The country in the center of the Frankish lands (the country between the Meuse and the Rhine with the cities of Aachen, Trier, and Metz) went to the son named Lothaire. A year later the three kings, meeting at Metz under pressure from the church prelates, vowed to preserve the peace and to heal the wounds that civil war had dealt ecclesiastical institutions. The unity of the Empire was to persist theoretically, with each of the new kingdoms carrying the name Francia and with Lothaire designated emperor. But "the regime of fraternity and mutual charity" did not last long. In 855 Lothaire, now at the Abbey of Prüm (only 25 miles from Luxembourg), gave up his crown and divided *his* kingdom among three sons. Disintegration continued. The hope of reconstituting the lost unity was dead.[5]

Sigefroid's situation in 963 when he acquired the site that was to become Luxembourg City epitomizes the circumstances of feudalism. Between 855 and 963 there had been at least seven kings who claimed the area that included Luxembourg. There were claims and counterclaims; for a time the Luxembourg area was divided in two on the demarcation that will continue to show itself in Luxembourg history. For a time King Arnulf governed the Lotharingian area from Carinthia in the eastern Alps. It can be argued that the local geographical sentiment grew stronger because the king was at a great distance. The people needed a strong local leadership, for they were beset not only by their neighbors. Within the Reims-Liège-Trier triangle the nobles and the bishops had to give mutual assistance in the face of Norman depredations that, in 882, came as far as Remich, a Luxembourg town on the Moselle. The Normans sowed desolation and death everywhere. In the monasteries of Trier the treasures and the holy relics were buried. The barbarians pillaged and burned the abbeys of Prüm and St. Maximin, perhaps Echternach and St. Hubert, ravaged the city of Trier and undertook the destruction of Metz. A Frankish army led by the Archbishop of Trier, the Bishop of Metz, and the lay abbot of Echternach was put to rout at Remich, but the Normans advanced no farther. But there was an onrush of barbarian Hungarians through the Ardennes in 911, 919, and 926, and again in the middle of the century. Malmédy, just above the Grand Duchy, was destroyed.

Lotharingia, the area that included Luxembourg, was, to a degree, ungovernable. It ceased to exist as a political entity. From the death of Charlemagne the decline of central control saw unleashed all the passions of human nature. "The great people of royalty," wrote the chronicler Richer, "pushed on by a burning cupidity, disputed over power among themselves and by whatever means possible augmented their possessions. . . . To acquire property at the expense of someone else was the supreme goal of each, and he did not know at all how to manage his patrimony who did not add to his own that of others." When power ceased to emanate from a central authority, anarchy prevailed.

Consider, then, a vast area over which no central power exercised effective control. Trade between large geographical units ceased to exist, so that each human group had to be self-sufficient in food and the objects and materials that made daily living possible as well as in defense against attacks by outsiders and neighbors alike. The flow of self-consciousness was inward toward the town, the village, the castle. Everything beyond the limits of group subsistence constituted a threat. Where interchange with other geographical groups stopped, the limits of identity went no further.

This is a generalization into which we shall fit the names of people and geographical areas. If there seems to be contradiction, we must keep in mind that where disintegration and separation were occurring strong men and groups were trying to make themselves stronger by imposing their will on other men and groups. To separation was opposed the counter force of amalgamation. Feudalism as we popularly know it was shaping itself out of these circumstances.

The general insecurity led men to look for the means of subsisting in the protection of the more powerful people. Legal loyalty became of less importance than the loyalty evolving from personal ties. The local strong man made himself a vassal by pledging his military support to the area leader, the lord or *dominus*, who was still stronger. The leader rewarded the military support with land. The land provided subsistence. There was no power without land. And land required a strong place or castle from which it could be protected.

Two social and political anomalies developed. Though a vassal pledged fealty to a lord, he might also pledge his fealty to a second and a third lord. To which of the three did the vassal actually give his military support when the three lords clashed? Then, too, when a vassal died, the original idea was that his property revert to the lord. But gradually the land passed to direct heirs, who exercised over the people of the land judgments dealing with property rights and justice. Local lordships became established when the landed proprietor's political responsibilities became hereditary. Old administrative divisions broke up; new ones took their places; each division became the nucleus around which were grouped many others. Political divisions that wiped out primitive boundaries were characteristic of the country between the Meuse and the Rhine, where Luxembourg was to take its shape. Rich and powerful lineages raised themselves above the local aristocrats.

One such lineage was the house of Ardenne, to which Sige-froid, the founder of Luxembourg, belonged.

Let us bring our attention back now to the present outlines of the Grand Duchy, with its river borders against Germany on the east, its borders against France on the south, and its contiguity with the Belgian Luxembourg on the west. This was a tiny part of the Lotharingia that went to Lothaire I in 843 and to Lothaire II in 855. In 870, by the Treaty of Mersen, all Lotharingia was divided between Germany and France, with Luxembourg cut in two, though by 880 it was again joined under a German king. Thus anciently the territory fought over by France and Germany as late as the twentieth century was naturally a bone of conten-tion between the two great powers.

As we keep our eye on the year 963, attempting to fit that year into a pattern and a sequence, one personality, from the Luxem-bourg point of view, comes clearly into focus. He is Wigeric, count palatine. We shall know him as Count of Ardenne, the father of the founder of Luxembourg.[6]

The word "palatine" connotes the power that the count wielded in the king's name. He was count of the palace. He, rather than the king, was the power, though he was vassal to the king. Wigeric was one of several counts in Lotharingia who brought the German King (of Lotharingia) Zwentibold to his death in 900, then managed to run that area in vassalage to both the king of Germany and the king of France, until in 925 the area of Luxembourg came into political and geographical dependency on the German empire alone, a dependency that would continue for centuries. Along the middle course of the Moselle there was no more powerful family than that of Wigeric. It was of royal stock tracing back to Charlemagne and united to the house of France.

The relations between the House of Ardenne, from which Luxembourg would evolve, and other powers exemplify the lay-church power relation of the time. Bishopric and abbey received much of their power from the emperor, and in turn the emperor received important strength from them. They constituted one reason that such powerful men as Wigeric did not administer their vast holdings as a unified sub-kingdom, for their holdings, which their own vassals and serfs inhabited, constituted affluent and powerful administrative units that could always be a threat to the lay nobles.

In regard to the future Luxembourg, Wigeric's power extended over the Bon Pays (the southern part of the country) and the western Eifel (on the eastern side of the grand-ducal frontier from Prüm to Trier). Trier was within its limits, but Trier took its power more from the bishop than from the count, the revenues from the mint, the *tonlieu*, and the monastery rents, among other sources, being paid to the bishop rather than to the king's man. There are documents extant that name Itzig and Mamer, two communities near Luxembourg City, as his possessions.

In Sigefroid, the son of Wigeric (there is some doubt even here), we see the secular and religious power come together. In 950 the Abbey of Echternach, which had been manned by secular canons for a hundred years, came to Sigefroid as an imperial fief. He was named its advocate, bound to protect the abbey's interests in peace and war and to serve as its legal representative. In this connection, as in many others, Sigefroid was typical of the regional leaders of northern Europe.

What Sigefroid did as he assumed his majority within the area where his father had wielded power was characteristic of all the nobles of Lorraine. He wanted to be the lord of as many properties as he could bring under his control, irrespective of old community boundaries or existing loyalties. The competing lords were all reworking the political and social geography of the area. Where each established his power over subordinate powers, each became subordinate to a power greater than his. In other words, each property became a fief to a larger power in the system called feudalism.

The domains to which Sigefroid laid claims are known:

a. The *Saargau*, which was the area of the Saar River. The church of Trier ceded Saarburg to Sigefroid, his wife, and his son Henry.

b. The *Rizzegowe*, which was the country running from Thionville to Sierck (at the very southeast corner of the Grand Duchy).

c. A part of the *Mithegowe*, which the Alzette watered. This was the Bon Pays, as far, at least, as to include Mersch.

d. A part of the country around Arlon, but excluding the town itself, which would come to Luxembourg later.

e. A part of Lorraine in the neighborhood of Gorze in the Moselle area of Lorraine.

f. A part of the *Bidgau*, in the area of Bitburg in today's Germany.

To these areas, which are considered to have been possessions of Sigefroid, must be added Echternach, which he held as a fief, Saint Maximin in Trier, of which he was solicitor, and their possessions.

If we keep our eye on the geographical dimensions of the Grand Duchy, we must note that of these six designated areas only one, the *Mithegowe*, with the possible addition of some of the Arlon area, belongs to that designation. They had no political unity whatever; certainly they did not constitute a county. There was no geographical center from which these scattered domains could be logically administered. Trier and Metz opposed with solid barriers not only an expansion toward the east and the south, but also the installation of military posts on the borders of the Moselle and the Saar. Sigefroid was stopped by the church also from expanding to the north. He had designs on territory near Stavelot in modern Belgium. But the abbot of Stavelot succeeded in incorporating into his own property the lands that Sigefroid coveted (the charter of Stavelot's acquisition uses the word), and Sigefroid of necessity sought his place of administration within the center of lands that he controlled.

Thus, in 963, he settled for a little fortress built on a rocky summit that the Alzette encircled—Lucilinburhuc, Luxembourg —and marked the location of a town destined to be a center of a new principality.

NOTES: Chapter II

[1]Such a linguistic condition has been achieved not necessarily by a natural evolution, but by the deliberate legal decision of the people in determining the education of their children. Still, might that not be considered natural?

[2]Luxembourg, Imprimerie Saint-Paul, 1966, p. 188.

[3]A. H. Cooper-Prichard, *History of the Grand Duchy of Luxemburg* (Luxemburg, P. Linden, 1950). See map, p. 32. Cooper-Prichard treats of the Gallo-Roman epoch and the Frankish epoch pp. 10-33. Also see John Allyne Gade, *Luxembourg in the Middle Ages* (Leiden, E. J. Brill, 1951). The first five chapters give a good summary of the centuries from the Romans to the tenth.

[4]"The century of the Merovingian saints was at the same time a century of iron." Joseph Goedert, *La formation territoriale du pays de Luxembourg depuis les origines jusqu'au milieu du XVe siècle* (Luxembourg, Imprimerie Centrale, 1963), p. 18.

[5]Ibid. See the chapter called "La dislocation de l'empire et la formation du monde féodal," pp. 24-28. In translation the first three chapters are "Our Country in the Roman World," "From the Frankish Conquest to Charlemagne's Empire," and "The Dismemberment of the Empire and Formation of the Feudal World" (my translation).

[6]The best list of sources for the founding of Luxembourg and the house of Sigefroid is in *La formation*, the Annexe, p. 37. The most accessible are the articles of *Hémecht*, a Luxembourg journal.

Chapter III

Sigefroid, Founder of Luxembourg
963-998

SIGEFROID[1] EXEMPLIFIED the centrifugal-centripetal forces of feudalism. As a vassal his strength moved outward to lords stronger than he, and his scattered properties invited appropriation by neighboring lords. As a strong lord with vassals of his own, strength flowed inward to him from all the properties and people that he could command.

The legal code of the Salic Franks required that the vast property of Sigefroid's father, Wigeric, be divided among Wigeric's heirs; no one heir could receive the property intact. As Count Palatine, Wigeric had exercised kingly authority over his possessions. The authority — which Sigefroid inherited in the possessions that fell to him — was the centripetal force. To stay in power Sigefroid needed to resist the encroachment of other lords — not to speak of attempting to add lands to his possessions — and he needed a central fortress from which to exercise his strength and to which subvassals could rally.

Sigefroid emerged into his position of power as lord of extensive lands after the threats from foreign peoples were ended. In a period of little more than sixty years the territory of which Luxembourg was a part had freed itself from the threat of foreign domination and destruction. As we have seen, the Norman incursions into Luxembourg territory ended in 891; the Magyars were finally defeated by the king of the Germans in 955 at Lechfeld in Bavaria. The threats to Sigefroid, then, just like the threats to all landed magnates in western Europe, would come from relatives and neighbors, from the king above him and from the lesser nobles below him.[2]

Thus the acquisition of Lucilinburhuc and its rather rapid expansion to a castle and fort of strength. If the property at Feulen (near Ettelbruck) that Sigefroid gave for it could support only one or two or three families, it was probably on just such a small scale that he started on the Bock. The original property containing the little fortress was less than 150 acres, stopping short at what is today's Fish Market. The second wall passed along what is now the Rue du Fossé and the Rue de Clairefontaine, a few hundred yards to the west. The little fortress almost certainly would have been made of wood, though possibly of stone, and probably the first additions to its strength and extent were of wood. It became Sigefroid's residence. To carry on his business of war and administration he needed a staff and soldiers. To feed them, house them, serve them in every way he needed the population of a village. Thus it was that Luxembourg became a town.[3]

Sigefroid cemented his power from his administrative center at a time when the German king was more powerful than any other monarch in western Europe. The king nominated the bishops and the abbots; from their lands he drew military forces. The kings were emperors, really, of the west. Sigefroid drew strength from being a vassal to the king; and the king drew strength from having such vassals as Sigefroid, who made it their business to bring the neighboring gentry under their control, granting fiefs and receiving homage. That is the way that feudalism worked: centripetally the power centered in the nobleman around whom lesser noblemen rallied; centrifugally the power flowed to the nobleman below or the king above him. When the tensions were all in play, there was a kinetic equilibrium that was vital and creative. At a time when towns were forming and the middle class of merchant and workman was growing, in the Germanic lands there were more of these free citizens than elsewhere in Europe. Groups of citizens took their homogeneity from the lords to whom they gave their loyalty or paid their taxes or served in the way of making a living. Around Lucilinburhuc, from the time of Sigefroid, this homogeneity (which turned out in the end, after a millenium, to be very small in scope indeed) began to shape itself. Still, despite the rather extended lands over which Sigefroid exerted his control, the area around Luxembourg reflected the condition of all the small communities clustered around the innumerable castles scattered across the land; the people's loyalty went to the lord in whose vicinity they lived—a very limited area —however widely the nobleman's power was flung. Certainly the citizen loyalty of Sigefroid's little realm in the area around his little castle was different in no respect from that around hundreds of castles in western Europe. Even so, we must speculate about how deeply the psyche of those distant ancestors was penetrated by a spirit that rallied them into a unity that would resist the eventual defaulting, either forced or willing, of those citizens on the French, German, and Belgian periphery.[4]

We continue to emphasize the fact of littleness. In Roman times the site of Luxembourg City was designated a *munitio*, a word meaning a fortified place smaller than a *castrum* or a *castellum*. Dinant, Ivoix, Namur, Huy, Bitburg—all these sizable communities, by comparison, were *castra,* and all were the location of mints. Outside the fortification proper, in the valley below and across from the promontory, upon the present plateau of the Rham, was developed as early as the third and fourth centuries a *vicus,* a Roman camp with numerous habitations. But Sigefroid's acquisition was strictly limited, a fact indicated in the document of sale *"ab alveo fluminis Alsuntiae usque ad illos veteres truncos qui stant ante munitionem eiusdem castelli"* — from the River Alzette as far as certain old tree trunks that stood in front of the fortifications.

But even as the fact of littleness comes to the fore, certain evidences of importance attach to Sigefroid's acquisition. In 959 all of Lorraine had been entrusted to Bruno, Archbishop of Cologne, by his brother Emperor Otto I of the Holy Roman Empire. Bruno, the most important and powerful man in that part of the world, was a witness to Sigefroid's deed of transfer. Bruno had divided Lorraine into two parts, High and Low Lorraine. High Lorraine, in which the site of Luxembourg City was situated, had gone to Sigefroid's brother Frederic as duke; Frederic was both Count of Bar and Count of Metz as well. Frederic was a witness, and also Archbishop Henry of Trier. Other brothers of Sigefroid—and it may be supposed that they did not oppose Sigefroid's acquisition — were Adalberon, Bishop of Metz; Gilbert, Count of Ardenne; and Gosselin, from whom came the dukes of Low Lorraine. In a time of military aristocracy, Sigefroid held his place as a powerful warrior and made his seat of operations the site of present-day Luxembourg City.

* * * * * * *

We make our way through the years following 963 with difficulty. Did Sigefroid die in 998? Or did a Sigefroid II become count in 987 upon the death of his father? We simply do not know. This ignorance, though, is not a serious matter. The personalities as far as we know were one; there apparently was one motivation — the aggrandizement that could come from military defense and conquest. And though this military aspect did not differ from the military aspect of every other stronghold and growing municipality in Europe, Luxembourg differed from other important strongholds in having no motivation other than military, insofar as the military activity and political administration were two aspects of one effort.

Luxembourg had its particularity in this respect. Unlike Trier, which had had a flourishing urban life in Roman times and continued to be an administrative and urban center, Luxembourg's Roman existence had been only peripheral to the larger centers. Luxembourg had had no royal palace, as Aachen had. It had not been an important place of commerce, such as the cities of western Belgium were. It had not been a religious center, like Liège, had drawn no saints or bishops to it, had never been an episcopal or abbatial seat. It had not been a river halting place. It had had no mint.

The geographical situation, however great the emphasis put on it by historians through the centuries, is hardly sufficient to explain Luxembourg City. After all, Sigefroid's first choice had been a spot near Stavelot. He needed a center from which to administer his landed domains, legal lordships, fiefs, and solicitorships. So scattered were they that they could not collectively be called a county, for they did not constitute a political or geographical entity. Since that was the case, Luxembourg could serve Sigefroid's purposes quite as well as his first choice could have done.

The decisive impulse that led men to settle on the site chosen by Sigefroid came from two circumstances connected with the personality of the founder. The most solid foundation of seigneurial power was the possession of a fortress, and Sigefroid needed power. Before his time possession of a fortress had been a royal prerogative, but Sigefroid typified the movement in the tenth and eleventh centuries of princes usurping the fortresses for their own military purposes. The *castellum* that Sigefroid devoted himself to enlarging rapidly became a more extensive fortress, a *castrum*, reaching out to take within its wall some advanced works on the rocky ridge and promontory, the farthest point of the high city itself. The word *castrum* appeared about 987 in a text relating to the consecration of the castle church. The *castrum* played the role of a preurban nucleus.

Besides its developing character as a fortified market town, Luxembourg City constituted from the end of the tenth century the fixed residence of the count. He sheltered in its walls the men at arms, charged with the defense of the castle, and the officers of the count. The life of the humble people, like that of the great, was regulated in terms of the residence, which made possible the organization of a steady administration. Thus the first counts gathered together separated territories with the aim of developing a viable political unit and threw up laboriously the foundations of a principality generating a new nationality. In that epoch of the formation of territorial principalities, there is little doubt that the autonomy, the nationality of Luxembourg shaped itself in the long continuing residential authority of the Sigefroid dynasty.

It must be remembered, though, that for Sigefroid's authority there was some precedent. The monks of St. Maximin in Trier had been in possession of Lucilinburhuc, as a gift from Charles Martel in 723, for 240 years when Sigefroid took ownership. Where the Romans had had a small fort, the abbey had built or rebuilt the fortress as a refuge for its subjects against incursions and attacks. Since Sigefroid was advocate of St. Maximin, whatever families lived in the vicinity of the Bock were not disturbed in their loyalties or in their sense of the genius of the place by

Sigefroid's advent. The cohesion that we have referred to as a centripetal force had been in effect now for centuries. We can only speculate about the self-consciousness induced in count and citizen by the name itself — Lucilinburhuc, Luxembourg — Little Fortress. That self-consciousness, through the centuries, was to turn back upon itself or expand beyond the limits of self-sustainment, in the end, in the twentieth century, to nurture the astounding strength of a minuscule independent nation.

*   *   *   *   *   *   *

In order to round out the picture of the Luxembourg of 963 to 998, we must make much of little; that is, knowing few facts, we have to assume the relative importance of the facts that we do know. Where the fact is not plain or is open to interpretation, we must draw a conclusion. Thus we take the position that there were a Sigefroid I, who died in 987 at the latest, and his son Sigefroid II, who died probably in 998.[5]

The orientation of Luxembourg within the German sphere in its first 35 years, as opposed to the French sphere, is important, especially as the power of the two Sigefroids to augment the strength of their support to the empire increased. The extent of the fortified castle was more than tripled, determining an access of armed warriors to the castle and of artisans and provisioners to the environs, the locale that would become the Grund, Clausen, and Pfaffenthal, suburbs that cluster below the promontory of Luxembourg City in the valley of the Alzette. The Sigefroids' relations with the church, on which their power was partly based, was strengthened. Sigefroid's positions (and their accompanying power) as advocate of the abbeys of St. Maximin and Echternach came to him from the German emperor. He exercised his powers over them as fiefs to strengthen the church and to aggrandize himself, both through his judicial function, which was great, and through the opportunities thus encountered to enlarge his properties.

Something of the growth of the castle — and thus of the community and of the count's power — is attested by the dedication, in 987, of an *ecclesia in castro Lucilenburco* — in a *castrum* rather than a *castellum*. The church, dedicated under the names of the

Holy Savior, the Holy Cross, and All Saints, included five altars and a crypt. At the same time the dedication of a second church took place, probably in the location of today's Church of Saint Michael, which is on the inner Bock within the original walls.

It is reasonable to digress here to amplify the episode of Sigefroid's first experience in Italy. From it we derive a clearer picture of two aspects of the Middle Ages.

In 962, shortly before Sigefroid acquired Lucilinburhuc, King Otto I of Germany went to Rome and in the midst of almost unbelievable pomp had himself crowned emperor. Details are not recorded, but it is assumed that Otto went through the same procedure of his predecessor, Berengar: "After the king had then put on clerical garments, he was anointed as a priest at the altar and thus, as a member of the clerical order, received the imperial crown and sword from the hands of the pope." Thus, both as emperor and as head of the church he was to exercise his powers. As we follow the prince-bishop, the secular and clerical abbots, and the abbatial attorneys, we can understand better how the joint power found reciprocating enforcement — how temporal rule from the lowest officer to the emperor found its religious fortification, and how religious rule could seek and use the power of armies.

This combination of powers resided in Sigefroid. In addition to that evidence, Otto expressed another development in medieval rule — the direct heritage of title and power. Before Otto I left Germany in 961 to become emperor, he caused his son to be crowned Otto II of Germany. And in 966, on his return to Italy, he placed the imperial crown on the head of Otto II, signifying the succession that would take place. The imperial pattern of the inheritance of land and power would be the one that Sigefroid would use in giving his possessions and power intact to his heir.

But besides the temporal religious power and the direct succession, Otto exemplified another aspect of the Middle Ages in which Sigefroid took part; that is the frightful cruelty with which that power could be exerted. Sigefroid, having accompanied Otto to Italy in 966, was charged with putting down an insurrection of Greeks. He and his partner Gunther succeeded in their mission and took revenge by depriving the prisoners of right hands, noses, and ears.

The warlike involvements of the Sigefroids were persistent. The son accompanied Otto II into Italy in 981 in an expedition against the Saracens. Otto died in the fighting. At the bedhead of the dying emperor Sigefroid received his last orders: Otto asked his vassal to intermediate with the Duke of France, who in fact governed the kingdom, in order that the alliance between the two dynasties should be maintained.[6]

But the history of the Sigefroids' part in the contentions between the French and German powers is confused. When the Bishop of Verdun had attacked Luxembourg territory, Sigefroid made him prisoner, but was forced to free him by pressures from the church and to pay a fine. After Otto II's death, Lothaire of France joined Henry the Quarrelsome of Bavaria to attack Verdun in an effort to acquire the Moselle country. Sigefroid and his nephew, Godefroid of Verdun, were taken prisoner and held in a chateau located on the Marne until their liberation in 985.

The contentions, animosities, and competitions of this period, involving the Luxembourgers, are difficult to disentangle. The end result was a firm friendship with the house of Saxe (Germany), strengthened, however, by friendship in France in the person of the new king, Hugh Capet, who had been instrumental in gaining Sigefroid's freedom from Lothaire in 985. The house of Saxe in Germany and the Capetians in France were allied.

Thus early in its self-conscious nationhood Luxembourg felt the tension of friendships and alliances extending in two directions of nationality fundamentally opposed, intermittently allied, and ultimately in bitter enmity. How, caught between two great powers, could Luxembourg maintain its own personality and identity?

There is still left for us to consider some facts concerning Sigefroid in relation to the church. Through the lifetime of Sigefroid the night of the Dark Ages was passing. Early in the kingship of Otto I the Great (he was crowned in 936), he was faced with the rebellion of the four dukes of the kingdom. Even though he placed counts palatine such as Sigefroid's father within the dukedoms to look after the royal interests, he needed more than secular help to secure his power and dominions, and he appointed some ecclesiastical lords to positions equal to or superior to the powers of the lay lords. He made his brother Bruno Archbishop of Cologne and his son William Archbishop of Mainz. Learned bishops came into Germany from Italy, bringing classical manuscripts with them, so that the study of Greek and Latin spread. Learning increased in court, church, monastery, and convent. Even though the tenth century has been called the age of barbarism, as the pall of ignorance lifted the civilizing effect of the clergy made itself felt in German nationalism, ecclesiastical discipline and monastic reform, the growth of justice, and the development of responsible society. Thus, all the while the leading clergy lent their strength to the king's battles.

Sigefroid played his part in all this. He had held the Abbey of Echternach as an imperial fief since 950. Two particular circumstances after 963 indicate both his interest and his power. In 973 he replaced the secular canons, who had exercised their influence there for a hundred years, with Benedictines under Abbot Ravanger. Sigefroid's brother Adalberon, Bishop of Metz, was a leader in the movement of monastic reform, and Sigefroid's action at Echternach was no doubt a reflection of his participation in the spiritual cleansing that was making itself felt throughout the area.

The second circumstance was Sigefroid's success in 992 in obtaining for Echternach the right to coin money. What conclusion should we draw from the fact that the first money coined in Luxembourg City dates only from the reign of Count Henry II (1026-1047)? Apparently neither the size of Luxembourg nor the extent of its commercial activity justified the existence of a mint.[7] The Echternach coinage reflected the power and the influence of the church within the Ottonian empire, as well as the prestige and influence of its advocate Sigefroid.

There is no doubt that the first phase in the history of Luxembourg was identified with the character of its founder. That phase came to an end with the death of Sigefroid—or of Sigefroid II— in 998. In 35 years Luxembourg had achieved an identity and a function. Its founder was characterized by strength, the ability to gain and hold possessions, favor with his lord, support from his vassals, a sense of responsibility toward the church, some impulse for learning and culture, and intrepidity.

In Sigefroid the new nation found its fulcrum and was balanced on it. Political power, military power, and church power were in equilibrium. If we think of it as an organism, it was a growing

organism and in a state of health. If we give it human characteristics and apply the measure of morality to it, it was as moral as
most political units and more moral than some. And if morality
is a test of a healthy national validity, then we may conclude that
Luxembourg by 998 had found an identity from which to prog-
nosticate a healthy maturity.

We have now noted almost all that is known about Sigefroid
(or Sigefroid I and II). But this is a history of Luxembourg, not a
series of biographies, even though it is more often than not
through people that the national lineaments can be seen. Those
lineaments must be discerned partly through people who were
not in the Luxembourg line. Those people are the brothers and
sisters of Sigefroid whose power in lands adjacent to Sigefroid's
possessions restrained the expansion that Sigefroid would have
wanted to make; so that the centrifugal impulse of the new state
was thrown back upon itself and Sigefroid found his power confined within a small area bordered by his powerful relatives.

It will pay us to contrast the heritage that Wigeric gave to Sigefroid and Sigefroid's brothers with the heritage that Sigefroid
passed on to his single heir.

Wigeric, who had royal blood and whose wife Cunegunde was
descended from the kings of France, had garnered extensive lands
in the Moselle region under the German king. In the division of
property following Wigeric's death, his sons took their individual
places of power as follows:[8]

1. Frederic became Duke of Bar, Count of Metz, and Governor of High Lorraine. He married Beatrice, daughter of Hugh the
Great, Duke of France, whose wife was Avoie, sister of Otto I of
Germany. High Lorraine included the whole ecclesiastical province of Trier, including the bishoprics of Metz, Toul, and Verdun,
and all of Luxembourg's Bon Pays.

2. Gosselin, whose son became Duke of Low Lorraine, which
included the archbishopric of Cologne and part of the bishopric
of Liège, as well as Luxembourg's Oesling. Gosselin's son Adalberon became Archbishop of Reims, confidant of the Saxon
emperors and of Hugh Capet, King of France.

3. Adalberon (do not confuse him with another of that
name), Bishop of Metz and leader of ecclesiastical reforms.

4. Gilbert, Count of Ardenne.

Add to these the possessions of Sigefroid and we see the very extensive holdings that Wigeric bequeathed to his sons. At the same time we see how the possessions of a great nobleman became, according to custom, scattered in pieces among his heirs. And we see too how Sigefroid was hemmed in on all four sides.

In Sigefroid we see that custom changed. The centrifugal force set loose at a nobleman's death is, in Sigefroid's case, reversed. At his death his title and the lands associated with that title went to one heir, Henry I, whose lands extended beyond the present Grand Duchy a good distance in every direction. These lands were small in comparison with Wigeric's lands that were divided among his sons. But now, at least, Sigefroid's lands, coming to a single heir, would not be divided. Political Luxembourg as an entity was taking shape.

The Luxembourg line had now put its anchor down in Luxembourg. Its centripetal strength, through direct and single heirs, was now established. At the same time in Henry I, who took on the dukedom of Bavaria, we see the centrifugal force that time and again, for centuries to come, will threaten to tear Luxembourg from its moorings.

* * * * * * *

It is recorded that in 993 Sigefroid and his wife expressed the wish of being buried in the Monastery of St. Maximin in Trier, before the altar of St. Clement. The epigraph on his sepulchre was found in 1608.

NOTES: Chapter III

[1] I choose the spelling "Sigefroid" because *La formation* uses it. According to a Luxembourg scholar, Edouard Probst, "Préférons Sigefroid!" I shall speak later of Godefroid. I use "Baudouin" instead of "Baldwin" because the King of Belgium is Baudouin; "John the Blind" because "Jean" is unnatural to Americans. For names I use the form that seems reasonable — Cologne, Aachen, Brussels, etc. The usage is that of the Merriam-Webster dictionaries.

[2] "La dislocation de l'empire et la formation du monde féodal" in Joseph Goedert, *La formation territoriale du pays de Luxembourg depuis les origines jusqu'au milieu du XVe siècle* (Luxembourg, Imprimerie Centrale, 1963).

[3]J.-P. Koltz, "Die Burg" in *Baugeschichte der Stadt und Festung Luxemburg* (Luxembourg, Sankt-Paulus-Druckerei, 1970), pp. 50-91.

[4]See chapters XI, XV, and XVI.

[5]*La formation*, p. 43.

[6]Ibid.

[7]John Allyne Gade, *Luxemburg in the Middle Ages* (Leiden, E. J. Brill, 1951), pp. 49-51.

[8]Ibid.

Chapter IV

The Sigefroidian Counts
998-1136

WHAT WE KNOW about Luxembourg in the 1000s and 1100s has to do with noblemen and geography, little else.

The title "Count of Luxembourg" did not really exist until Gilbert carried it a century after Sigefroid appeared in history. Whatever territory Luxembourg City was the nucleus of did not, for at least a century, have anything like a national character. In the chaos of the times whatever existence Luxembourg had was chaotic. But the counts (we have little choice but to call them counts of Luxembourg) who followed in Sigefroid's line held their own, kept what they had, and acquired more. They were men of their time. In the Moselle country they held first rank. They allied themselves to the houses of France and Germany as their purposes served. Count succeeded count as follows:

Sigefroid (or Sigefroids I and II, father and son)	963-998
Henry I, son of Sigefroid	998-1026
Henry II, nephew of Henry I	1026-1047
Gilbert (Giselbert), brother of Henry II	1047-1056/1059
Conrad I, son of Gilbert	1056/1059-1086
Henry III, son of Conrad I	1086-1095/1096
William, brother of Henry III	1095/1096-1129
Conrad II, son of William	1129-1136

With Conrad II the direct line of Sigefroid came to an end.

Exactly in the character of the century the children of Sige-froid were avaricious, violent, and warlike. Since Luxembourg as a country did not yet take an identifiable shape, and since appar-ently no one person was exactly identifiable as count of an iden-tifiable country, we must be conscious of all the Luxembourgers and of Sigefroid's sisters.

Loyalties must have swirled and mixed and separated and merged like the currents of converging streams, clear and muddy, both, and turbulent. Apparently the parts of what we think of as geographical Luxembourg were subsumed under the count of Ardenne on the west, the duke of Low Lorraine on the north, the duke of High Lorraine on the south, and the king of Germany on the east, with even some necessary loyalties to the king of France. Nor were the problems of loyalty merely political, for the church had its claims, certain Luxembourgers had their claims on the church, and others made themselves quite free to appropriate to themselves certain church properties. All this was done in a state of constant war.

Henry I, Sigefroid's son, participated in the campaigns of the kings of Germany. In 1004 he was awarded the dukedom of Bavaria as a fief and raised to the importance of Prince of the Empire. His appointment came from the new king of Germany, who had been Duke of Bavaria and whose wife was Henry's sister. In 1009 he lost it. He became Duke of Bavaria again in 1017. At his death in 1026 Bavaria did not go to his heir, but Henry II did become Duke of Bavaria in 1042. Look at the map. It is a long way from Luxembourg to Bavaria, with powerful men and places in between. The centrifugal force was exerting itself here. Two loyalties — or more — were in competition. Since hegemony was impossible, it would have been quite reasonable for the amor-phous Luxembourg to yield its personality to the long-established and powerful dukedom.

But we must not forget those other offspring of Sigefroid, whose various strengths surrounding Luxembourg were like but-tresses to an ill-built building.

The whole of Lorraine, both High and Low, came into the Luxembourg family by the gift of Emperor Conrad II after 1024 (to be lost, to be sure, to Emperor Henry III's son a quarter of a century later). Or consider some of Sigefroid's offspring: Henry II of Luxembourg, Duke of Low Lorraine, Count of Salm and Longwy; the Bishop of Metz; the chosen Bishop of Trier; the wife of Baudouin IV of Flanders and wives of other powerful men. Then there were Cunegunde, crowned Empress of the Holy Roman Empire with Emperor Henry II; Liutgard, wife of Arnulf of Westfriesland and Zeeland; Eva, wife of Gerhard of High Lorraine; a famous abbess and the mother of another abbess. These places of power were often won at the expense of warlike competitors, as High Lorraine was won at the expense of the churches of Verdun and Toul. Thierry (or Theodoric) usurped the bishopric of Metz from his cousin Adalberon, son of Thierry of High Lorraine. Adalberon rent Saarburg and Berncastel from domains belonging to Trier, was elected Bishop of Trier but deprived of the office by the emperor, who wanted to keep such appointments in his own hands.

In this flood of names and events, common to all the histories — inevitable, really — we tend to lose sight of that geographical area called Luxembourg. Let us keep it in mind, but turn for a short while to the daughter of Sigefroid, sister of Henry I (died 1026) and aunt of Henry II and Gilbert, Luxembourg counts. This was Cunegunde.[1]

In those days of rapine and villainy, the Empress Cunegunde's light shone clear and bright. Most importantly, after years of her brothers' plotting and intriguing, after their open rebellion against the emperor, her influence sustained them and in the end restored them to much of their possessions and power. She was a good woman. She was educated. She had some taste for politics and some aptitude for dealing with affairs of state. After the imperial coronation, in 1014, she was called *imperatrix augusta*. After the death of her husband she was made regent along with Thierry of Metz and Henry of Bavaria (both Luxembourgers). This arrangement was all the more remarkable in that the rebellion of the brothers had held out until 1015, in the course of which time large parts of Lorraine had been devastated by the fighting.

We should complete her story as an example of another aspect of the Middle Ages. Cunegunde and her husband the emperor were interred together in the cathedral at Bamberg. By using her dowry for the building of that church, he had brought on the rebellion of her brothers, who feared to be deprived of her heritage. The pious foundations in which the sovereigns had taken the initiative and their liberalities with regard to the church helped bring about one of the most brilliant periods in the spiritual life of the church. They were rapidly honored as saints, Henry in 1167 and Cunegunde in 1200.

Succeeding counts — Henry II (1026-1047), Gilbert (1047-1056/1059), and Conrad I (1056/1059-1086)[2] — continued to be in the German orbit. Henry and Gilbert were brothers, nephews of Count Henry I. Henry II's lands spread widely in the Moselle region and probably on both sides of what would be the present border to the north, through the Ardennes, and in the region of Liège. He was often at the side of Emperor Conrad II; he accompanied his sovereign in the campaign against the Magyars in Hungary in 1030 and fought in the Burgundian war of succession. In 1042 Bavaria again came to the Luxembourg count, but again as a fief rather than as a family appanage.

If we liken Luxembourg to an edifice and the various relatives and feudal connections to buttresses, it was a building subjected to repeated shocks, and the buttresses were often unsure and unreliable. Gilbert's rapaciousness was as much a threat to the welfare of his own country as an assurance of its continuance and strength. He found his major conflicts with the church. While being attorney of Echternach he appropriated some of the abbey's lands to himself and distributed them among his vassals. The abbott had to appeal to the empress. While the Archbishop of Trier was in the Holy Land, Gilbert invaded the archbishopric in an attempt to take back the property that his cousin Adalberon had willed it years before. The Archbishop sought help from both emperor and pope, and only the intervention of Gilbert's brother, the Bishop of Metz, saved him. He was killed during a battle in Italy.

What must be particularly noted about Gilbert is that he was the first of his line to be denoted Count of Luxembourg in the records, being called *comes de castello Lucelinburg* and *Gilbertus Lucenburgenses comes*.[3] The power pulsing outward, inviting destruction of the identity wielding the power, had evidently generated still greater and more exactly identifiable power in the person of the count. The expansion and strengthening of the stronghold of Luxembourg provide the physical evidence of the title and the power. The walls as of 1050, including 12 towers, enclosed more than 12 acres, three times the area of the original castle.

The next count, Conrad I (1056-1086), pursuing his father's policies toward Trier, came to an unhappy end. After he seized and imprisoned Archbishop Eberhard of Trier, he was excommunicated, just as Emperor Henry IV was excommunicated by Pope Gregory VII. Significance derives from this fact in that attitudes and events on the small scale of Luxembourg paralleled attitudes and events on the scale of the empire, indeed on the scale of all Europe. The emperor and the pope clashed over the source and the order of power, the pope insisting that the temporal power should be subject to religious power. When Henry IV was excommunicated, the princes of the empire withdrew their loyalty from him. When Count Conrad persecuted the abbotts and bishops, when he seized church property as scattered as Cologne and Trier and Echternach, he was excommunicated; and his vassals thus were freed from all loyalty to him.

The punishment of Count Conrad was severe.[4] He was required to walk barefoot to Trier cathedral dressed as a penitent, kneel before the high altar, and confess his sins. More, he was required to build a new church at Luxembourg and make a penitential journey to the Holy Land. He did both, but died in Italy on his way back from Palestine.

One result of those troubles was a politically strengthened archbishopric of Trier, which, in its temporal capacity, was able to protect its interests with its own vassals and soldiers. As a consequence, such pestiferous noblemen as the Luxembourg counts found it more difficult now to pillage church possessions.

Out of these crimes and tribulations at Luxembourg came something good. At this time in the eleventh century when the church was reforming itself Conrad founded the Abbey of Altmünster (Notre Dame) in Clausen, directly beneath the castle. From 1082 until 1796 the abbey that the wicked Conrad founded was an important source of virtue and learning, not only for Luxembourg but for all of Europe. Out of battles and theft and cruelty came a religious equilibrium that would sustain itself through the political and social distress of the centuries. There can be little doubt that centuries later the character that separates little Luxembourg from all its great neighbors derives in part from the character that shaped itself in the often wicked events of the eleventh century. A reminder, however: though parish churches were being established, though the abbeys of Echternach and Münster would flourish, the various geographical parts of Luxembourg, larger then than now by far, would through the centuries belong to different bishoprics. And the bishoprics, powerful as they were, would pull the fabric of Luxembourg in different directions.

After Conrad I came three more counts in the line of Sigefroid — Henry III (1086-1095/1096), William (1095/1096-1129), and Conrad II (1129-1136). With Conrad II, who died childless, the direct line of succession ended. The counts' policy throughout the 173-year period remained consistent: geographical aggrandizement by whatever means, however cruel and rapacious; alignment generally with Germany and the emperor; conflict with the church, particularly Trier, with occasional armistice. At a time when the crusades were beginning to seize the imagination of Europe the Luxembourg counts apparently held themselves aloof from the enthusiasm; their purposes lay much closer to home than the Holy Sepulchre, and their motivations were more selfish than the freeing of Palestine from the heathen. There were some Luxembourg crusaders, however: Adalbert, the brother of Count William; Henry and Godefroid of Esch-sur-Sure, Walter of Vianden, and Francis and Sigismund of Grevenmacher.

The Luxembourger counts acquired church lands, some by purchase, some as emoluments, some by machinations. Count William, however, received in goodwill a generous award of properties in the 1090s from Trier during a period of peaceful relations between the count and the archbishop. When William offered Archbishop Egilbert his assistance against all adversaries except the emperor, he received in fief 600 manses. How great this acquisition was we recognize when we recall that the measure of Sigefroid's Lucilinburhuc was one manse — enough land to maintain one family.

The peace between Luxembourg and Trier lasted less than a quarter of a century. Dissensions, incursions, and ravages began again. The right of protection that Count William promised he made the fallacious pretext for attack. When he tried to enrich himself at the expense of the Abbey of St. Maximin in Trier, he submitted only when threatened with excommunication. When the Bishop of Metz fought with the Bishop of Verdun, William sided with Verdun. In reward he was denominated Viscount of Verdun and was given the towns of Stenay and Mouzon, well to the west of the Grand Duchy. The portrait of Count William is more favorable in his capacity of negotiation with the pope for the lifting of excommunication from Emperor Henry V and for his part in helping to settle the War of Investitures. For Luxembourg itself William completed Notre Dame of Münster, begun by his excommunicated father.

There is little to note of Count William's son and successor, Conrad II (1129-1136). Conrad was the last of the direct Sigefroidian line.

* * * * * * *

In 1083 the formal title of Count of Luxembourg was imprinted on the seal appended to the charter of foundation of the Abbey of Notre Dame (Altmünster) as *Conradus comes de Luccelemburc*. By the twelfth century the name Luxembourg had become a great one between the Meuse and the Rhine. The Luxembourger lands were now largely contiguous and continuous. The separation between Trier and Luxembourg was now a fact, a fact not to be denied through the centuries to come, up to the late twentieth century. But on the north the attorneyship of Stavelot won by Henry II brought that area into the Luxembourg orbit, to join Salm-in-Ardenne, won as early as 1030 by Gilbert. On the south and west Longwy, Stenay, and Mouzay were Luxembourger. Thionville was completely Luxembourger at the beginning of the twelfth century.

Yet, when Sigefroid's line came to an end, the principality was still incoherent. There is no map of it because no text exists that gives an exact description of it. We do not know if there was a council to advise the count, who were the domestic officers, who were the men who gave him military service, collected his rents, supervised his serfs, drew up his documents, maintained his property. The legal relations between prince, land, and vassal have never been worked out.

What was the peculiar virtue, what was the peculiar morality, of this early county of Luxembourg? If it shaped itself into some kind of unity, it must have had one. If among all the first counts one can identify a strain of action common to all, it must have had one. As a fact, its virtue had nothing to do with commerce. Its motivation was really not that of religion. It was not agricultural, except as agriculture had to provide subsistence. It was not its overall loyalty to the Holy Roman Empire. As far as we know, it was a ruthless aspiration to power and possession. Within the spirit of the age the Luxembourger counts were as virtuous as most and more virtuous than many, for their efforts met with success. They reckoned with themselves, and they were an identifiable people to be reckoned with by others. This last statement one might say of Luxembourg in the twentieth century. Of the countless princes scattered across northern Europe and quarreling among themselves at the beginning of this millenium, what other family house gives its name to its nation a thousand years later? None.

NOTES: Chapter IV

[1]Joseph Goedert, *La formation territoriale du pays de Luxembourg depuis les origines jusqu'au milieu du XVᵉ siecle* (Luxembourg, Imprimerie Centrale, 1963), pp. 44-45.

[2]Ibid, pp.45-46.

[3]John Allyne Gade, *Luxemburg in the Middle Ages* (Leiden, E. J. Brill, 1951), p. 55.

[4]Ibid., pp. 56-57.

Chapter V

A Century of Disintegration and Recovery
1136-1247

AWILD, CHAOTIC, sanguinary scene" — thus Motley speaks of the times of which we are writing. Such excursions and alarums, such clashes of arms, such cupidity and perfidy, such conscienceless alliance and betrayal, such gain and loss of people and property and allegiances!

We seek to identify that tiny spot of territory called Luxembourg that struggled to life in the late 900s, survived the afflictions of the first two hundred years of its infancy, found a personality through participation on the larger international scene, and then lost its political identification for 400 years. There must have been a vitality stronger than that of the sovereigns whose efforts were largely destructive, such as the first count in the new family line of Namur-Luxembourg, Count Henry IV, whose long reign lasted from 1136 to 1196.[1] History has found some good things to say about him, but for the most part he was a dastard whose unprincipled machinations almost brought his little country to annihilation.

Luxembourg survived — even thrived — under Henry IV's daughter Ermesinde (Hermessend), to whose reign we assign the dates 1196 to 1247, though certainly those dates are open to contradictory interpretations. It was a woman who rescued Luxembourg from the cataclysms of the decades that preceded her reign. Under the leadership of Ermesinde, Luxembourg participated in

the intellectual, artistic, and religious renaissance that characterized western Europe. When the ideal of the feminine was exalted
into a cult, she showed herself to be a noble woman with the
spirit and talent to mould a nation that, through the centuries,
would retain much of the character that she gave to it.

At any time in the High Middle Ages Luxembourg might have
swung out of its own orbit and been absorbed in some other political entity. After Henry IV became count, it was only three years
until he became Count of Namur; and some years later the counties of Laroche and Durbuy came to him also. These contiguous
areas lay to the northwest of the grand-ducal area. It was not until
1190, though, that the counties of Namur, Laroche, and Durbuy
were all to be united into one marquisate under Count Baudouin
of Hainaut. The point is that Luxembourg was a minor political
unit in comparison with the other units. This fact is further borne
out by the muster of the knights that the various counts could rely
on. Hainaut at the beginning of Count Henry IV's reign could
count 700 knights, as could the Bishop of Liège; and the Count
of Namur could count on at least 250 knights as compared with
Luxembourg's much smaller number.[2] Once when Count Baudouin came to Henry's aid against the Count of Limburg, he
brought with him 350 knights and 1500 foot soldiers.

The county came to Henry IV by the award of the emperor,
Luxembourg having fallen into escheat through the lack of a
direct heir. Henry was first cousin of the last count, Conrad II,
and grandson through his mother of Conrad I. Along with Luxembourg came the fief of Thionville and the attorneyships of
Saint Maximin and Echternach, fiefs of the empire, to which
later the attorneyship of Stavelot was added. In addition, he possessed the county of Longwy.

When the young Henry of Namur-Luxembourg became count,
he was a powerful prince of the Meuse-Moselle region. At the
end of his long reign all of his possessions were dispersed, he was
blind and abandoned. Luxembourg itself existed only as a fief
within the disposition of the emperor. Like leaves in a small
whirlwind, counties and attorneyships had spun away from their
center; whatever elements of greatness it had had some decades
before were totally dispersed by the time of Count Henry IV's
death in 1196.

How profitable will it be to try to follow the steps by which Henry attained his possessions and then lost them? And then follow the steps by which his daughter Ermesinde brought possessions and power back to Luxembourg? Between them they ruled Luxembourg for more than 100 years, a long enough time to contribute to the character of the nation that would emerge from centuries of turmoil into the little nation that exists today. We cannot ignore the events of the two reigns; we can only try to give some clarity to the confusion of the times compounded by the immense distance of centuries.

The traditional trouble with Trier continued. In a contest against the Archbishop of Montreuil, who wanted to incorporate the Abbey of Saint Maximin into his own principality, Henry put the Trier country to fire and blood. Henry lost Echternach and the castles of Soleuvre and Manderscheid to the imperial army and had Luxembourg taken away from him in 1145. The counts of Luxembourg were evicted from Trier territory, Saint Maximin lost its autonomy, and the attorneyship of that monastery disappeared. Thus the separation between Luxembourg and Trier that remained final and continuous.

It was two years before peace was concluded. In 1147 Henry was absolved of excommunication. He received back most of his fief, except the castle of Manderscheid.

Henry involved himself in troubles to the southwest at Verdun and to the north with the Bishop of Liège, who had extended his hold on a part of the county of Namur. Eventually the whole of the Meuse basin was caught up in the war. Henry made repeated incursions, seized and burned Fosses, burned the town of Ciney, and in 1151 lost to Liège the decisive battle of Andenne. In the course of these overlapping follies Henry had exhausted his resources in men and money. His vassals left him or, deceived in their hopes, even revolted against him.

Henry's greatest troubles, however, came in connection with the question of his heir. His first marriage was childless. His second wife, Laurette or Lawrence, daughter of the Count of Flanders, left him and took refuge in a monastery. The marriage was annulled. In 1168 he married Agnes of Nassau, daughter of the Count of Gueldres. She too fled to a cloister, and even the threat of excommunication could not move her to return. There was no heir.

For a period of almost four decades the process of disintegration went on. The centrifugal impetus set going by Henry IV spun off property after property, until at his death practically nothing remained. The seeds of disintegration were planted and nourished in the first 30 years of Henry's reign. They came to fruition in the final 30 years. Lacking an heir, in 1163 he secured to his sister Alix, Countess of Hainaut, and to her son Baudouin, the inheritance of property that he owned outright in the counties of Namur, Laroche, Durbuy, and Luxembourg. Shortly after, Baudouin became Count of Hainaut. Namur and Luxembourg as political units belonged as fief to the emperor, who alone had the power of assigning them to a vassal.

Baudouin helped his uncle time after time in battle after battle for 20 years. The rewards, he knew, would be great, and he meant to have them. When Henry fell gravely ill in the winter of 1182-1183, Baudouin came to Luxembourg and received the homage of many vassals. He was anxious to eliminate the claims of all other pretenders. He had the advantage of the help of armed strength from the king, Philip Augustus, who favored him. In 1184 the emperor, Frederick Barbarossa, in express terms granted him the succession in its entirety, freehold and fief alike, confirmed him in the terms of Henry's promises, and projected the erection of a new principality or marquisate combining indissolubly the four counties of Namur, Luxembourg, Laroche, and Durbuy into one unit, promoting Baudouin to the rank of *princeps imperii*. One speculates about the disappearance of Luxembourg from history 800 years ago if the emperor's projection had become reality. The potential power and importance of this new political unit, along with those of Hainaut, are indicated by the emperor's making Baudouin's daughter his empress.

But the power was too great a threat to Baudouin's neighbors. The Archbishop of Cologne, the Count of Flanders, the Duke of Brabant — see on the map the extensive lands represented by these titles — undertook to thwart Baudouin. They succeeded in restoring Agnes to Henry's bed, after a fourteen years' absence, and he succeeded in fathering a child, Ermesinde, in 1186 at the age of 72.[3] The consternation of Baudouin and all the other covetous rulers of neighboring areas was profound. But there was no suggestion that Ermesinde was the daughter of any other father than Henry.

This birth set in motion vast disturbance in Lorraine country. Henry revoked the donation to Baudouin, and Baudouin took up arms. Ermesinde was the excuse for another miscalculation. Henry engaged her at the age of one year to Count Henry II of Champagne, who took the child to his own court at Troyes to educate her and protect himself from a change of mind by Henry. The engagement angered the emperor, who saw in it a Frenchman getting a footing in an important fief of the empire. Baudouin had his way, and at the Diet of Worms in 1188 the emperor invested him with the marquisate of Namur and conferred on him the title of Prince of the Empire. The county of Luxembourg, a male fief, was omitted from the marquisate and was bestowed on the emperor's brother Otto.

Henry still had allies, but they were defeated in their last attack on Namur. Henry had no more Luxembourg, no more political possessions. And Luxembourg no longer had identification as an entity deriving from Sigefroid. In the swirling turmoils of decades all had spun off and away. Henry died, abandoned by all, in 1196 at Echternach.

* * * * * * *

The death of Henry IV could have marked — did all but mark — the demise of Luxembourg. The calculating, judicious, and shrewd manipulations of his daughter Ermesinde drew the pieces back into the Luxembourg orbit. By the time of her death (1247) Luxembourg was a strong political entity again. In the millenium of Luxembourg's history Ermesinde's name will rank with the name of only one other great sovereign.[4]

Functioning within the disintegration of the county was a force that for centuries would make itself felt. Henry seemingly was always slipping out of the domination of Germany. Blocked on the west, unwilling to submit himself unreservedly to the emperor on the east, he opened himself to influences and alliances on the south. Here of course was France, and the French king was not averse to getting a foothold in German territory. This became a disturbing possibility when Henry turned over the heir of Luxembourg to a French court with an alliance through marriage shaping up. The French-German opposition in Luxembourg, the dichotomy that would mark Luxembourg through all its future, was throwing its shadow far ahead. Ermesinde's alliances would make those French influences even stronger.

Ermesinde was sent back to her father when marriage to her no longer offered advantages to Champagne. Henry promptly found a French replacement (Ermesinde was now three years old) in Thibaut of Briey, younger son and brother of the counts of Bar. This turned out to be a brilliant move in favor of Luxembourg. Thibaut assigned as a dowry to Ermesinde (the document called her "his wife") the *châtellenie* of Briey and all its fiefs; and he promised to add to it the castle of Saint Mihiel when his brother the count should die.

That very year, 1189, Thibaut became Count of Bar. Though Ermesinde was still an infant, she was beginning the revivification of Luxembourg.

* * * * * * *

Ermesinde reaped the fruits of her father's folly. It was a mighty thin harvest. Henry IV of Luxembourg, Count of Namur, had lost Namur entirely. Luxembourg as a fief of Germany returned to the control of the German king, so that to Ermesinde came only some freeholds. What had for a few years been the most important principality west of Germany was in the 1190s practically nonexistent.

Ermesinde was ten years old when her father died. Within a year she was the wife of the Count of Bar. And then began the all but incredible assembly of lands and powers associated with the reconstitution of Luxembourg as an important principality. The blood of Wigeric flowed in the veins of both Ermesinde and Thibaut. The spirit that animated Sigefroid was strong enough still not only to reverse the process of disintegration but to assemble a political property more extensive and powerful than Luxembourg had yet known. The centrifugal-centripetal process, so early begun, so long to manifest itself, expressed itself in Ermesinde and Thibaut who, like magnets, attracted disparate properties to themselves.

Note how deep into the French sphere the Luxembourg ties now extended—to Pont-à-Mousson on the south, to Bar-le-Duc, a good 90 miles southwest of Luxembourg City; north through Briey and Clermont-en-Argonne and Stenay; farther north to Chiny in what is now the Belgian province of Luxembourg; to Marville, Arrancy, Gorze, Vaudremont, Grandpré. The various nobles declared themselves, one after another, the liege men of Thibaut. It was Thibaut, of course, who was the strong force; the child Ermesinde could not have brought all this about. But apparently her name and heritage helped provide persuasion. With the passing of years much of the leadership became hers.

Ermesinde developed her knowledge and strength in a rough school. At ten years of age she became the wife of a 38-year-old man who had already had two wives. Thibaut was described as faithless, unscrupulous, and cruel. At 14 she was considered to have attained her majority and signed her name as Countess of Bar and Luxembourg, as her husband signed his as Count of Bar and Luxembourg. At 28 she was a widow with one living child, a daughter. In those years of her first marriage Thibaut bought back Luxembourg. Just as importantly he settled matters with Namur. By the Treaty of Dinant in 1199 Thibaut confirmed his ownership of Durbuy and Laroche and the part of Namur on the east side of the Meuse that made of Luxembourg once again an important principality. And once again Luxembourg was defined as lying between the Meuse and the Moselle rivers.

In 1214 Thibaut died. Because there was no male heir, Ermesinde was cut off from inheriting many of the properties that had been hers and his together. Her position was threatened by the thieving desires of every prince of the region. Thibaut's only male heir, the new Henry of Bar, could justify some pretensions to Luxembourg. The frightened vassals of Luxembourg forced Ermesinde's hand. Before Thibaut had been dead three months she married again. The integrity of her property required that she have male children.

Ermesinde married Waleran, Duke of Limbourg. Over the scattered and numerous properties that schooled around the territory of Luxembourg the two of them threw their net wide and drew in a big catch. First, Waleran brought her as dowry the marquisate of Arlon; thus the German Luxembourg and the French-speaking area of Belgium were joined in a union that would last for centuries and that would determine to a large extent the linguistic culture of the Luxembourg that we know.

The terms on which the gift was made were these:

1. Only vassals of Durbuy, Laroche, and Luxembourg would constitute the guard of the castle of Arlon.
2. The succession was regulated in all details.
3. Waleran promised not to build any other castle that was not dependent on those three counties.
4. Waleran looked forward to the creation of a council of 10 vassals who would superintend the three counties.
5. Waleran promised to maintain nobles, knights, and free citizens in their liberties.

And then followed a series of acquisitions in ownership or in fief or in income that gave weight and security to the name of Luxembourg. Waleran and Ermesinde made a feint toward reacquiring Namur; but, frustrated by the Archbishop of Cologne, they were forced to consider that settlement final. They were astute and circumspect, keeping themselves on the side of the winner in the conflicts between the larger powers, Germany and France.

1. The Duke of Bar awarded them the moiety of the towns of Arrancy and Marville (in French Lorraine)
2. A throng of secondary lords, short of money or looking for more powerful protectors, declared themselves vassals of Waleran and Ermesinde:

    a. Philip of Hauterive (near Liège)

    b. Simon Muraut (to the east of Damvillers)

    c. Agnes, Duchess of Lorraine, held the castle of Stenay in fief

    d. The Archbishop of Trier put in fief to Ermesinde and her children all the fief that Waleran held from Trier

    e. Werner of Bolanden (in the Palatinate) accepted 200 livres to be Waleran's liege man

    f. Wildgrave Conrad (of the Nahegau) and the Rhingrave Embricon (of Stein) promised to serve Waleran and Ermesinde

    g. Count Henry of Daun (in the Eifel)

    h. The castles of Florange (near Thionville), Beauclair (near Stenay), and Orchimont (near Dinant) became fiefs.

Nearer home, within the county proper, relations were cemented with strong, local lords. Robert, seigneur of Esch-sur-Sure, had the count and countess participate in supreme justice in the valley of Diekirch, and revenues were divided. Frederic of Ehnen ceded half of the mill of Eich, on the northern edge of the present city, and a division of profits. Among the vassals were the lords of Wiltz, Rochefort, Septfontaines, Looz, Chiny, Salm, Linster, Bourscheid, and Berg. She owned Frankenstein, Falkenberg and Bitburg and Daun (in the Eifel), and Poilvache (in Namur, east of the Meuse) — properties near at hand, but some also scattered north, east, south, and west. In the twentieth century the castle ruins that crowd upon one another as one drives swiftly through the countryside seem too numerous to have been independent strongholds deriving sustenance for lord and retainers and peasants from so little property. But we must picture them as they then were in their full strength, populated and busy with the activity of husbandry and the constant maintenance of a readiness for war. They were the western extension of the area most thickly planted with castles of all of Europe.

In the actions and circumstances of Ermesinde we see expressed all the aspects of chivalry and feudalism. A vexed point is the question of her sovereignty. Under Salic law she could not, as a woman, inherit the Luxembourg property. Only as the wife, first, of Thibaut, and second, of Waleran could she really call herself Countess of Luxembourg. But as wife and countess she shared the fealty of all the vassals that acknowledged fealty to the house of Luxembourg. The question was moot during her wifehood. But what of the sovereignty when Waleran died in 1225, leaving a male heir, another Henry?

Henry came of age only in 1234. From 1226, then, until 1234 Ermesinde's right to function as sovereign, at least in the capacity of regent, could hardly be questioned. But Henry did not become count in 1234. Ermesinde only now became officially Countess of Luxembourg and so reigned until her death in 1247. There were precedents, but not conclusive ones. In 1240 the Countess of Bar announced that Henry — Henry the Blond or the Fair — would have the county only after the death of his mother.

Circumstances in the empire favored Ermesinde's increase of power. The emperor, Frederic II, in 1231 gave over to the major princes important privileges reserved in principle to the royal power. The Pragmatic Sanction promulgated fiefs to the princes of the empire: they became truly *domini terrae,* Ermesinde among them. Given the strong leadership that she offered, the diplomacy that she knew how to wield, and a reserve of military strength apparent to all challengers, the fealty that she now received logically followed. The pendulum of history continued to swing. As the pendulum of history swung away from imperial strength, it swung toward the strength and favor of just such territorial princes as Ermesinde.

Of course no minor lord would pledge his fealty to the countess except as he could derive benefit from his vassalage. When he put his land in fief to Ermesinde, he was confident — at least hopeful —that some other count, warlike and voracious, would not swallow him up. The more vassals united in service to her, the greater their combined strength and thus the less likelihood of attack. The greater the interrelationship and the more concentrated the allegiance, the less anarchy and internecine confrontation. As the sovereign received payment from the fief in the form of rents, say, she guaranteed a specific income to the vassal. And for the guarantee of an assured income, the vassal pledged his support in martial ways. If a vassal wavered in loyalty, the sovereign could withhold payment.

Certain problems presented themselves in the possession of scattered or ununified holdings. A nobleman might be vassal to one lord for one property, vassal to another lord for another property, and so on. It was necessary for a vassal to declare his "lige" seigneur, the lord who would receive his first and primary obedience.

The principal service required of the vassal was military service. The lord could levy a tax for war or call men into his armies. Often the lord forced a vassal into the service of guard in one of the lord's castles, as at Arlon, or required him to open up his castle to the lord and his party. The vassal assisted the lord in holding courts of law. Specifically, the vassal was bound to help his lord financially on four occasions: when the lord left for a crusade, when he knighted his eldest son, when he married off his eldest daughter, and when, being held prisoner, he was forced to pay a ransom.

Ermesinde was a capable governor, choosing her subordinates wisely and distributing duties. In 1224 the lord of Daun was made Marshal of the Nobility, to be in command in case of war. The office was hereditary and with the right of fief. The lords of Thionville, Larochette, Soleuvre, Wiltz, Fentsch (in Lorraine), Arlon, Septfontaines, Bourscheid held their castles in fief from her and were charged with specific duties. The castle of Falkenberg came under her sway. She bought back from the Duke of Lorraine certain hereditary rights on Thionville. She received the moiety of Sarreguemines and administered the laws of Sierck. She acquired the moiety of Dèle and the income from Nives. She received from the Archbishop of Trier all the rights that he held in Bitburg; they would fortify the town and raise it again into the fief of Trier; starting with 1248 the provost of Bitburg would have jurisdiction over Echternach. Ligny came under her sway when Bar gave it as a freehold to her son Henry the Blond, who would marry Bar's daughter in 1240.

Under the developing sway of feudalism freeholder and vassal alike were drawn together in the customs of chivalry and the rights and duties of a military aristocracy. The knight was the warrior with complete armor, fighting on horseback. Later, the noble became by right a knight. The old nobility and the families of knights gradually merged by the ceremony of dubbing and by the knighthood's becoming hereditary. As the hold of the empire weakened, the institution of chivalry served the purpose of such a princess as Ermesinde in drawing loyalty about her from all the nobles in her geographical area of dominance and even from nobles at a considerable distance who could profit by the tie.

Feudality was a two-way street, of course. A Ghibelline, Ermesinde was loyal to the German empire; relations were comfortable and peaceful. The old thorn Trier did not prick now. Ermesinde and her son promised help and support to the archbishop against all opponents except the emperor and the Duke of Lorraine. In 1237 they found peace in the north and northwest borders when they swore faith and homage to the Prince-Bishop of Liège. The Count of Champagne, the King of Navarre, and the Archbishop of Cologne all sought and obtained the alliance of Luxembourg. The entire periphery of the country was protected. The advancing and receding tides of Luxembourg history were, in Erme-sinde's time, at the flood.

Within the bounds of her country Ermesinde administered affairs with wisdom, discretion, and firmness. She took advice, and she delegated authority, even as she insisted on disciplining feudal excesses and increasing her princely authority. When as a mere child she had married Thibaut, he was already receiving advice from a group of chosen advisers. Evidently she allowed herself to be instructed in this type of government, for when she married Waleran, the marriage contract made specific mention of a self-perpetuating council of men who were locally powerful, including the following vassals: Henry of Esch-sur-Sure (well to the north); Gautier, seigneur of Wiltz and attorney of Arlon; Gilles of Ouren (on the very northeast border); Conon of Reu-land (to the northeast); Thierry of Houffalize (to the northwest in Belgium); Henry of Mirwart (northwest of St. Hubert in Bel-gium); Arnould of Larochette; Arnould of Rodemacher; Rodolphe of Kahler; and Erard of Meysembourg. See how far-flung this representation was; how comprehensively self-interest was enlisted in seeing to the welfare of the country; how the des-ignation of points of power and defense tends to define the geog-raphy out of which a later Luxembourg would grow.

We probably are justified in concluding that Ermesinde's gov-ernment was the very model of county government throughout the Meuse-Moselle-Rhine country. Her council included partic-ular officers: the seneschal, the most eminent officer and princi-pal counselor; the gentleman carver, the first chamberlain, the chief huntsman, the treasurer, the knight-banneret. The offices had evolved from simple headships of various exterior services, such as supplying the provisions, supervising the wine cellar, maintaining the battlements, controlling finances, etc. The offices tended to become hereditary, as was the case of the lords of Daun, marshals of nobility.

For purposes of administering justice there was a bench of nobles (*Rittergericht*), which had its roots in ancient times. It was Ermesinde, however, who fixed the powers of it. That court brought some order into the relations among the feudal leaders themselves and regulated relations with the sovereign. It was pre-sided over by the marshal, later by a chosen justiciary from among the nobles. This court existed until 1795, carrying out pretty much the same duties that had animated it for 600 years.

We are familiar with the title "attorney" or "avoué." Sigefroid, it will be remembered, had been attorney of Saint Maximin and Echternach. The title and the function remained in force in Luxembourg for more than two centuries. For instance, the seigneurs of Soleuvre-Bertrange served as attorneys for the property owned by Saint Maximin within Luxembourg territory; and in Luxembourg City a noble family residing there and carrying the patronymic of "Luxembourg" administered the domains of the crown and served as the count's lieutenant in the administration of justice. An advocate (avoué) named Wery even carried the title of "vicomte" (vice-comes) in a charter of 1182. These attorneyships were or tended to become hereditary.

The court of feudal justice, the bench of nobles, was probably very ancient, but it was Ermesinde who fixed the powers of it. It was instrumental in regulating relations of feudal leaders among themselves, with the suzerain or the countess and with the emperor.

She created in the place of the attorneyships revocable offices and removable officers, bailiffs or provosts, on the model of French practice. Provosts represented the prince in various territories, exercising judiciary, military, and police powers. Some posts went to non-members of the nobility, but parts of the countess's *familia*, designated by the term *ministeriales* (*Dienstmannen* or *sergents*). These were the collectors, the preceptors of toll and *tonlieu*, foresters, mayors. Originally socially inferior, little by little they became important men and ended by being intermingled with all the chivalry. Such a process of equalization was widespread in the feudal system.

Despite Ermesinde's use of council, court, provost, and functionary, her strength derived in great part from her refusal to let her authority or power leave her hands. She had been endowed with a lively sense of property, which she evidenced particularly in relation to her own family. Though she made Thionville the dowry of her daughter Catherine, married to the Duke of Lorraine, she bought it back in 1236. She assigned Marville and Arrancy to her daughter Isabelle-Elisabeth, married to Waleran of Montjoie, but reserved to herself the lifetime possession of them. Her son Henry received, on the occasion of his marriage to Marguerite of Bar, the counties of Luxembourg and Laroche and the marquisate of Arlon. But in 1236 Ermesinde denominated herself actual Countess of Luxembourg, not merely spouse, or mother, or regent, and this after Henry was already of age; and she declared that Henry would receive Luxembourg and Laroche only after her death.

She was an enlightened woman of her time in yet another way, that of giving a charter to towns. In 1182 the Archbishop of Reims had granted a charter to the town of Beaumont, southeast of Sedan. The practice of granting town charters spread rapidly and widely. How important the charter movement was in changing and liberating the social character of western Europe appears in the general terms of the Charter of Beaumont, which became the model. It guaranteed the rights of

1. the burghers or leading townsmen to move about as they wished, to dispose of their goods and chattels, to marry independently of the permission of the lord
2. exemption from forced labor
3. exemption from extraordinary taxes
4. justice except in criminal cases.

It imposed the obligation to bear arms in time of war and the obligation to pay only a quitrent of a certain amount for their house as feud.

With the Charter of Beaumont civilization took a great step in its long march toward freedom and democracy. In the provinces of the Netherlands there had been small steps taken toward freeing the town and the town citizen already, as trade grew and independent income increased; certainly the news of those freedoms had spread to Luxembourg. Such news had come up from the south, too, as charters became more and more common in France. There were no municipalities of major size in Luxembourg territory, but there were municipal foci of government and military operations that took their importance from their size relative to other town settlements. Echternach received its charter in 1236, then Thionville in 1239, then Luxembourg City in 1244.[5] In its small terms Luxembourg was expressing the same individuality of nationality as the large nations with their great cities that lay upon its borders. Sharp in our attention must be the fact that Luxembourg preserved its identity through many centuries, when its characteristics generally would have indicated its reasonable absorption into the major powers on its flanks. But even as it kept pace with evolving modernity, so that it could hardly be set apart from its neighbors, still it expressed its own character so as not to have its identity lost in the identity of a neighbor.

There is no existing evidence to identify the exact topography of Luxembourg City of the twelfth and thirteenth centuries. It is important, though, to be aware of just how small it was. When we read about city freedoms, we tend to think of Trier or Metz, of the great cloth cities of Flanders; we tend to think of real cities of 100,000 or even more inhabitants. When we consider that in 1900 Luxembourg City counted 20,000 people, and we remember that at no time in 700 years before that did it have a larger population, we bring the medieval town into focus as, at most, an overlarge village. In the 1300s it had only 5000 inhabitants. It had no commerce to speak of. Its workshops — millers, weavers, fullers, dyers, tanners, brewers — produced mostly for local consumption. But to maintain itself and its environs it did develop all the crafts that it needed, it supplied itself with its food and clothing, it ran its markets, and it developed its local government like that of any other town. Its inhabitants gradually became self-consciously citizens. There were elective offices that had their own dignity. The merchant clergy identified their own peculiar financial responsibilities. The market became the essential element of the city. Men who were neither nobles nor clergy came into possession of freeholds. Property values grew.[6]

All this was a contradiction of feudalism. In the economic prosperity that went along with the growth of the town and its suburbs, the merchants and craftsmen developed their own aspirations. They became conscious of their strength. They wanted naturally to protect what they had, to pay less and earn more, to restrict the exploitation by which feudal customs menaced them.

In a certain measure these developments favored the sovereign too, for as the town grew more prosperous his rule, through his rents and levies, became more lucrative. Gradually the town was withdrawing from the feudal regime by a natural process. Emancipation would eventually be achieved either by agreement

77

arrived at between the prince and the group of *burgenses* or by compulsion and violence.

Ermesinde's competence expressed itself through adjustment and agreement, rather than through compulsion and violence. By granting the town freedoms, in conformity with the social spirit of the times, she extracted commitments from the new freemen that assured her income and strength, and she affirmed her authority in the form of agreement. The citizen continued to be subordinated to the prince. The community of magistrates and citizens would choose for one year the justicior (the chief political officer), but the count would install him. The magistrates themselves were named for life by the count. The *justiciarius* and magistrates were bound to protect the rights of the count as well as those of the citizen.

Confirmation of citizen prerogatives entailed financial and military obligations spelled out in detail. Funds were collected from fines. Taxes were imposed on merchandise. In their military service citizens were obliged to equip themselves and to provide for their nourishment and that of their horses for the first eight days; that period having passed, the count had to feed the troops. By contract now the citizens preserved their ancient rights of use of waters, pastures, and woods. But taxes and penalties, along with military obligations, were severe. It was the cost of freedom.

The charter of 1244 would serve as the constitutional law for Luxembourg for centuries to come. Legal status was founded no longer on the feudal contract of man with man but on an agreement that bound the sovereign and a social group in mutual responsibility.

Still another marked characteristic of Ermesinde was a religious devoutness that found expression in religious foundations and gifts to the church, even as she held the church at bay, in a sense, in its grappling acquisitions. The church may have had in freehold possession as much as one-third of Luxembourg's overall area. Even so, it took to itself no powers that she wanted to keep for herself.

Ermesinde contributed either to the founding or increased strength of no fewer than nine religious organizations. Though she herself does not deserve all the credit for them, there is little doubt about her contribution:[7]

Clairefontaine, 1216 (near Arlon)
Useldange, 1217 or earlier (west of Mersch)
Luxembourg City, 1223, 1224 (at least three houses)
Bonnevoie, 1234 or earlier (south of Luxembourg City)
Houffalize (in Belgium off the northwest border)
Differdange, 1235
Roth — the Templars (in Germany, near Vianden)
Vianden — the Trinitarians

Add to these Echternach and Münster and no doubt others. Collectively they helped define geographically the essential nation that remained after all its territorial expansions expired in the grasp of her neighbors. Education in Luxembourg and the care of the sick were largely intrusted to these houses. The Abbey of Münster, first charged with its educational duties by Henry the Blind, became a center of learning for all of western Europe, maintaining its importance for four centuries. It taught in both French and German, giving expression to the bilingual aspect of Luxembourg and putting down the linguistic roots that would flourish up to this very day. From Ermesinde's time onward the French character of the nation would be accentuated in language and custom. French marriages succeeded one another. The French language would become official, even as the daily use of their Germanic language would persist in the very soul of the people.

When Ermesinde came to die in 1247 her preparations had been thorough. The great countess, under whom geographically the country had grown fourfold, solvency had been attained, loyalties had been cemented, peace had been fostered, and cultural idiosyncracy had continued to define itself, revealed in her will the concern for the individual person and the attention to the smallest detail to which may be attributed much of her success.

From the will of Ermesinde:[8]

> . . . To the building of the convent, which in the French is called Beaulieu (= Clairefontaine), I give all my mares, 64 in number, with their new foals; forty sacks of wheat according to the measure of Arlon, forty pounds (?) in Luxembourg denares; all the sheep from the four best sheepfolds; oxen and horses for two plows. As heirlooms for said cloister and for the maintenance of the inmates I give the tithe of Attert, similarly the ground rent of Hobscheid, likewise a half of that from all that is

belonging to Dèle, likewise the rents in Beckerich, Hesperingen, Sand-weiler, the right to gather wood just as the people of Eischen have it.

To Cunegunde I give 15 pounds (gold), to Beatrix 10, to the servant Hugo 10, Bartholomans 10 and a cock, to Watrinus 100 sous . . . , to Pepitpas a hundred sous, to Albertinus a hundred sous and a cock, to the heirs of Lambert of Dinant and Hans the clowns 10 pounds, to both fal-coners 40 sous and two sacks of corn, to the tailor Walter 100 sous and two corn-measures of corn, to each of the other domestic servants 60 sous, to the chaplain Henry 100 sous, Sara and Mechthild whatever seems good to the executors, to the gentleman Godfrid and his brother 60 sous and three sacks of corn.

To the Church of our Beloved Lady in Luxembourg 100 sous, to the Cloister Bonnevoie 60 sous, to the Holy Ghost Cloister 60 sous, to Mar-ienthal 60 sous, to Differdingen 60 sous, to the clergymen in Verdun 60 sous, to the minor brothers of that place 60 sous. . . .

She was buried in the Abbey of Clairefontaine.

NOTES: Chapter V

[1]"L'avènement de la maison de Namur: Henri IV" in Joseph Goedert, *La formation territoriale du pays de Luxembourg depuis les origines jusqu'au milieu du XV*ᵉ *siècle* (Luxembourg, Imprimerie Centrale, 1963), pp. 49-53.

[2]John Allyne Gade, *Luxemburg in the Middle Ages* (Leiden, E. J. Brill, 1951), p. 62.

[3]*La formation*, p. 53.

[4]Ibid, "La restauration de la dignité comtale par Ermesinde," pp. 56-66.

[5]Ibid., "La ville de Luxembourg reçoit sa charte constitutionnelle," pp. 71-76.

[6]Paul Weber, "L'Etat féodal" in *Histoire de l'économie luxembourgeoise* (Luxembourg, Chambre de Commerce, 1950), pp. 21-38.

[7]Gade, p. 83.

[8]Paul Margue, *Luxemburg in Mittelalter und Neuzeit (10. bis 18. Jahrhundert)* (Luxembourg, Editions Bourg-Bourger, 1974), pp. 37-39. My translation. This is Vol. II of *Manuel d'histoire luxembourgeoise*.

Chapter VI

From Henry V to John the Blind
1247-1346

CAST YOUR EYE FROM AFAR, as with a spy-glass, over the capitals of western Europe. We think of them in the twentieth century as naturally the capitals of the countries that they serve. But through the centuries there was often the possibility that those countries would not be countries at all; and had they not become the countries that they are, quite possibly other cities could have become capitals. Madrid is an artificial political creation. If Paris reasonably would have been a capital under almost any circumstances, its country might have become a geographical entity different from what it is. Certainly it was not inevitable that Berlin be the capital of more than 300 principalities become united as Germany; nor is it even the capital of an inevitable Germany today. Bonn, the capital of one of the three greatest nations of western Europe? Until World War II not to be thought of. Ghent and Bruges and Antwerp could not have expected Brussels to be their capital, nor could Rotterdam and Middelburg and Utrecht have expected Amsterdam and The Hague to take political precedence.

But Luxembourg City was the planted seed that grew into the present capital entity. Except as Luxembourg were to lose its identity entirely, it was almost inevitable that Luxembourg City be its nucleus and capital. It was always small — tiny by comparison with the other capitals. The heart could not really beat for a body larger than it has, though from time to time the nation developed an obesity beyond the health and the capacity of its nationhood.

The tendency to shape itself as the nation that we know was evident early on. We must recognize that if the Luxembourg that we know today included also the Belgian province of Luxembourg and territory on both the French and the German perimeter we should be making the same point. Luxembourg still would be the natural capital, and the extended nation would still be the natural country with Luxembourg City as the capital.

It seems geographically and politically reasonable that Count Henry V (1247-1281)[1] should call these powerful lords and vassals to his aid when he warred against Bar in the 1260s: the lords of Vianden, Durbuy, Bourscheid, Koerich, Esch-sur-Sure, Ouren, Meysembourg, Bertrange, Rodemacher, Larochette, and Huncherange. Other vassals were the lords of Amblève, St. Vith, Mensdorf, Diekirch, Neuerburg, Betzdorf, Spanheim, Aywaille, Orchimont, Arlon, Bolland, Linster, Salm, Septfontaines (Simmern), and Veldenz. We need not remember such a cluster of names; we specify only to be aware that they pretty much defined geographical Luxembourg, at the same time extending its borders almost to Liège on the northwest, to the north, into the German Eifel, and almost as far west as Virton and Sedan.

Noteworthy particularly was the accession of the Count of Vianden to Luxembourg as a vassal in 1264, when Henry succeeded in liberating the count from imprisonment by the count's nephew.[2] Vianden had been a powerful rival, but from now on its union with Luxembourg as the acknowledged master, tested of course from time to time by opposition and rebellion, resulted in a strength and geographical definition that would continue till the present day. By way of balance, during the 1260s Namur went to the Count of Flanders when he married a Luxembourg daughter, pointing to a distant future when Belgian Luxembourg and Luxembourg proper would be separate. In somewhat similar circumstances Ligny, some distance to the south, went to a Luxembourg son, by virtue of which the French branch of the Luxembourg family was founded. If not to be likened to a pendulum, the figure that is time and again appropriate, Luxembourg might be likened to a bellows, inflated and deflated, the fundamental apparatus of government keeping its familiar shape even as its outlines are modified again and again.

There were wars, of course. How could that multitude of castles, located only a few miles apart, one from another, otherwise justify itself? Or those thousands upon thousands of armored and sworn knights, divided in their tens and hundreds among their castles? There were captures and imprisonments, ransoms, arbitrations. Count Henry himself was captured and imprisoned by the Count of Bar over the lordship of Ligny. Only the intervention of the pope released him. Coming clear out of this warlike confusion was the lack of responsibility, on the part of Germany, for contentious Luxembourg and the growing influence of France in the person of Louis IX (St. Louis). It was his arbitration that established some sort of peace. Count Henry accompanied French Louis on the sixth crusade, which came to a deplorable end in the spread of pestilence and the death of Louis. In the troubles of the mid-thirteenth century over the German kingship Henry supported William, Count of Holland, against the Hohenstaufen. We see in the thirteenth century the erratic swinging of the Luxembourg pendulum, hardly defining a regular arc but jerking now toward Germany, now toward France, now toward the Low Countries, exactly as it would be doing six hundred years later in regard to the same three political entities.

Accompanying that erratic oscillation was the further identification and strengthening of a political citizenry centered in the towns. One by one, during Henry V's reign, they won their charters or letters of freedom: Grevenmacher (on the Moselle) in 1252 after having been fortified in defense against Trier; Bitburg (30 miles into present-day Germany) in 1262; and Bascharage, Linger, Marville, Pétange, Virton, all in the south and southwest. What little municipalities they were, none of them then or destined to be up to the present time larger than a village. Needing almost a magnifying glass to be identified in comparison with the urban centers that would ring them about as great cities, still under the glass their lineaments showed strong and plain in identification and personality, just as they do in the twentieth century.

With Henry VI (1281-1288) we may still identify geographical and political Luxembourg with its count. The Luxembourg that

Henry VI received consisted of the county of Luxembourg (a kind of bloated geography compared with today), Durbuy and Laroche, and Arlon. He coveted Limbourg (a geographical unit directly north and west of Luxembourg, not the Belgian political unit of the 20th century) and staked all on its acquisition. The battle of Worringen, in which he lost his claims, illustrates to the most horrifying degree the barbarity of medieval war. Twenty thousand soldiers fought there, among them 4,000 knights.

Henry VI died in the atrocious battle. His brother Waleran of Ligny died; his half-brothers Henry of Houffalize and Baldwin died. The seigneurs of Brandenbourg, Meysembourg, Bourscheid, Mirwart, Van Oesning, Vianden (this time on the side of the enemy, Brabant) — all died.[3]

All Luxembourg pretensions to Limbourg were at an end.

By way of summary we note that by this time Namur, Bar, Ligny, and Limbourg would no longer figure in the geographical definition of Luxembourg. At the end of new centuries of turmoil, of defeat and subserviency, of artificial political unions—at the end of five and more centuries when today's Luxembourg would assume its selfhood, those political units would not be a part of the Luxembourg body politic. The separations of the thirteenth century, though at the time seeming to be only new vagaries in a series of confusing amalgamations and dissolutions, were definitive.

* * * * * * *

If we are to know Luxembourg leaf, branch, trunk, and root, we shall do well to keep its counts and dukes in only partial focus. Because of the tendency to write history in the form of biographies of a country's sovereigns, the general tends to be absorbed into the biographical particulars with a consequent loss of accurate perception. Beginning with Sigefroid the history of the man is the history of the country, and that condition remains true for the rulers of the next 300 years. But the situation begins to change with the death of Ermesinde; with the election of Luxembourg counts to the emperorship and with the sovereignty of John the Blind the opportunity for misunderstanding intensifies.

Some ten years before her death in 1247 Ermesinde had preempted the title of countess and ruled Luxembourg as its sovereign until its heir, Henry V the Fair, was 30 years old. Henry had a long and fruitful reign, until 1281. During that time the power and independency of the citizens grew, pointing to a future quite removed from the serfdom and vassalage of all in a hierarchy topped by the count. The short reign of his son Henry VI provided Luxembourg with seven years of conflict and turmoil that left it reduced in size and threatened by insurrection, proof and sign of the weakening of the feudal ties that had kept the common people in sure subjection.

Then, in a few years, came a series of circumstances that changed the direction of Luxembourg's destiny. The boy who was to become Henry VII when his father died in 1288 was only 14 years old. That boy was to grow into the king of the German nations, emperor of the Roman Empire. His heir, too, John was only 14 years old when he became Count of Luxembourg — by default, as it were, for his father turned over the county on becoming emperor. The boy John became not only count, but also King of Bohemia in the same year, 1310, and was married to boot.

With Henry VII and John, Luxembourg set foot on the big stage of European events. Or was it, rather, that Henry and John acted their parts in the big drama, while the nation of Luxembourg settled its feet more firmly among its fellow nations and grew corpulent in the process, absorbing parts of the Low Countries, Germany, and France into itself on all sides, tending toward the period of its greatest geographical extent toward the end of the 1300s.

The time span that we are concerned with here was only about 100 years.

Henry VII's reign and the regency of his mother were not long begun when the burghers of Luxembourg rose in revolt—a Luxembourg shaking if not a world shaking event.[4] The lord of Esch-sur-Sure, to whom the countess mother had entrusted the rule of the country during the count's minority, had threatened the hard-won enfranchisement of the towns. So fierce was the threat that Henry and his mother had to seek refuge in the Abbey of Marienthal until peace was reestablished; the count's sovereignty was acknowledged by the citizens' paying a sum of money to him, and the towns' freedoms were reaffirmed by the count. Thus, early, the spirit of independency that would flash in the European scene repeatedly through the centuries, and flash most brightly in the nineteenth and twentieth centuries, revealed itself.

But we must keep all this in scale. The town of Luxembourg after 300 years of existence had fewer than 5000 inhabitants. The other towns were much smaller. Viewing the site of Marienthal today one cannot conceive of a retreat that could repel an attacking mob by the strength of its walls or the numbers of its armed men. Sovereignty and contention were on an extremely small scale, finding their equilibrium much as Grand Duchess Marie Adelaide and her people were to contend and find a settlement 600 years later. Is it too much to perceive thus early the genius of a tiny people asserting an individuality that would never be destroyed?

The strengthening of citizens' rights was to continue through the next reign, John's, which lasted until 1346, even as both Henry VII and John found the larger fields of their successes and contentions outside geographical Luxembourg — in fact, at vast distances, usually, from their native land. The town freedoms already granted were confirmed once more by Henry and yet once more by John. The mortar that held the stones of independency together was being more thickly applied, so that when terrible assaults came against the structure later it would continue to stand in ruins that could afterward be rebuilt. The towns of Laroche, Bastogne, Bellain, Laferté, Villers, and Dudeldorf all received charters from John (these were in the extended Luxembourg of that day).

The root system of the little nation continued to strengthen itself. Roots had gone out and died or been cut off in all directions, while the tree itself had maintained itself even when most seriously threatened. In the period of 1288 to 1346, when Henry VII's ambitions toward domination of the empire were opening and John was largely an absentee sovereign, Luxembourg was shaping itself toward the largest extent that it would ever attain; the tree was sending out branches too extended and too heavy for the mother tree, too distant from the roots called on to sustain them. At the same time, certain alliances were being made that would counterbalance areas lost to the Luxembourg sovereignty.

Limbourg was gone, but Henry VII became the husband of the Duke of Brabant's daughter; thus a strong friend dominated matters on Luxembourg's west flank. On the north a friendly cousin was Bishop of Liège. On the east flank conflict with Luxembourg's old enemy Trier flared. Henry had a tollbooth established on the Moselle, but the troops of Trier demolished it and ravaged the surrounding country. Henry retaliated, devastated the area of Trier and prepared to lay siege to the city. Out of the peace that was established in 1308 with Henry's cousin Baudouin, Archbishop of Trier, came money and honor to Henry.

Along with the development of a degree of commercialism came the enhancement of the French influence in Luxembourg. Henry VII's mother was a Frenchwoman; he was born in France. He was knighted by the King of France after receiving the best possible education in chivalry and in general learning in France. He knew the French, German, and Latin languages equally well. It is not surprising that, even as he kept his country oriented with Germany, the French taste and influence grew stronger. Along with this intensified culture went a sharper sense of justice, supported by the increase in education as religious foundations spread in Luxembourg City (the Hospital of St. John in the Grund), Arlon (the Carmelites), Thionville (the Augustinians). If the citizens of the essential core of Luxembourg spoke their own language that was to become Letzebourgesch, the knights and nobles — and we may suppose those burghers who earned their living in commercial intercourse with their neighbors — made use of French and German as a matter of course. What was essentially the Luxembourg nationality in economics, religion, culture, and language sent its shadow far ahead to be measured in centuries, prefiguring the modern nation in which the characteristics remain largely unchanged.

By his character and keen abilities Henry VII could justify his election to the emperorship. The election honored him. In his instance the election honored the country. His remaining loyal to Germany, even as he nurtured his French connections and proclivities, paid off. His episcopal brother at Trier and cousin at Metz and the pope himself gave the support that resulted in his election as King of Germany. A negative factor also played its part. His chief rival was the brother of the King of France; the

German princes wanted none of him. In the few years that remained to Henry VII, though, his personal history and the history of Luxembourg were separate. In the case of both Henry and John it seems to be imperative that consideration of the man be separated from consideration of the country. Henry recognized that he no longer belonged to Luxembourg when, upon his election, he turned over the sovereignty to his son, only 14 years old.

It was John the Blind, Henry's son, who extended Luxembourg in a national way.[5] We must give careful attention to him. For one reason, he was a major romantic figure in medieval Europe. For another, Luxembourg has made him its own particular hero. In its political hagiology John ranks in first place.

John's reign was a history of making war, playing in warlike games, grasping territory, losing it, fortifying his lands, and mortgaging them. We are told that he "passed only four springtimes without setting out to make war in some direction or other in Germany, in Bohemia, in Belgium, in France, and on the banks of the Oder, the Vistula and the Po." All this waging of war was set going by Count Henry VII's marrying his adolescent son to the heiress of the throne of Bohemia. At fourteen, John was a king and a husband before he was a man. He could maintain himself in rebellious and strife-ridden Bohemia only by warfare for other conquest.

Our concern is with his conquests for Luxembourg. He fortified Diekirch and Koenigsmacher. He built the castle of Freudenburg. He became sire of Falkenstein and provost of Bastogne. He came into ownership of Ivoix, Virton, Laferté, Nassogne, Belvaux, Damvillers, Mirwart, Han-sur-Lesse, Reuland, Dudeldorf. Again, we need not identify these towns except to know that most of them were in territory that lay contiguous to but beyond the extent of grand-ducal Luxembourg. At John's death he was planning to own more. He received as vassals the lords of Koerich, Blankenheim, Manderscheid, Schoenecken, and others. And a good thing, too. For before he died his outlays on war, his extravagance and princely show, and his expenditures to make his son emperor brought him to the edge of bankruptcy. He needed these possessions in order to pawn them.

It is almost incredible that John should have moved among the vast concerns of international politics with something of a sure foot while younger than twenty years of age. Had he been a little older, he might well have been elected King of Germany, and thus, emperor, with the help of his powerful uncle, the Archbishop of Trier. But to buy that help he had to cede to his uncle all pretensions, personal and royal, to the county of Hainaut, a rich area well to the west that, centuries later in Luxembourg's period of steel production, would have meant much to its prosperity. He played an important part in the election of Louis of Bavaria as king; from Louis, then, John was to receive important help, including support in Brabant and Eger and possession of Kaiserslautern, a considerable distance to the east of Luxembourg. On the other hand, the king frustrated John in his claims to Carinthia, Brandenburg, and the Tyrol. Out of the conflict, though, ending in the deposition of the king, came the election of John's son to the German throne.

In the roll call of the possessions that he added to Luxembourg and that of the lords who owed him fealty we see how the parts of the very core of the Grand Duchy were already adhering like a piece of conglomerate rock. He succeeded in protecting the essential core of Luxembourg on all its flanks. He held the routes of the Eifel and was protected against the unruly lords of Vianden. He controlled the approaches from Namur and Liège. He was adequately guarded against Trier.

Two important circumstances weigh heavy in the determining events of these times. The one has to do with trade; the other has to do with France.

Never was Luxembourg a commercial country until the twentieth century. What its fate would have been had it been able to compete with the commercial cities of Western Europe we cannot know. One guess is that it would have ceased being an independent entity. But fundamentally it remained agricultural, supplying agricultural produce to its neighbors. On the other hand, the growing independent spirit of the town citizens indicates the presence of some trade. Trade meant commercial rivalry. Trade was involved in the minting of money, the levying of taxes, the raising of tolls on trade routes, such as the Moselle. Trade had been at the root of Henry VII's difficulties with Trier and the subsequent establishment of a peace that lasted many a year; we can conclude that both sides were satisfied in terms of money. Trade became important enough that in 1340 John established a fair called the Schobermesse that brought foreign traders to Luxembourg City every August.[6] Six hundred and more years later the fair and the term both exist.

John brought Luxembourg to a position of such military security that its enemies were afraid to invade it. Within the country the brigandage of feudal lords was greatly reduced. John was only 21 years old when he joined Cologne, Trier, Mainz, Speyer, and Aachen in a treaty eliminating taxes on the transport of merchandise, and a few years later he extended his protection to all merchants crossing his lands. He, Brabant, and Limbourg negotiated free access to the fairs of those lands.

At what a cost were all John's wars fought and all his acquisitions made! He became known as the most famous counterfeiter of the epoch. In England his debased coins were known as *lushbournes* or *lussenbergers*. He paid thousands of *louis* or *livres* or *esterlins* or *florins* here and more thousands there. He had the lands of Ivoix and Virton ceded to him for the immense sum of 100,000 gold florins. If he could not pay his debts, however, how could he hold on to his acquisitions? In the tangle of exchanges over what was he lord and under whom did he become vassal? What he acquired from Liège in 1334 he sold in 1343. He gave up the provosty of Poilvache in 1342. He was in debt to the Metz financiers and engaged himself with others in an attack on Metz to rid himself of the burden. His financial troubles were unsolvable.

Very early John became indebted to his uncle, the Archbishop of Trier, and he began the disastrous process of pawning his Luxembourg lands. He gave up to the Archbishop the provostships of Echternach and Bitburg and the law court of Remich. He borrowed from the Archbishop 30,000 florins and sold to him the towns of Echternach, Bitburg, Grevenmacher, and Remich (on the Moselle and in the Eifel). The citizen Arnould of Arlon, by lending to John, became not only immensely rich but immensely powerful and drew vast sums from the territories in the south of Luxembourg with the consequence of impoverishment of their people.

John repeatedly found his attention torn away from Luxembourg to find its play in Bohemia, Poland, Lithuania, Germany, Italy, Switzerland, France. However much modern Luxembourg identifies itself with the romance of John the Blind, King of Bohemia, the identification is somewhat romantic. The histories of Luxembourg consider John's history to be Luxembourg's history. One speaks of the kingdom of Bohemia as being an appanage of the Luxembourg dynasty. Appanage? John no doubt kept his Luxembourg loyalty. He had the country fortified on all sides. But in the long course of his reign he visited it only four times. The Bohemians did not see in John the glory that Froissart attributes to him. To them he was a brutal, overextravagant, overweening king who brought no happiness or welfare to them. In a way he was an anachronism. The knighthood that he epitomized, the chivalry by which he died, were making their turn toward extinction even as he exemplified the flower of their principles. In the end much of the territory that he had shaped as Luxembourg was alienated or pledged or pawned to Trier, Liège, Hainaut, Namur. For all practical purposes at John's death on the battlefield of Crécy in 1346 Luxembourg was bankrupt.

* * * * * * *

The marriage of John with Elisabeth of Bohemia was anything but a happy one. From the age of fourteen when he attained his majority, became Count of Luxembourg and King of Bohemia, and married and through the years of his young manhood he was a bad king and a bad husband. Though his wife left him several times and actually fought against him in battle, she bore him nine children.

Is it far-fetched to liken John of the fourteenth century to a national or international athletic hero of the twentieth? It is difficult to find any action or incident connected with his kingship that can be viewed as favorable toward his intellect or character or good sense. He was an abominable administrator of Bohemia. His attempts to be King of Poland and conqueror of Lithuania were failures. He was equally a failure in Italy. Who knows how many bastards he fathered? But from boyhood he was a jouster. He moved from tournament to tournament, arranging and participating in knightly contests that used hundreds of knights and lasted for days. He was constantly on the move across Europe, to the north, south, and west, to take his part in the constantly recurring wars. Whatever his personal characteristics were, in the imagination of medieval Europe he was dressed in light, admired, sought-after, adulated. However much in debt he was, he lived in magnificent style while burdening Bohemia with taxes and levies too heavy to bear. All the while his aura of romanticism grew brighter.

All this is important for Luxembourg in that he did not demand from it impossible sums of money, even as he bought contiguous properties, built castles, and added important vassals and provostships to his county; and he spread the influence of the Luxembourg house (as differentiated from the county itself) through the marriages and political advancement of his children. But the Bohemian money did start to dry up. The acquisitions that he had made so triumphantly now had to be pawned, sold, or liquidated. Thus he gave up Durbuy, Poilvache, Thionville, and a dozen other places that had expanded Luxembourg to the west and the south.

Still, through his sons and daughters the Luxembourg line extended its fame and influence. Son Charles, to become Emperor of the Holy Roman Empire, married Blanche of Valois. Daughter Bonne married the Duke of Normandy and died only a year before she would have become Queen of France; her son did become Charles V (the Wise) of France, another son founded the Naples branch of Anjou, and yet another became Duke of Burgundy. One daughter of John married Henry of Bavaria, and another daughter married the Duke of Austria.

The child of John that mattered for the country of Luxembourg, however, was Wenceslas, born of his second marriage of 1334 to Beatrice of Bourbon. An important aspect of that marriage is the part that the Estates of Luxembourg played in it. The Estates, a kind of count's council, consisted of the appointed representatives of the nobility and the free cities.[7] These men were called upon by John to subscribe their approval of the stipulations of his marriage contract, thus sharpening and continuing the participation of Luxembourg's constituencies that had started with Ermesinde.

It was stipulated that Luxembourg should go, on John's death, to the oldest son of this new marriage, that children of his first marriage to Elizabeth should not participate in the Luxembourg heritage. In 1340 John drew up a will that appointed a seneschal to defend Luxembourg and named Wenceslas his successor. The nobles and free towns of Luxembourg were to elect representatives to govern the country until Wenceslas should be old enough to assume his responsibilities. This provision in itself is unofficially important in establishing the shared responsibility for administering the affairs of the country. Particularly interesting, in view of the linguistic history of Luxembourg, is the fact that from 1313 onward separate seneschals had been appointed to administer the Germanic and Walloon sections of the country. French, however, would continue to be the official language for some time to come.

John spent a total of perhaps eight years in Luxembourg territory in the 36 years of his reign.[8] We are informed about his years as count by some 3000 documents that record his transactions of all kinds. As we give him his due, we find it difficult to substantiate the affection and adulation that have been paid him through the centuries. He did extend the franchise to many Luxembourg communities. He gave communities and vassals certain rights of representation. He extended ecclesiastical foundations and protected them.

But the towns did not grow. Trade did not much increase; the Schobermesse declined into a local celebration. Trade routes bypassed the county. The produce of the land was its chief concern, and farmers still used the two-field system dating back to Merovingian times. There was much wasteland, and the poverty of serfs was terrible. Iron production was only a household occupation. Even Luxembourg City had no regular garrison — this after four centuries of being a fortified place and a center of government. Its population was still less than 5,000 as compared with the 100,000 of Paris. Among these were a few Jews, whose occupation was moneylending at usurious rates, whose numbers shrank to zero by 1424.[9] The powerful nobles bore the same names that designate towns and castles in the Luxembourg of today.

Such a listing calls to mind cognate situations of the Luxembourg of the era of 1900 and even that of today. Until very recent times agriculture provided the economic base for the country. It was poor then as it was to remain until the twentieth century. Iron is a concern now as it was then, except that its importance after 1870 grew to be much greater than that of any other product. Luxembourg City has continued to be the same size in comparison with other capitals. It is no more now a trade center than it was then; and though it is labeled a crossroads of Europe, it is a crossroads as a spot on the map rather than as an actual focus of international activity. The European Economic Community has changed much; but remove that, and leave out of account the banking development only a decade and a half old in the 1980s, and the character of Luxembourg relatively has not much changed. After almost 1000 years of history Luxembourg received its own bishopric. But the days when the church wielded great economic and moral and military power are long gone, so that the church determines Luxembourg's destiny no more now than in the days when its church foundations took their direction from foreign bishops. If we likened Luxembourg to a physiognomy, we should say that its lineaments are little changed.

* * * * * * *

Luxembourg had less than a century of self-government ahead after John's death. After John came four more counts or dukes, and then the extinction of the independence of the nation. Between the bankruptcy at John's death and the subservience of 1437/43 oddly enough Luxembourg reached the greatest geographical extent that it was ever to know. Under one foreign master or another this inflated national entity was to remain almost entire for four hundred years. Searching for a spiritual identification of all those separate parts of the single geographical identity one with another or among all together, one seems to discover with surprise that no vestiges of such an identity seem to remain. In most parts of Europe the national lines between peoples laid down arbitrarily by contending parties at their peace tables have continued to divide peoples whose loyalties flow across those lines in a familial sympathy and ethnic heritage that have not yielded to new national loyalties. Not so with the extended Luxembourg of 1400. Are we justified in inferring that through those centuries ties were tenuous if they existed at all, that culturally and socially there never was a Luxembourg of that size?

However self-consciously John was a Luxembourger, his national loyalty certainly was not confined to a Luxembourg narrowly defined by geographical limits. What he wanted seemed to be defined by what he could get. His willingness to risk what he possessed in one egregious campaign after another was not restrained, apparently, by sentiment or loyalty or patriotism. His motivation appears to have been an ill-defined megalomania. He seems seldom to have been directed by common sense. He flew his flag flamboyantly and indiscriminately; he chose his goals according to the dictates of an inflated ego. And though history has ascribed an attractive romanticism to the gallantry of his final act at Crécy, it gained him and his cohorts exactly nothing — except death. It was one final act of undiscriminating foolishness that excused him from any more responsibility for all the troubles that he had made for others. His escapades were not the history of a small nation; they constituted merely the biography of a man.

NOTES: Chapter VI

[1]John Allyne Gade, "Henry V, The Blond (1247-1281)" in *Luxemburg in the Middle Ages* (Leiden, E. J. Brill, 1951), pp. 91-110.

[2]A. H. Cooper-Prichard, *History of the Grand Duchy of Luxemburg* (Luxemburg, P. Linden, 1950), pp. 48-49. Translated from Arthur Herchen, *Manuel d'histoire nationale.*

[3]Gade, pp. 105-109.

[4]"Henri VII, comte de Luxembourg, roi d'Allemagne et empereur" in Joseph Goedert, *La formation territorial du pays de Luxembourg depuis les origines jusqu'au milieu du XVᵉ siècle* (Luxembourg, Imprimerie Centrale, 1963), pp. 95-103.

[5]"Jean de Luxembourg, roi de Bohême," in *La formation*, pp. 107-116.

[6]Paul Weber, "La foire de Schober," in *Histoire de l'économie luxembourgeoise* (Luxembourg, Chambre de Commerce, 1950), pp. 32-38.

[7]Ibid. pp. 149-150.

[8]Gade, p. 141.

[9]Ibid, p. 158.

Chapter VII

Feudalism and Expansion: The Groundwork of Decay
1346-1383

JOHN IS DEAD. The Luxembourg pendulum continues to swing. Where is the nation's destiny? Though it may be unreasonable to foretell its future, certainly it is not unreasonable to seek the nation's definition now. But the definition eludes us.

With his death at Crécy in 1346, Count John came to the end of his romantic feudal contests, his temerarious assaults on the peaks of power and fame, his gambling sorties from one end of Europe to another, his desperate financial shenanigans, the bullying flamboyance that found its most flamboyant gesture of all in his final futility.

Still, we should sound a note of caution. These simplistic pejoratives may be as far off the mark as Luxembourg's adulation of John as a national hero.

If the welfare of a nation can be defined by an extension of its borders and possessions, then the county benefited. Under the two next successors the borders would be pushed farther than they would ever be pushed again. What later would become parts of Germany, France, and Belgium were brought into the Luxembourg orbit. The pendulum in its slow swing would incline to strength and order and affluence for a time until, having gone as far as it could from its center while Wenceslas I was sovereign, it began its backward swing with his death in 1383.

John, Charles, Wenceslas, the second Wenceslas, Sigismund
— all carried the Luxembourg name proudly in the world scene.
Three of them were emperors of the Holy Roman Empire. And
though for a time the country of Luxembourg was among the
strongest of the European states, it was for a time only. Europe's
attention was directed to the name, not the country. It was the
house of Luxembourg that bestrode much of the European continent. Even as John extended the country's limits, he impoverished it by pawning most of it to raise money to be spent
elsewhere and by taxes for the same purpose. His son Charles the
emperor was to impoverish it still further. And though under
Wenceslas it was to find an extent and affluence greater perhaps
than it had ever known before, its enjoyment of that state was
precarious. With Wenceslas II it began an uninterrupted slide
toward the extinction of its independence. The erratic swinging
of the pendulum would cease in 1443 for almost 400 years.

The money that John extracted from his hapless subjects he
spent, in part, to make his son Charles Emperor of the Holy
Roman Empire. Having provided for Charles by making him
King of Bavaria and Emperor, and for another son by making him
Margrave of Moravia, he designated his son Wenceslas his heir as
Count of Luxembourg. But Wenceslas was not of age. Charles
the Emperor, as guardian, made himself Count of Luxembourg
and turned the revenues to his own use until 1353, when Wen-
ceslas assumed the sovereignty. Luxembourg, then, had a Count
Charles I from 1346 to 1353.

As Luxembourg plays its part in the high Middle Ages, as it
enters the throes of its loss of independence, we should take time
now to search out and identify characteristics that would survive
the outrages of centuries and would reveal themselves hundreds
of years later in the lineaments of a small independent state, sin-
gularly identifiable in the midst of its large and powerful neighbors. Impossible as it is to close our eyes to the personalities of its
sovereigns, we can yet determine aspects of national physiognomy that outride the centuries, even as on the face of a human
being essential physical characteristics outlast the decades.

Consider the castles. In the late twentieth century they rear
above the landscape, romantic now in their wreckage, but
remindful of the realism of medieval times when the power that

they represent was needful for Luxembourg to establish and keep its national identity against the assaults and machinations of all Europe. Their remains have outlasted the foreign domination of centuries. Starting from Luxembourg City, where the counts' castle topped the Bock, in whatever direction one rides one sees the broken towers and walls betokening a noble's stronghold in the Middle Ages.

Imagine them whole again. Imagine them the bastions of strong defense that they were. Imagine them housing the lord and his family and near retainers, villagers' houses clustering at the base of the walls, stables for the horses that would carry the knights into battle, flags flying from the turrets, the business of daily life in which fifty, a hundred, a few hundred fighting men had to be provisioned; the athletic and warlike training in which they made themselves ready for battle; the providing of food, the making of garments and armor; the breeding and training of horses; the coming and going of warriors, always getting ready for campaign, involved in war, or returning from battle; the domestic life with wives and children that we can only guess about. Within the confines of Luxembourg's 1000 square miles are the identifiable sites of at least 76 of these foci of domestic, social, and government life and of warfare. Lying on the immediate borders of the Grand Duchy are the remains of another 20 or 30 such castles, so that in a Luxembourg only slightly enlarged were some hundred strong, rugged, and threatening battlemented dwelling centers within view of the Luxembourg hills. In many areas the smoke of at least three castles could be seen from the battlements of another.

Across the little river from Vianden were Falkenstein, Neuerburg, and Roth. Across the Moselle from the castle of Remich were the castles of Bübingen and Freudenburg. Push the borders outward and find, in the enlarged extent of Luxembourg, more than a hundred of these busy places in a state of readiness for war even as the routine business of living went on day by day. The territory of the archbishopric of Trier, right next door and snuggling against the Luxembourg border mile after mile, contained another hundred armed castles where the knights rallied under this or that local lord before coming together under count, duke, prince, or bishop to wage war.

But back to our point. The Count of Luxembourg found in these castles the rallying points of the citizens that made up his little country. Whether in residence or as an absentee the count had governmental power such as to sustain him in his seat of authority and to resist the challenges that ambitious neighbors on every side were ready always to throw at it.

The castle strikes the eye immediately as a place of centripetal activity. It is a place built to keep other people out. It does not beckon in welcome; it repels. Its extent within the walls, the extent of the fields and the forests on the outside, that supply it, are sufficient only for those who turn to the castle's lord to support them and to receive support from him. When the lord's people are not engaged in war elsewhere, all their energies are directed toward feeding the vitality of the social unit that the castle signifies.

We are struck with surprise at the relative smallness of these units. Yet on reflection we realize that we should not be surprised. At a time when the population of Luxembourg City was fewer than 5000, it was not in the interest of the Count to have within shouting distance, as it were, ambitious lords who might get the idea that they were stronger than he. The Count of Vianden was such. His adherence to the Count came late; he rebelled; his title and country disintegrated early. Of the castles in the Grand Duchy only Vianden reveals in its remains a strength that might encourage its lord to challenge Luxembourg himself. Nor was it in the interest of the lord to display a strength that appeared to challenge the overlord whose protection he wanted. There was functioning here a social vitality akin to the balance of nature. Had the lords within the grand-ducal area been at one another's throats, the result would have been annihilation, and the county would have been absorbed into one of its powerful neighbors. The social units, organized around the castles, together made up a unit in which a character and a personality matured that would be identified, apart from the sibling entities on its borders, as Luxembourg.

The nation, then, adhered within itself by the centripetal force of self-interest. Counter to that were the centrifugal forces of the counts' personal ambitions. These took expression in two forms: (1) the impulse to war and aggrandizement by conquest;

(2) dynastic marriage. The two were intermingled. Both war and marriage were a form of politics, and John was an exaggerated embodiment of the fact.

Not only John but his son Charles contributed to the wealth and power of Baudouin of Trier. Charles was a learned and accomplished man. But he turned his talents to political uses elsewhere, manipulated Luxembourg into poverty and dependence, and turned over great pieces of it to others. Charles wanted not so much Luxembourg as what he could get out of it. Baudouin of Trier was the real power.

As early as 1314 Baudouin had been lieutenant of Luxembourg with the power to appoint officers and sheriffs. Eventually he owned outright Echternach, Bitburg, Grevenmacher, and Remich — a great piece of the Moselle territory. Charles gave up to Baudouin ownership of the three castles that John had constructed to protect Luxembourg from Trier. Charles made Baudouin vicar general of the empire for Germany, Burgundy, and Luxembourg. Baudouin received power over all the Luxembourg revenues not already pledged or sold. His control extended over the counts and the coinage of money. He had the power to fix and collect tolls and other taxes. He received from Charles power of attorney over all matters not expressly foreseen. Finally, in 1349, Charles ceded to Baudouin, who carried the title of *engagiste,* all the lands that constituted Luxembourg.

Had Baudouin not been one of the important members of the Luxembourg family, had he acted solely in his own interests, had he wanted for one reason or another to see Luxembourg divided up and scattered, the dissolution of the country could have taken place then and there. But he added to it and kept it all together. He bought back the county of Laroche, the *avouerie* of Stavelot-Malmédy, the towns of Marche and Bastogne, and the lordships of Durbuy and Reuland. He had Luxembourg join surrounding principalities in protecting commerce and travel. He checked brigandage and extended justice. He extended protection over the life and property of the Jews. He saved Durbuy for Luxembourg when he bought it back after Charles had sold it. From the Meuse to the Moselle and from the Moselle to the Rhine commerce and property and the person were probably safer than they had been for years.

Perhaps the pendulum figure tends to fail us here. Certain it is, though, that the pendulum was not hanging on dead center. It is a happy irony that the policy of Charles, which tended to bankruptcy and dissolution, led instead to circumstances of solvency and power. No matter for the moment that Luxembourg's solvency and power preceded by only a few decades the disappearance of its sovereignty. It was to be now for a time a part of one of the most powerful states of the empire.

The sovereign was Wenceslas I, youngest son of John, designated heir of Luxembourg, but only nine years old when John died. His half-brother Charles (Charles IV of the Empire and Charles I of Luxembourg) seized the title of count for himself and kept it for nine years, a period sufficiently long for him to compromise the county in every way. But with Wenceslas came compensation. The compensation came in two forms. One was marriage. The other was Luxembourg's rank as a duchy, which Charles as emperor gave to it in 1354.

Now begins a period of prosperity and power for Luxembourg. But it is an unhappy irony this time that the prosperity and power are but a bridge to new debts, new mismanagment, new profligacies, all compounded by contests for ownership and domination, the position of duke disputed by powerful contenders, and finally absorption of the duchy into another dynastic and geographic entity. We are pointing now to 1443, when Luxembourg's independence would be lost to the Burgundians. To arrive at that point we shall start again with the accession of Wenceslas I to the throne in 1353 and the denomination of Luxembourg as a duchy in 1354, both auspicious events from which one, at the time, could only have augured good for the little nation. As duke, Wenceslas was a prince of the Empire.

Wenceslas was Duke of Luxembourg by right and Duke of Brabant and Limbourg by marriage. The marriage was a brilliant one, for it enabled Wenceslas to pay off the debts incurred by John and Charles and bring alienated properties back under his control, among them Durbuy, Echternach, Bitburg, Remich, and Grevenmacher. Friendship was cemented between Brabant, Luxembourg, and Jülich, commercial relations were developed, security of the subjects was guaranteed. Treaties were made with

Cologne, Aachen, Liège, and Trier. Luxembourg and Trier minted gold and silver coins in common. Wenceslas's recovery from the impecuniosity of John and Charles was remarkable. In 1364 he acquired the county of Chiny by purchase. For hundreds of years henceforth the sovereign would be known as Duke of Luxembourg and Count of Chiny. He increased the number of his vassals to the largest that any sovereign of Luxembourg could number. Among them — and most powerful of them — was the Count of Nassau-Vianden. The geographical names and sovereignties became linked when the last heir of Vianden, Adelaide, married the Nassau count. This merger points ahead to events hundreds of years later when Luxembourg grand dukes would stem from this union. In all directions the Luxembourg sovereignty extended itself under Wenceslas to a geographical extent four times greater than it commands today. These extensions did not always come peacefully. In 1371 Wenceslas was taken prisoner by the Duke of Jülich (to the north of the Duchy) during Wenceslas's efforts to suppress robber knights who were distressing the country. He fought over Verdun and again over Trier in his effort to tax the clergy. But for the most part the expansion of the Duchy was peaceful, and along with the relative peace went a growing prosperity and developing social freedoms.

All this must be brought into perspective properly. When we speak of "greatest extent" and "growing prosperity" and "developing social freedoms" we must know whereof we speak. Look first at the geography. The Brabant of which Wenceslas was duke consisted of the North Brabant province of the Netherlands and the Brabant and Antwerp provinces of Belgium. It included the cities of Brussels, Antwerp, Tilburg, Eindhoven — cities then as well as now. But what cities were there in the Luxembourg of those days, extended to four times its present size? None. Range the map. Except for the casual and haphazard recognition of a municipal name, we see no municipality to rank in size, activity, and prosperity with the important cities — and even those of second and third level of importance — to the north, east, south, or west. In terms of numbers, in terms of product, in terms even of trade routes, Luxembourg was a place of almost no particular importance. It would not be long before it would be very important indeed as a bone of contention between great powers. But Wenceslas, Duke of Luxembourg, made his residence in Brussels, as Duke of Brabant. He came home — that is, to Luxembourg — only to die in 1383.

We have made much of castles and defense and the occupation of knights in war. What else was there to do? Failing the occupations of peaceful citizens, Luxembourg had for its occupations agriculture and war. Anyone with social pretensions — that is, knights and their superiors — would know agriculture only by its fruits; war of necessity was their resource. Virtue for them was perforce defined by war.

And for a time agriculture failed them. Perhaps no country suffered more from the great plagues of 1348 and 1360. The rural areas throughout the Ardennes were depopulated. As many as 60,000 people died. Whole villages disappeared from the countryside. With today's population of 365,000 in mind, think what 60,000 dead, almost all at one time, meant to it. This was decimation doubled. This was threat, fear, and sorrow comparable to — indeed, greater than — the effect of saturation bombing of a city in wartime.

But as Luxembourg was to do time and again through the centuries, it found a means of strengthening itself, of sending its individualistic roots deeper.

The strengthening — pointing to the distant future —came in the form of a degree of economic prosperity and of social freedom. Feudalism was breaking down. The free man was becoming more numerous. With the rural population of the Ardennes and the Moselle region sharply reduced, measures to repopulate and restock those areas were necessary. The right of mortmain was eliminated; by so much the liberties of the farming population were increased. Up to this time by feudal practice the local lord could, upon the death of a subject, take possession of that subject's best chattels and best piece of cattle. But no more. Production, and thus trade, received an impetus, sustained by the development of fairs for the exchange of goods. Traffic along the Moselle increased. Foreign financiers — money lenders or bankers — saw an opportunity for their services and came, scattered among the larger towns of the Luxembourg area, in which Thionville, Luxembourg, Arlon, and Bastogne marked off the stages of the route from Italy to Flanders. Craftsmen and workmen began the process of organization into guilds. Towns one after another received charters of freedom. Under the necessity of raising money Wenceslas drew representatives of nobility, clergy, and free men together as the Assembly of the Estates. Thus began a representative body that would last as an entity until 1795 and remain in the citizens' consciousness as a model for reestablishment of representative government later.

Then came 1383, the death of Wenceslas I, the separation of Luxembourg from other political entities of the Lowlands, a new duke, new entanglements by marriage, new debts and mortgages, financial entanglement beyond clarification, and finally absorption by a foreign power.

We must trace now if we can the loss of Luxembourg's freedom.

Chapter VIII

The Loss of Luxembourg's Freedom
1383-1443

THE FIGURE OF THE PENDULUM will not serve us now, nor will that of a balloon or bellows, inflated and deflated. With the death of Wenceslas I in 1383 Luxembourg entered a period of shocks and distresses sad to relate. History deals with dukes, princes, kings, and bishops — and to a considerable extent that will be our concern here. But one wonders about the peasant on the farm, the artisan, the little dealer in wares, and above them on the social scale the land holder, the merchant, the minor official, their wives and children. Certainly no concern was shown for them, unless through the church and its offices there was some amelioration. We may wonder if even in the Dark Ages those in power showed less concern for the happiness and welfare of their subjects than did the sovereigns of the 1300s and the 1400s. We have seen that in John's long reign of 36 years, 1310-1346, the longest estimate of his time spent in the Luxembourg area is eight years, divided among a maximum of four visits. Even then his time was not spent in only the territory of the present Grand Duchy. Wenceslas I, who became count at the age of 16, gave most of his time and attention to Brussels and Brabant. Wenceslas II, duke for 36 years, 1383-1419, visited Luxembourg only twice, and his successor Sigismund, duke from 1419-1437, never once set foot on Luxembourg land. For a century and a quarter, then, the sovereign's identity with the nation was so attenuated as even to disappear for decades at a time. If the citizens of Luxembourg did not know the presence of their sovereigns, neither could they have known the sovereign's concern for even their basic welfare.[1]

Luxembourg remained behind its neighbors in population, liberties, and wealth. True, it had its guilds like the other parts of the lowlands, to the number of 13.[2] But the many nobles still held the power, while the commercial classes to the west were becoming stronger and stronger. Luxembourg simply did not have commercial resources. When the Estates requested participation in government from Wenceslas II in 1388, 76 nobles and 15 towns signed the request.[3] But with fewer than 5000 inhabitants in Luxembourg City, with every other municipality being much smaller than that, with the rural areas still greatly depopulated, there was little in the way of wealth or business or martial strength to give force to the request.

We make our way with difficulty through the period beginning with the death of Wenceslas I in 1383 and ending with Luxembourg's absolute loss of self-government in 1443. What other sovereign state of Western Europe was so constantly rent and buffeted for so long a period of time with total insensitivity to the people most concerned, the citizens?

For the next fifty years Luxembourg will be treated like a chattel, or a country estate, or a stash of gold bullion, or a city skyscraper — like something owned that can be bartered or sold or pawned; a property removed from the human values of love or loyalty or birthright. It had been treated this way before by John and Charles, but its integrity had always been secure within the grand-ducal limits, however much its sensibilities might have been affronted. Beginning with Wenceslas II its personality is ignored, its body is torn, its soul is violated.

"Shameful," "miserable," "disorder," "anarchy" — these are words that are readily called on to depict the times that we are dealing with now. The legitimate sovereigns Wenceslas II (1383-1419) and Sigismund (1419-1437), both emperors as well as dukes of Luxembourg, were unprincipled profligates, with no sense of honor. To them Luxembourg was the security for money to be poured down the drain, or stakes to be flung on the gambling table, or pawns for which there was no power or plan of redemption. No wonder that nobles, threatened with the loss of all that they possessed, rebelled and connived, were caught up in intestine embroils, plotted and cheated. The old habits of the Middle Ages, gradually controlled over two hundred and more years, broke out in all the unrestrained malevolence and brutality of feudal times. Sovereign in name, Wenceslas II and Sigismund yielded their ducal powers to others who in their turn, sometimes, yielded them to still others.

Our target date here is 1443; that is, as we take up the Luxembourg story at the death of a good sovereign, Wenceslas I, in 1383, we shall make our way as best we can along the tangled path that leads to its loss of independence in 1443. We must be prepared to encounter new names, Goerlitz and Burgundy in particular. When Burgundy finally annihilated Luxembourg sovereignty by the imposition of her own, Luxembourg had tested subserviency in those 60 years many times.

We should move slowly through this Luxembourg turmoil. We should remind ourselves first that it takes place in the context of a high civilization. In Belgium, France, and Germany the great cathedrals were abuilding; what imagination conceived technologists and artisans were able to bring into reality. We cannot suppose that the supersophistication of architecture existed alone among all the aspects of social life. Intercourse among the political units of Germany was unremitting. Communication was on the highest cultural plane. We have not made a pretty picture of Emperor Charles IV as far as Luxembourg is concerned, but for the Empire he was enlightened. He spoke Latin, German, French, Czech, and other languages. He was widely read, and he mingled with wise counselors. He was an astute statesman, a subtle politician. Excellently educated at the court of France and the University of Paris, he founded the university at Prague on the Paris model, attracting thousands of students from all over Europe. His long arm of influence extended to England, Poland, Italy, as well as to the countries of Western Europe.

Evidence in Luxembourg of the high-mindedness of which he was capable exists in the Golden Bull of Luxembourg, which he executed in 1356.[4] By the Bull he regulated the judiciary, ameliorated the police powers, restricted the cruel exactions by the nobles upon the peasants, and made a move to lift the serfs above their lot of slavery. In the exactions of his international involvements he was, however, too seldom conscious of the human dimensions of that ducal property.

Charles's half-brother Wenceslas, as Duke of Brabant as well as Duke of Luxembourg, maintained at Brussels one of the most brilliant courts of Europe, opulent to the highest degree, the gathering place of wits and poets, among them Froissart. Why was it that his death took place in the castle at Luxembourg? Because there, where nothing went on, he could find peace and contentment. In other words, in Luxembourg he could die without the excitement and disturbance of bankers, merchants, architects, writers, painters, flaunters, challengers, jewelers, furnishers, etc., etc., etc. Luxembourg — the town and the areas within the grand-ducal limits — was still a quiet, rural backwater, taking its culture above the subsistence level from its neighbors, but in the intercourse of daily life maintaining itself in language and preoccupation and viewpoint within the self-conscious limits of 1000 square miles, without even the self-conscious pride of its own bishop. It had nothing with which, really, to compete. It became a kind of sedimental entity beneath the stormy surface of international conflict, cupidity, and intrigue. Above it and around it now those storms would rage for the next 400 years, while Luxembourg essentially stayed the same. As other nations emerged from the Middle Ages into the Renaissance, from the Renaissance into the Reformation and the Enlightment, from the Classical Age into Romanticism and from Romanticism into the Industrial Age, Luxembourg's essential nature would be contained within the limits that it knows today; its natural borders, once they were finally imposed, would lead no one on the outside to clamor to get in; its population would be essentially unchanged; its economic system would remain essentially rural and self-centered; its loyalties would be to itself. Only when the Industrial Age went into full swing would it develop a commercial character that would change its nature of 800 years.

* * * * * * *

Luxembourg's survival of the late Middle Ages is almost a miracle. The family dynasty was played out. It produced nothing of international importance. Its commerce was negligible. In art

and architecture it lent no personalities or movements or monuments to the times. It had no weight within the church. But like
a ball that has been set in play it bounded and rebounded, while
the game played itself out into the twilight of medieval times.
The stakes of the game were high. The players were motivated
only by the stakes, by neither patriotism nor loyalty nor familial
custom.

Let us try, beginning with Wenceslas I, to make our way
through the tribulations of Luxembourg for the ninety years following his marriage to the heiress of Brabant in 1334. Always we
shall be conscious of the Luxembourg that fitted approximately
within the confines of the country as we know them today. We
should keep in our awareness, too, the name of Brabant and, ultimately, the name of Burgundy. The fundamental question for this
period is this: How did Luxembourg come into the ownership of
Burgundy?

By his marriage Wenceslas I became Duke of Brabant, Duke of
Limbourg, and Marquis of Antwerp. He was owner of the counties of Durbuy and Laroche, both of which he gave in dowry to
his wife, Jeanne. In 1364 he became Count of Chiny. Now here
is the point: Each of these functioned, to a great extent, as an
independent entity. Though they belonged to the Duke of Luxembourg, he did not administer them collectively as the Duke of
Luxembourg. They were not Luxembourgian. It follows, then,
that their later dispersal played no great part in the fate and history of Luxembourg itself. As the dispersal takes place during the
succeeding decades, we shall see the centripetal force that governed Luxembourg in full and fateful play.

1. As early as 1357 Wenceslas's wife Jeanne[5] promises Brabant to Charles IV or his nearest male relative if she dies
childless.

2. Wenceslas I dies in 1383, leaving his wife in sole possession of those properties not Luxembourgian. When she is
attacked by the Duke of Gueldre, she appeals for help to the
Duke of Burgundy, Philip the Bold, who was the husband of her
niece, Marguerite of Flanders.

3. Jeanne, in 1390, renounces possession of Chiny, Laroche,
and Durbuy. She acknowledges Marguerite as her successor to

Brabant and Limbourg, transmits those lands to Philip of Burgundy so that he might be in possession of them when she dies.

4. 1386. Wenceslas II appoints John of Goerlitz his lieutenant, with all the rights of justice, concluding treaties, declaring war, and making peace.

5. 1388. Wenceslas pawns the entire Duchy to Josse of Moravia. Josse gives over Luxembourg to incompetent governors. The soldiers of France and of Ligny put everything there to fire and blood.

6. 1402. Josse confides the administration to Louis of Orléans, the brother of the King of France, who becomes pawn holder for 100,000 gold ducats. (By now the pawn is twice removed.) Louis is assassinated by Burgundy. Anarchy is now the permanent condition of Luxembourg.

7. 1411. Elizabeth of Goerlitz (niece of Wenceslas) has married Antony of Burgundy, Duke of Brabant. The King of France secures her dowry by Luxembourg. The citizens are ordered to obey Elizabeth and Antony. (The pawn is now three times removed.) The rightful heir presumptive is Sigismund, King of Hungary and Emperor, who encourages the towns to revolt.

8. 1415. Antony is killed. Elizabeth continues to hold the pawn. Sigismond, in 1419, to hold back Burgundy, now reconciled to Elizabeth, gives her in marriage to John of Bavaria.

9. 1419. Wenceslas II dies. Sigismund becomes Duke of Luxembourg. Since he cannot repay the debt of 120,000 florins, with Luxembourg as security, Elizabeth keeps possession of country and title alike. Disorder, quarrels, pillage. She is quite incompetent.

10. 1437. Sigismund dies. Ownership of Luxembourg goes to his daughter Elizabeth and her husband, Albert of Austria.

11. 1439. Albert dies, leaving a son, Ladislas, yet to be born. Thus Ladislas would be the rightful Duke of Luxembourg. The widow Elizabeth makes over the rights to Luxembourg to the Duke of Saxony.

12. 1441. Elizabeth of Goerlitz makes Philip the Good, Duke of Burgundy, her heir in exchange for money, jewels, and an annuity.

13. 1442. The rightful Duchess of Luxembourg (the other Elizabeth, mother of Ladislas) ratifies the 1441 agreement. Fac-

tions oppose, fighting follows, Elizabeth of Goerlitz flees. The Duke of Saxony takes over Luxembourg by force.

14. 1443. Burgundy attacks the Saxons and takes Luxembourg by storm. Pillaging, suppression of freedoms. All rights to Luxembourg are ceded to Philip of Burgundy for 120,000 Hungarian florins. The pawn is now four times removed. The King of Germany authorizes the Luxembourg Estates to recognize Philip as their sovereign while giving assurances that the rightful heir, King Ladislas of Hungary, only three years old, will remain suzerain lord of the Duchy with the buying back of his rights when Elizabeth of Goerlitz dies.

15. 1451. Elizabeth of Goerlitz dies.

16. 1457. Ladislas dies. Burgundy is now the owner as well as ruler of Luxembourg.

* * * * * * *

The sixteen steps of the scheme through which we have just gone are simplistic. We are looking at 100 years of unimaginably complicated history as if through several layers of dirty plastic.[6] We can discern only the blackest of lines, the most assertive of events. Whoever prospered by these divagations of financial chicanery it was certainly not the Luxembourg citizens.

Again we marvel at the survival of an entity attacked by one enemy and another, torn by the contending forces of avarice, starved by the very powers — the only powers — that were and could be responsible for its nurture. But again Luxembourg did not become French, did not become German, did not amalgamate with its sister entities to the west in the Netherlands. It is as though it became annealed. The arrows of affliction bounced off its tough hide. No weapon could get at its core.

Its integrity penetrated the inflictions heaped upon it. Toward the end of the 100 years of the *engagistes* the little nation began to lift its head before its latest conqueror, Philip of Burgundy. Philip granted a pardon to the inhabitants of Luxembourg. He pronounced a general amnesty and restored their goods, save for 25 persons pointedly excluded from his generosity. He returned to the city its privilege of administering justice. It established a new magistracy, set up a new system of taxation, and provided for the upkeep of the fortifications.

113

The process of healing continued. In 1451 the Estates declared their willingness to take their oath of homage to Burgundy, provided the rights of the natural heirs would be protected. (Remember: Philip still held Luxembourg by right of pawn and manipulation, rather than by heritage.) The Estates asked to be confirmed in the old liberties that, despite all, had been shaping for 200 years. Philip granted the requests.

With Philip came order. Law was reestablished. The sovereign (Philip) and the Estates worked together. Parts of the country that had collaborated against the assaults of fortune continued in close association. The lineaments of the little nation took on the firmness and identity of national health, even as it was forced to function under the domination of a national government extended far beyond Luxembourg's restricted borders, a government that thought of itself, not as Luxembourgian, but as Burgundian.

* * * * * * *

Because the history of the last hundred years before the triumph of Burgundy in Luxembourg is so complicated, we may serve our purposes of clarification best if we recapitulate, in capsule form, the sixteen steps leading from Wenceslas II to Philip the Good. Let us borrow and adapt the schematic of Arthur Herchen, as presented in Cooper-Pritchard's translation:[7]

Sovereigns of the Dukedom of Luxembourg, Legal and Engagiste

Legal Sovereigns

1383-1419: Wenceslas II

(1386-1388: John of Goerlitz, Lieutenant)

1419-1437: Emperor Sigismund

1437-1439: Albert of Austria and Elizabeth of Luxembourg

(1439-1443: William of Saxony and Anne)

1440-1457: Ladislas the Posthumous, King of Bohemia and Hungary

1461-1467: Philip of Burgundy (It was only in 1461 that the Estates of Luxembourg recognized Philip as the legitimate sovereign.)

Engagiste Sovereigns

1388-1402: Josse of Moravia

(1401   : Philip the Bold, Duke of Burgundy, his Lieutenant)

1402-1407: Louis of Orléans

1407-1411: Josse of Moravia

1411-1451: Elizabeth of Goerlitz

(1441-1451: Philip the Good, Duke of Burgundy, as *mambour*)

1451-1461: Philip the Good as *engagiste*

With Philip the Good, Burgundy inaugurated the long domination of Luxembourg and its incorporation within the Burgundy state. Burgundy's domination of the Netherlands was less than 100 years old when it absorbed Luxembourg. That domination began only in 1384 when Burgundy's Philip the Bold acquired Flanders and Artois by marriage to the heiress of the Count of Flanders and niece of Wenceslas I of Luxembourg. Then the duke purchased Namur in 1429, inherited or usurped the duchies of Brabant and Limbourg, inherited the counties of Hainaut, Holland, and Zeeland in 1433, and became titular master of Friesland. The merging of Luxembourg with the neighboring territories and its separating from them had flowed and ebbed with the tides of war and marriage for hundreds of years. The tide of amalgamation was now at full flow, seemingly the product of the inevitability of history as much as the ocean tides derive from the inevitability of nature.

NOTES: Chapter VIII

[1]"Les derniers souverains de la maison de Luxembourg" in Joseph Goedert, *La formation territoriale du pays de Luxembourg depuis les origines jusqu'au milieu du XVe siècle* (Luxembourg, Imprimerie Centrale, 1963), pp. 158-170.

[2]Paul Weber, *Histoire de l'économie luxembourgeoise* (Luxembourg, Chambre de Commerce, 1950), p. 29.

[3]John Allyn Gade, *Luxemburg in the Middle Ages* (Leiden, E. J. Brill, 1951), p. 191.

[4]*La formation*, p. 161.

[5]Ibid, p. 165.

[6]This is succinctly put in Paul Margue, *Luxemburg in Mittelalter und Neuzeit* (Luxembourg, Editions Bourg-Bourger, 1974), pp. 89-95. This is Vol. II of *Manuel d'histoire luxembourgeoise.*

[7]A. H. Cooper-Prichard, *History of the Grand Duchy of Luxemburg* (Luxemburg, P. Linden, 1950), p. 91.

Chapter IX

Foreign Domination: Burgundy and Spain
1443-1579

I N THE MIDDLE 15TH CENTURY Luxembourg was pawned, sold, and conquered — pawned and sold like any chattel, raped like any piece of valuable real estate. In these deceits and frauds the citizens who called themselves Luxembourgers, noble and common alike, had nothing to say. While living in the old homestead, as it were, they did not own title to it, but continued to pay the rent, through taxes, to a succession of rapacious landlords.

Why was Luxembourg, as a political entity, not subsumed, absorbed, blotted out? Why did it not become merely the name of a place instead of the identification of a people and a personality? Practically all the other areas termed counties and lordships and dukedoms that we have been mentioning were destined to surrender their identities to larger identities — Durbuy, Laroche, Bar, Lorraine, Trier; the list is interminable. They became a part of something, a part of France or Germany or Belgium.

Now, in 1443, Luxembourg is a part of Burgundy, later will be a part of Spain, later a part of France, a part of Spain again, later a part of Austria, a part of France again, later a part of the Netherlands. But the foundation on which it rested never crumbled. The wings of its edifice to east, south, and west were lopped off, but the central mansion stood. Its various sovereigns did not take up residence for 400 years while the demesne itself maintained its integrity.

We must continue to look for the reasons.

Part of the reason lies in the same process that determined the municipal character of the great cities of western Europe — Ghent, Bruges, Antwerp, etc. But whereas they remained only parts of larger political units, Luxembourg with its small rural appendages remained itself alone. Feudal loyalties continued their centripetal adhesion. For seigneuries to continue their existence in the closely compacted circumstances that characterized Luxembourg, a peaceful coexistence was imperative. As the seigneuries or lordships continued to exist, citizens found an increasing power in the bourgeoisie of the trades and commercial exchanges. Affluence among them increased, as elsewhere, and responsibilities for self-government grew.

We recall that the solidarity of the bourgeoisie was first ratified in the form of communal autonomy that Ermesinde gave Luxembourg in the charter of enfranchisement of 1244. By it private families, such as the Asfelts, grew rich and powerful; so rich and powerful, in fact, that they aspired to the perquisites of the nobility and acquired them in both riches and title. Their independent welfare was inextricably related to the independent welfare of the Duchy. Pressing on the heels of these entrepeneurs were the artisans and businessmen of a more everyday variety, quite willing to rebel and demand in order to establish their own perquisites and consequently concerned that the political circumstances — in other words, the Duchy itself — that made their security possible should not be absorbed by political groups with powers greater than their own. Affluence led to power, as in the granted privilege that every other year the judge would be chosen from among the common people.

The church contributed to the cohesiveness of the area.[1] The Abbey of Münster in Luxembourg City had a monopoly on teaching. And note, in view of the Luxembourg of today: instruction was bilingual. The Clares, the Franciscans, the Beguines, the Dominicans, the Trinitarians, all established in Luxembourg by the 1200s, received their members and adherents from the free bourgeoisie. They acquired property, collected rents, built buildings, bought from the workmen and merchants. As they strengthened themselves they gave economic impetus to the city and to the Duchy. These religious and economic activities tended to adhere in mutual strengthening — the centripetal principle again and still functioning.

We may suppose that prosperity and peace go together; in the Luxembourg of the Middle Ages such was the case. In a period of constant wars the territory of Luxembourg was not often violated. The warlike Luxembourgers took their wars elsewhere. They did not have to suffer any important battles on their own ground or in and around their fortified city. Neither force nor temptation, then, prompted the citizen or the monk or the nobleman to play renegade to his own native land. This point calls for some amplification.

The amalgamation of Luxembourg into Burgundy was slow and troubled,[2] but no slower and no more troubled than one would expect in the surrender of sovereignty, a surrender that would last 400 years. Consider the full extent of the possessions that the Duke of Burgundy ruled: Burgundy and Upper Burgundy in France (since called Franche-Comté), along with Charolais, Nevers, and Artois; Flanders, in the Netherlands, along with Antwerp, Mechlin, Brabant, Limbourg, Namur, Hainaut, Holland, Zeeland, and Friesland.[3] Luxembourg was only a relatively small segment of all this. Its citizens were slow to capitulate. It was not until 1451 that the Estates took the oath of homage to Philip of Burgundy as sovereign *engagiste;* even then they did not consider him their duke, who legitimately was Ladislas, King of Bohemia and Hungary. In 1461 the Estates did recognize Philip as their legitimate sovereign. A further step in amalgamation came in 1473, when Philip's son and successor, Charles the Fearless of Burgundy, established Mechlin as the center of high justice for all his possessions, including Luxembourg. Charles's daughter Mary, who succeeded him as Duchess of Luxembourg, cemented relations still more firmly. France had coveted Burgundy, including Luxembourg, and sought to acquire it by marrying its Prince Charles to Mary. But once again Luxembourg failed to become French when Mary married Maximilian of Austria, a Habsbourg, who became Emperor; and once again Luxembourg remained within the German orbit. Mary had the ramparts of Luxembourg strengthened and furnished with cannon, a move that again helped frustrate France when France launched an attack on Luxembourg in 1479. This abortive attack resulted in firming up the Burgundy connection, for some Luxembourg nobles who had inclined to France gave up that adherence, and Luxembourg was drawn to a firmer unity.

Before she was 25 years old Mary had won Luxembourg loyalty to Burgundy by restoring to Luxembourg City its city hall; by ratifying or restoring the granted privileges of towns, monasteries, and corporations; by designating certain taxes for strengthening the ramparts; by restoring the confiscated seal; and by giving to Luxembourg City the lower course of the Petrusse. At the age of 25, when the Burgundian possession of Luxembourg had lasted some 40 years, Mary died.

Two important facts, among those that we have been articulating, come into focus. The first has to do with the Duchy's success in maintaining its identity. Within the Burgundian federation of dukedoms, marquisates, and counties listed above, Luxembourg had its own governor and administrative council to manage its affairs; it continued in its customs and local institutions the habits of centuries; the three Estates continued to function as representatives and spokesmen of the country; it maintained its Court of Nobles.

The second fact is of monumental importance. Not particularly noticeable at the time of its occurrence, it determined the fate of centuries. We can put it into a capsule thus: Mary of Burgundy in 1477 married a Habsbourg (German) instead of a French prince; of this union was born Philip the Fair in 1478; at the age of 18 Philip married the Infanta Joanna, daughter of Ferdinand and Isabella of Spain. Thus it was that Luxembourg was to leave the orbit that it had, to an extent, independently maintained within the hegemony of Burgundy and, under the mastership of Spain, become only a segment of a unit known as the Low Countries. The comparative ease of the 40-year process of becoming Burgundian now gave way to destructive threats and stresses.

* * * * * * *

In the 16th century Luxembourg entered a long period that we shall designate the Middle Years, a term that we apply only to

Luxembourg in contrast to the Europe-wide application of the terms Middle Ages earlier and then the Renaissance.

We remember that Luxembourg came into being in 963 when Sigefroid built his castle on the rocky promontory called the Bock in Luxembourg City. In 1543-1544, almost 600 years later, the castle of Luxembourg, along with the Abbey of Altmünster, was destroyed. This act of destruction, which came about when France seized the city and then was forced to surrender it to the German or imperial forces, was a kind of watershed in the affairs of the nation. It symbolized the reversal from national integrity to national absorption. The imperial finger would from now on dispassionately move the Luxembourg pawn.

Even so, that pawn would never be swept from the chessboard of Europe. Now, for long years to come, it is the fortress, rather than the city and the geographical area, that will define Luxembourg's international importance.

The fortress took its significance, not from its national character, not from its being Luxembourgish, but from its international or extranational character. The fortress meant much to Germany, to Austria, to France, to the Low countries, to Spain. But apart from its being a market for local services and goods and a place of employment, what possible national significance could it have had in those long centuries of foreign ownership? In the twentieth century we may find the paradigms of the Luxembourg of the Middle Years in the European occupied countries of the World Wars' aftermath. Germany was no less Germany during the Allied occupation of the 1920s; indeed, the German national consciousness coalesced into the Hitlerian nationalism of the 1930s. France of the occupation years during World War II only became more self-consciously French. The East Germany of the late 20th century is probably not Russion in spirit, however much it has become communistic in the Russian manner. We have no reason to suppose that the Duchy of the 15th, 16th, and 17th centuries — of the Middle Years — became Burgundian in spirit when Burgundian princes were dukes of Luxembourg, or became German when emperors were also dukes, or became Austrian, or became French, or became Spanish.

Whatever the reason, the foreign sovereigns gave themselves the title of Duke of Luxembourg along with their more grandiose significations as prince and king and emperor. It was a matter of property, of course, and a matter of income. Property and income could have continued to adhere to them had the title itself lapsed, but the title did not lapse. We are justified in making much of the symbol.

* * * * * * *

After the death of Mary of Burgundy, Duchess of Luxembourg, in 1482, let us make our target date now the year 1555, when Charles V abdicated his dukedom in favor of his son Philip. This Duke Philip a year later would be Philip II, King of Spain. Within those years, (1) the German orientation of Luxembourg was confirmed and (2) the Spanish mastership of Luxembourg was tragically imposed.

Mary's son Philip the Fair and her grandson Charles V both acceded to the dukedom when they were very young. Philip's father Maximilian, King of Austria and German emperor, acted as regent and exercised the ducal powers. When Philip died at the age of 28, his heir Charles spent his minority under the regency of his capable aunt, Margaret of Austria. Despite, then, the immensity of the geographical powers to which Philip and Charles both acceded, their rearing and their point of view were Germanic. We must remember that at this time, and ever since the domination of Burgundy, the Duchy of Luxembourg was a part of the Low Countries. Administration of the Low Countries centered in Brussels. This identification, which was arbitrary and unnatural, would lead to desperately unhappy circumstances for Luxembourg.

The symbolic designation of the dukes of Luxembourg significantly continued in full force, giving the Duchy a continuing individualistic identification through the turmoils to which it would now be subjected. When Philip was 16 years old he had himself declared Duke of Luxembourg. When he was 22 (1500) he came to Luxembourg to receive the oath of homage from the Estates. When he was 27 (1505) he came again to Luxembourg, at which time he declared the Court of Nobles the high legal authority of the Duchy, its decisions without appeal. His son Charles V (known in European history as Charles-Quint) was declared Duke of Luxembourg when only six years old, upon the death of his father Philip. Such designation served notice on France that Luxembourg was and would continue to be within the Empire. Charles was declared of age when he was only 15 years old (1515); by the age of 16 he was King of Castile and King of Aragon; by the age of 19 (1519) he was Emperor. The destinies of Luxembourg and of the European world were in the hands of a mere boy. History does not attribute the troubles of Europe at this time to the immaturity and inexperience of its most powerful leader. Yet one wonders about the intestine ambitions and machinations of the strong men under him, and about the presumptions and egregiousness of his enemies, counting upon their own acumen to challenge the powers of an untried adolescent. Certain it is that embroils and martial clashes followed upon Charles's assumption of European powers. We may make the generalization that the martial clashes involving Luxembourg at this time derive in large part from its identification with the Low Countries.

We may search in vain for any natural explanation of the political phenomenon of the Low Countries. No geographical features, other than contiguity, explain a single political identity for the sweep of territory from the North Sea to the Moselle and the Rhine Rivers. The monotonous alluvial and marine plains in the western half have the identity of like terrain. To the east of the Meuse River the Ardennes Mountains take their rise and undulate in forest, range, and ravine across half of Belgium, across the width of Luxembourg, and into Germany (with the name of the Eifel). Geography, then, divided the Low Countries in half.

History divided up the two sections further. In prehistory apparently, in the days of the Celts, at the time of the Romans, in the Merovingian and Carlovingian epochs these areas had been subdivided among contending tribes, each of which developed its own patois and mores; as time passed contiguous tribes made comfortable or uncomfortable accommodations into larger groups; and then there were conquest and marriage to complicate relationships in such a way that peace was impossible. Out of all this evolved the Low Countries, in which political unit no subunit had less natural reason for being a part than Luxembourg. In the twentieth century the name Pays-Bas for the Netherlands, and the name Netherlands itself, makes sense. One general reference that puts the Netherlands and at least part of Belgium together under the term Low Countries makes sense. The term Low Countries employed to include the old Duchy and the present Grand Duchy except for political reference in centuries past makes no sense whatever. Yet by marriage and conquest Luxembourg was a part of the Low Countries, subjected to the same overall laws and edicts and levies and restraints as the other parts; and caught up in the armed conflicts, the attacks and counterattacks, like an innocent citizen caught in the dark streets between fighting gangs of ruffians. Thus it was that its castle, a national nucleus, was destroyed, and its fortress, an unnatural and unnational concoction of foreign powers, became a fulcrum between those powers that was the focus and the battleground of international contention.

* * * * * * *

Let us be reminded that we have been making 1555 our target date for this section. We should note, though, that a decade earlier, in 1545, Count Mansfeld became Governor of the Duchy of Luxembourg. In personality and in action he was a strong man. Though only an agent of the Duke-Emperor, he fixed his personality on the Duchy as its leading man. A ducal palace no longer existed; therefore he built his own palace, one of the great palaces of Europe apparently; we must say apparently, for it too was destroyed completely. He inherited the administration of a going concern, there was a major fortress, and there was a Council of 10 members that administered Luxembourg under the authority of the central government in Brussels. All this added up to a continuing Luxembourg identity within the larger administrative unit, consisting of seventeen provinces, that constituted the Low Countries; if Luxembourg did not have real autonomy, at least it ran its own affairs within the structure of the imperial unit. For a time there appears to have been a kind of prosperity for Luxembourg City, if not for the province as a whole. Where the old town hall, destroyed in 1554, had stood was erected in 1572 the new town hall that one day would be converted into the present-day grand-ducal palace. In 1563 Mansfeld built the magnificent palace to which we have alluded.

But all in all the long years of Mansfeld's governorship (he died in 1604) and the century after were a time of stress and suffering for the Luxembourg people. Prosperity came to the capital city as an administrative center for the Spanish domination and military rallying point; but that prosperity was more foreign than native. Moreover, outside the capital the farms and towns of the Duchy had to bear the merciless sweep of plundering armies, the cruelties of oppression and the poverty brought on by preemption of crops and money.

We are always confronted by the problems of perspective. When we speak of Philip II of Spain as Duke of Luxembourg, we must remind ourselves that the Duchy was to the empire of Spain as a copper penny is to a one hundred dollar gold piece. Philip commanded a full half of the world, west and east, and was a claimant to still more. His riches were vast beyond comprehension. Even within the Low Countries, of which Luxembourg formed a part, Luxembourg was the poorest of poor relations. We have noted that Luxembourg City had 13 guilds; Brussels had 52. Have we ever heard of tapestries of Luxembourg, of armor, of paintings, of gold work, of churches, of flowers and gardens, of stained glass? The population of Brussels was 100,000; that of Luxembourg, fewer than 5000. The population of the 17 provinces of the Netherlands was at least 3,000,000; of the single province of Luxembourg, possibly 500,000, more or less (one estimate puts it at only 150,000). The seven provinces from which the modern Netherlands derived contained 12,600 square miles; the Grand Duchy consists of 999 square miles. The circling walls of Ghent measured nine miles; those of Luxembourg, three miles.

Having mentioned the seven — and the 17 — provinces, we should take some care to explain. In the 17 provinces there were "208 walled cities, many of them among the most stately in Christendom" — Luxembourg City would hardly have ranked among the most impressive of them. In the Netherlands there were six universities by 1648; in Luxembourg, none.

A pragmatic sanction issued by Charles V in 1549 established 17 provinces as one governmental unit under one central government located at Brussels. Of those 17 provinces, 11 retained their own individual governmental organizations, among them Luxembourg. Even as centralization and subordination wrapped them round, there struggled within the official cocoon the spirit of local freedom that would take, before long, the shape of rebellion. Motivating the rebellion was the desire for civil liberty and independent religious affirmation. The high level of culture that made of the Netherlands the leading area of the world in learning, business, and art was obvious and incontrovertible evidence to the citizens themselves of the rightness of their expectations and demands.

In 1549, at the instigation of Charles V, the provinces were required to swear fealty to his son Philip, and for his part Philip swore to maintain all ancient rights, privileges, and customs. One might say so far so good. Except that throughout the provinces to the west and north protestantism had established itself as the very kernel and seed of the spirit of freedom. By 1549 the conflict between the protestant republic and the Catholic emperor had been exacerbated, and in 1550 Charles undertook to burn heretical men at the stake and bury heretical women alive. In his Catholic fervor Philip II perpetrated the iniquitous inflictions of the Inquisition upon the Netherlands. The Netherlanders' republican spirit grew inflamed; their instinct for self-government found action in arms. The presence of Spanish troops, the intensified Inquisition, the cruelties of Alba, the reorganization of the bishoprics as a means of eradicating heresy — all these were the bitter and painful stimuli of the rebellion that flared and worsened in the 1560s.

Presenting the Netherlands thus, we tend to view Luxembourg out of focus. Let us sharpen our lens. Luxembourg was only one-seventeenth of the Netherlands. Of all the provinces, though, it was the most extensive. It was the most distant from the center of those issues that moved the united 17 to revolt. While the condition of the Catholic church in Luxembourg was hardly strong, because of weakened institutions and a careless clergy, protestantism had nothing to with the Catholic weakness; protestant tendencies there were less than negligible. No activities of the Inquisition whatever manifested themselves in the Duchy. In respect to religion, then, Luxembourg was without motivation in opposing itself to Spain.

Other factors weighed more than religion. Most important of all, perhaps, is the fact that Philip was not king of the Netherlands. Not king, the man who began all his communications to the Netherlands "Yo el rey"? No, for in the provinces he was merely duke of this one, or count of that one, or lord of the other one. The individual provinces had no king, wanted no king, would have no king, though collectively they were under one sovereign. Thus Philip was Duke of Luxembourg, King of Spain, but not king of the united country. We cannot make too much of this point, for it goes a long way to explain the Lowlanders' self-justification in their resistance to regal restraints and exactions. They were willing enough to have a head of government with the title of king, but the rights remaining to him would be only the rights left after the people had defined all their liberties. They were republicans, not monarchists. And when the exactions employed unimaginable cruelties and the most unreasonable demands, offending the conscience and appalling the spirit, the people had recourse only to revolt. They paid a prodigious price for their independence.

*　　*　　*　　*　　*　　*　　*

We began this chapter by asking, "Why was Luxembourg, as a political entity, not subsumed, absorbed, blotted out?" We shall come to the conclusion that the reasons were geographical, political, and religious. It is best to arrive at those reasons slowly.

First, let us fix Luxembourg geographically. As firmly fixed in the national consciousness as the fact of Sigefroid's founding of the nation in 963 is the fact of the nation's being reduced to its present size by three partitions of a much larger national entity. As we accept the first fact as much by faith as by proof, so must we accept the other.

What was the national entity from 1555 to 1659, the date of the First Partition? Charles V declared 17 provinces to be one nation in 1549. Motley introduced his great study thus: "The north-western corner of the vast plain which extends from the German ocean to the Ural mountains is occupied by the countries called the Netherlands. This small triangle, enclosed between France, Germany, and the sea, is divided by the modern kings of Belgium and Holland into two nearly equal portions."

Where is Luxembourg? Such a generalization and such an omission are characteristic of the histories that deal with western Europe. It is Belgium that is referred to, leaving the reader to infer the inclusion of Luxembourg and, too, leaving the reader uninformed.

As a part of the Netherlands, Luxembourg was in union with those provinces in revolt. The sequence of the first cruelties against protestants by Charles V, the policies of suppression by Philip II, the introduction of the Inquisition, the infliction of unimaginable barbarities, the increasing number of insurrections, armed revolt and pitched battle and extended campaign — this sequence involved the Duchy of Luxembourg as one of the 17 provinces, yet left her peculiarly removed from the heat of the fray, the clash of arms. For Luxembourg, secure in her Catholicism, was free of the Inquisition. What sufferings she endured — and she endured many — were not those of murders and reprisals; so that she herself was not in a condition of revolt against Spain. So pronounced, then, did her separation from the revolutionary spirit of the Netherlands become that she, along with nine other provinces, henceforward known as the Spanish Netherlands (but often referred to by modern historians as Belgium) abandoned the cause that was to make the ensuing nation of the Netherlands great, and began the process of dissolution that eventually would lead to the poor and reduced nation out of which the Luxembourg of today would evolve.

The seven provinces that remained in revolt against Spain were, from January, 1579, known as the Union of Utrecht or the United Provinces. The Spanish Netherlands were known as the obedient provinces; with them we have to deal.

During the very years that the glories of the Netherlands were being dimmed, its cities sacked, its churches desecrated, the city of Luxembourg was taking on such luxuries as it had not known before. We have mentioned the magnificent castle built by the governor of the province, Count Mansfeld. We have mentioned the new city hall, which was to become the grand-ducal palace that we know today. The building of the Jesuit College took place in the early 1600s; today it is the National Library. Next door rose the Jesuit church; today it is the cathedral. The Neumünster Church and the reconstructed Hospital of St. John rose in the

Grund below the Bock. A church called the Mother of God Chapel was built in the 1620s near the west end of the walled town. The Dominicans built in the 1630s. St. Michael's Church was enlarged. None of these impresses by size or grandeur, but they all have a certain elegance, a certain affirmativeness that seems to speak of the self-confidence of their builders. In a time of trial and tension what could that self-confidence derive from?

Luxembourg was loyal to Spain. It was totally Catholic. It was the bridgehead from which Spain made its approach to the Netherlands and the staging point from which troops were directed against the Netherlands. Its governor-general, Mansfeld, was one of the most powerful leaders of the Spanish authority; he rallied in little Luxembourg City an opulent and arrogant staff. Alba as governor-general of all the Netherlands (1567 to 1573) gave way to Requesens (to 1576), to Don Juan of Austria (to 1578), and to the Prince of Parma (to 1592). All these rank among the most brilliant generals of history, as they rank among the cruel and perfidious. In their power they shed some sort of glory on the little Duchy, which formally in 1579 declared its separation from the Netherlands and its adherence to the ten provinces that were called the Spanish Netherlands. Prince William I of the Netherlands spoke of these ten as the disunited provinces; Motley speaks of the "epidemic treason" that motivated them. Within these collective circumstances Luxembourg City built and grew stronger and fed itself on the frightful costs of the Netherlands war, while the countryside suffered from the deprivation and rapine of mercenary soldiers unrestrained by civilized discipline.

Whether disunited or actually treasonous, Luxembourg was not inviting for itself a happy future. Wars would claw at it and strike at it for decades to come. Spain's mastery would continue to lay its blight on the Duchy, only to be yielded to another mastery and a loss to the Duchy of some of its richest territory.

* * * * * * *

It remains for us here to look at the religious reason that Luxembourg was not "subsumed, absorbed, blotted out" in those Middle Years.

Luxembourg remained unequivocally Catholic. Had protestantism been a strong, moving force, she would have found herself sympathetically stirred by the religious impulses sweeping the Low Countries and would have been caught up in the martial enthusiasms that supported those impulses. Because she did not invite religious vengeance and repression, as they identified the Inquisition, she was spared the horrible exacerbations of torture and death that scarred the United Provinces. When the day of Spain's weakness came and other powers took her possessions from her, Luxembourg was still a Catholic duchy in its entirety and so remained.

Perversely, though she was a political entity and Catholicism was totally her religion, she was not a religious or Catholic entity; and this seeming contradiction was a powerful element of her independence. She had never been herself a bishopric or come under the jurisdiction of a single bishop. In church administration over the years she belonged to Trier, Metz, Cologne, Liège, Verdun, Reims, and Namur.[4] What a confusion! Except that this very diversity wove a kind of lifeline to her individuality. Had she been one bishopric she might have been appropriated by another bishopric or duchy or county or kingdom on one side or the other as an entirety. But Liège was jealous of Trier, Trier of Metz, Metz of Liège and Trier, and so on. Each wanted to continue the money tribute that it had grown accustomed to receiving; each had no intention of lessening its revenues by allowing the part of Luxembourg under its jurisdiction to be taken over by another jurisdiction.

Philip II perhaps was reasonable in projecting the redistribution of the four Netherlands bishoprics under 14 new ones, including one for Luxembourg. But the project failed as far as Luxembourg was concerned, and in 1564 the administrator of the change, the villainous Cardinal Granvelle, was forced to leave the country. Thus the very perversity of conflict of interests favored by the jurisdictional divisions clouded the vision of the political predators, and Luxembourg continued to be a political unit through the foul political weather of those troubled times.

NOTES: Chapter IX

[1]John Allyne Gade, "The Monasteries" in *Luxemburg in the Middle Ages* (Leiden, E. J. Brill, 1951) pp. 32-46.

[2]A. H. Cooper-Prichard, *History of the Grand Duchy of Luxemburg* (Luxemburg, P. Linden, 1950), pp. 92-99.

[3]Ibid., p. 94n.

[4]Albert Calmes, *Histoire Contemporaine du Grand-Duché de Luxembourg* Vol. I. (Luxembourg, Imprimerie Saint-Paul, 1971), p. 479.

Chapter X

F

The Seventeenth Century: Part I

OR ALMOST 150 YEARS NOW, in the last quarter of the twentieth century, the Grand Duchy has sat securely on the face of Europe, reeling under dire threat and danger, but anchored there as a political entity to be reckoned with. For 400 years before that it stayed alive as a much more extensive duchy, even as great powers, one after another, imposed their power and their will on it. Wounded to the death, it could not die. We have said earlier that the reasons for its perseverance were geographical, political, and religious.

Geographically Luxembourg was far enough removed from the other provinces of the Netherlands in the 16th and 17th centuries that it could not rally its interest or spirit to support of the Netherlands cause. It had no indigenous impulse to commerce, to art, to manufactories, to architecture strong enough to compete with the domination that Spain imposed on it. Its agriculture, its material resources, its population were not copious enough to compel it to competition. Its agricultural land was poor. Its forests were vast, a hindrance to communication, a barrier to east, north, and west. What is more, the prince-bishopric of Liège held territories from north to south that split Belgium in two and hindered the flow of influence from west to east.

Coveted and dominated, still Luxembourg felt its own personality and yielded itself to no other power. The Netherlands would have been glad to keep it within the Netherlands orbit. In the abstract one might suppose that all of it might have become a part of greater Belgium by a kind of absorption. France coveted it voraciously. Germany considered it reasonably to be German. And of course for 178 years and more Spain considered it to be its own. Politically there are the factors of its continuing to be an entity. No one of the powers could reconcile itself to permitting any one of the other powers to absorb it. It was a cynosure, alluring and defined. Each power wanted to hold it in its hand, as it were; and held in the hand it was solid enough to be clasped, not filtering through the grasp like water or sand.

But in those years preceding and following its separation in 1598 from the United Netherlands Luxembourg was sore beset. The plague ravaged the Duchy time after time — in 1514, 1555, 1604, 1612, 1626, 1636-37. As the stronghold of the Spanish and Royalist party, its capital became a target of the protestant Netherlands' opposition. After the assassination (arranged by Philip II) in 1584 of the Netherlands' great leader William, Philip had awarded William's Luxembourg property, including Vianden, St. Vith, and Dasburg, to governor Mansfeld. An attempt at revenge was inevitable. The Dutch twice ravaged the country to the north of Luxembourg City. During the second marauding by the Dutch the French attacked the south and occupied Ivoix, Montmédy, and Virton. In 1597 the French made two more attempts to take Luxembourg. The Dutch continued their marauding in the Duchy: in 1604 much of St. Vith, Bastogne, and Mersch was laid waste.

The ill and aging Philip gave up neither his claims to sovereignty of the troublesome Netherlands nor his Catholicism. But their situation, continuing to be unsettled, prompted his designing a new and final move: he transferred the Netherlands as an independent kingdom to his daughter Isabella and her husband-to-be, Archduke Albert of Austria, who was already serving as governor-general. The joint sovereigns would be known as the Archdukes. In the event that there was no heir, the Netherlands would revert to Spain.

We should look ahead now to 1659. In that year the Duchy of Luxembourg saw its territories reduced on its southern border. France, by the Treaty of the Pyrenees, took that territory. What concerns us is (1) the series of events, from the Archdukes to the 1659 treaty, that brought that treaty about; and (2) the character of the country at that period.

First, the series of events: the advent of the Archdukes in 1598, the refusal of the seven northern provinces to give their fealty to the Catholic Archdukes, devastation of the country by the Dutch, a truce from 1609 to 1621, consolidation of law under the title of the Belgian Law (the *Droit Belgique*), the growth of Catholic foundations, the death of Archduke Albert in 1621 and the reversion to Spain, the Thirty Years War, and the Treaty of the Pyrenees. In those years the tribulations far outweighed whatever amenities the Duchy may have enjoyed. Attack, suffering, and deprivation prevailed over the shorter periods of peace, some little surge of building, some new roots of Catholic education. Chiefly the Duchy played its role grown familiar through the centuries, that of a self-conscious entity attacked from without, dominated by a great power, and nurturing its Catholic religion to the exclusion of any other spiritual and intellectual influence. In contrast, the United Netherlands, defying all the other powers, asserting its independence of Catholicism, competing on the high seas and in the Far East, was living its greatest, its most inspired, its most fruitful century. It was the century of Grotius, Rembrandt, Spinoza, Vandyke, Hals, and dozens of other scholars and artists who drew their spirit from their country and fed it back enlarged and enriched.

Whose names can we adduce from Luxembourg? Far to the west in Belgium were Rubens and Teniers at Antwerp, but in Luxembourg there are no names and no evidence of work to put beside the names and work that came from the west and the north. Fundamentally loyal to the Spanish king, it was more enervated than stimulated by the political situation and by its Catholic loyalty. Ravaged repeatedly through its countryside, with a population of no more than 5,000 citizens in its capital city, it lacked a critical mass for an excited and productive imagination. Loyal to Catholicism, it had no impulse to reexamine itself in its spiritual beliefs and observations; religious cults and superstitions were as strong as ever. Invaded repeatedly by troops and their leaders bent on flinging their attacks against the rebelling provinces, it was hardly hospitable to men bent on stimulating the arts and practices of peace.

Even so, the self-consciousness of Luxembourg continued to set it apart from its friends as well as its enemies.

The first of the series of events listed in this chapter was the advent of the Archdukes. Philip II had a daughter Isabella. Proposing to make of the Low Countries an independent kingdom, he gave them to her, along with Burgundy, in 1598 and promptly died. That very year she had become engaged to Archduke Albert of Austria, nephew of Philip. They were to rule the ten southern provinces together until Albert's death in 1621. After the Dutch ended their maraudings in Luxembourg, it was not on the whole a bad time for Luxembourg, especially during the 1609 to 1621 peace. Of course the good times were not long in coming to an end.

The reign of the Archdukes gave Luxembourg an opportunity to rediscover and reassert its individuality, so that its future resistance to impingement and absorption was strengthened. The renewal began when Albert inaugurated his reign in Brussels in 1598 before his marriage and before Isabella came from Spain to assume the sovereignty at his side. The scene invites the bravura of a Rubens on a vast canvas in a monumental setting, a picture big enough to do justice to the Luxembourgers' asseveration of pride and independence.

Picture the scene in Brussels: Albert on the throne, the Knights of the Golden Fleece on his right and then the twelve deputies from Luxembourg. The Luxembourgers remain covered. They take the oath of fidelity, but in the German tongue, not the French. They raise their hands, extending only one finger, not two. The representatives of the other provinces protest; Albert replies: "What do you complain of? You have been rebels against God and your king. The people of Luxembourg, faithful to their religion and to the king, can do me honor with a single finger, and even by a simple glance of their eyes, as sufficient witness of their loyalty."[1]

It was now that the ten provinces began to be referred to as Belgium, but at the very start Luxembourg set herself apart, and Albert confirmed her in her individuality. He confirmed to her the privileges that had become fixed by use. A little later, when the States General met at Brussels, the representatives of Luxembourg protested that their country was a distrinct principality, and they refused to participate in the common deliberations. They made their financial support contingent on the Archdukes' oath that they would respect the privileges of the Duchy, and the oath was taken. *Mir wëlle bleiwe wat mir sin* was not to make its appearance as a national motto for another 200 years, but its spirit in 1600 was very much alive.

For a few years, under the relatively enlightened rule of the Archdukes, Luxembourg, along with the rest of the Spanish Netherlands, would enjoy some peaceful progress economically and intellectually. But the death of Albert in 1621 put into fateful operation the agreement by which the Netherlands would revert to Spain in the event that Albert and Isabella had no children. In 1621 the Netherlands again went to Spain; Philip IV at the age of sixteen became king; Spain and France went to war, and operations against the United Provinces burgeoned again; the Thirty Years War (1618-1648) ground its long course in devastation and suffering. The suffering in Luxembourg in death, starvation, and plague was as great as at any other period in its long history. Along the Moselle the towns were laid waste. The soldiers, living in undisciplined disarray upon the country, consumed, pillaged, burned, raped, and devastated. Some localities, to the number of more than a hundred in the small grand-ducal area, were laid waste, some never to exist again. It made no difference whose soldiers they were: the citizens were at their mercy.

Luxembourg was caught between the two jaws of a gigantic pincers—weakening Spain and a France that was equally threatening. If Louis XIV married the infanta of Spain, as was proposed, Luxembourg and the other Spanish Netherlands provinces would go to Louis as a marriage portion. There were further illogical complications: when Spain and the United Provinces (the Netherlands) signed the Treaty of Münster in 1648, those localities held by the Provinces in the Spanish Netherlands were confirmed to the ownership of the Provinces. Spanish power, to which Luxembourg had remained faithful, was steadily draining away.

These tragic circumstances worked their inglorious way to the fateful Treaty of the Pyrenees in 1659. Spain had lost the war.

Now she had to give up to France — Luxembourg had to give up to France — large parts of Luxembourg's southern area.[2] Already under Charles V she had had to give up Thionville, the Johannisberg, and Soleuvre to France. The territory lost by the peace treaty included the towns of Montmédy, Ivoix-Carignan, Damvillers, Chauvency, and Marville. The Luxembourgers refer to their losses as the First Partition of their country; they call it a mutilation. France, on the other hand, considers it the acquisition of a large part of Alsace-Lorraine, a natural continuation and rounding out of a territory naturally French. However this new alignment is looked at 300 years later, those northern areas of France show a French character, rather than a Luxembourg one, merging wholly into France, French rather than Frenchlike. What is an incontrovertible fact is that the rich agricultural area (as well as some districts that became prosperous by industry) of the south of Luxembourg was drastically reduced, so that its economy would be affected ever after. The modern Grand Duchy was beginning to shape itself.

This long era of affliction gave issue in 1666 to an event of major importance in shaping the individualistic character of Luxembourg. With the atrocities of the twentieth century on the world's conscience, still the sufferings of little Luxembourg in the seventeenth century stir awe and sympathy even now. At one period famine and disease wiped out two-thirds of the population. Those who remained alive had to find hope somewhere. Many found it in one aspect of the religion to which they and their forebears had remained faithful.

In 1666 they named the Virgin Mary their patron saint under the title *Notre-Dame Consolatrice des Affligés*. Such she has remained. Their afflictions year after year had put a great burden on their faith. Now their hope of a happy issue out of their afflictions was brought clearly into focus in the Lady of Sorrows, whose own afflictions provided her with a measure of theirs and justified intercession on their behalf.[3] The adoration of the Consoler of Sorrows became something of a cult in the country. Then began the celebration of the Octave, a period of pilgrimage, penance, and celebration that brought all the faithful of the country to the Church of Notre-Dame in Luxembourg City. This veneration and observation gave still more character to Luxembourg City as the capital of the nation; they drew the people together as a nation, so that those faithful who did not actively identify themselves with the participants in the Octave helped define the division between what was Luxembourg and what was not.

Though Luxembourg remained Catholic at the time of the Reformation, it would not be correct to assume that she was purely or strongly so. In the hundred-year period that spanned the sixteenth and seventeenth centuries her churches and monasteries were beset by the same weaknesses and offenses that invited reform elsewhere. The clergy were neglectful, both in the sacraments and in parish work. Institutions lost patronage; in 1600 the Abbey of Münster had only nine inmates. The nobility had gained control of many church institutions, took their income, and manned them sometimes with unworthy relatives. Priests held multiple parishes and neglected them. Attendance fell off seriously; seminaries had poor attendance and ill served those who did attend. At the same time practices that could be labeled superstitious grew — the cult of religious, witchcraft, and concomitant persecutions. Now it was that the famous dancing procession of Echternach, having begun as early as 1100 and kept alive through the centuries, became truly fixed in the Luxembourg calendar of holy days and observations. The procession in honor of St. Adrian and St. Sebastian, deriving from the plague and taking place still in our day, had its beginnings in 1637.

Improvements came about slowly following the decrees of the Council of Trent. The Jesuit fathers established themselves in Luxembourg late in the 1500s. In 1603 they opened their college, which gave a Christian education to Luxembourg youth until 1773. They expanded their missionary work; they set up a new society, the Sodality of Mary. Early in the 1600s the Congregation of Our Beloved Lady began their work in Luxembourg, undertaking the education of girls, a work that continues in this century. Their founder was Sister Monica, born in Luxembourg. They sent out their women to found new houses in Germany and the Netherlands. At the same time the mendicant Capuchins founded cloister and church in Luxembourg City and gradually extended their work throughout the country. From them came missionaries to Louisiana in America.

Tried and threatened by church venality and neglect, as the rest of the European world was, church and nation survived in a unity that has dignified and defined Luxembourg to this day. The Lutheran influence invaded the Eifel; the Calvinist influence made itself felt in the French areas below the southern border of the Grand Duchy. But the Catholic integrity of the Luxembourg core pointed toward the definition as we know it today.

NOTES: Chapter X

[1]A. H. Cooper-Prichard, *History of the Grand Duchy of Luxemburg* (Luxemburg, P. Linden, 1950), p. 113.

[2]It amounted to 2,435 square miles (the present Grand Duchy is 999 square miles).

[3]Cooper-Prichard, p. 121.

Chapter XI

I
The Seventeenth Century:
Part II

S IT ONLY PLAYING WITH WORDS to suggest here that we refer to Philip IV of Spain as Duke of Luxembourg? Or can we thus focus our magnifying glass more clearly on that one small segment of Western Europe that is our concern? Certain it is that the long war from the 1630s to the 1680s between France and Spain had a concentration on Luxembourg, on which Louis XIV cast his covetous eyes. In a very real sense it was the Duke of Luxembourg against whom Louis was fighting, and the dukedom was the prize for which he was fighting.

Before we become more particular about what occurred, we should note who some of the dramatis personae were. Cardinal Richelieu[1] was one of them; it was his resolution on the part of the French that put the play into action. General Beck and General Aldringen on the Spanish side were two others. In 1642 Beck became Governor of Luxembourg and Chiny. Those two men are important to us because, major actors in Luxembourg drama as they were, they had both been born in Luxembourg, in the Grund. There was the Prince of Chimay, the Governor of Luxembourg who had to surrender Luxembourg to the French; and there were the French generals, Créqui and Vauban, who brought Luxembourg to her knees. These were all great men in the European theater who played out some important acts on the little Luxembourg stage.

The drama for the people of Luxembourg was a very sad one. It ended with the demise of the nation in 1684. There would be a resurrection, but in 1684 it was a kind of death-sleep for the Duchy.

We continue to ask questions. When thousands of Luxembourgers were dying of starvation, who were the Luxembourgers who stayed alive? Which of the women were most likely to be raped? When Luxembourg men were counterparts of today's guerilla fighters, which men evaded death? Which men joined the fighting armies, never to return? Did the strongest among those citizens live, or did the strongest die? Were the people owning some kind of property most likely to be struck down or those who had nothing to attract the thieving soldiery? Some directing force stronger than happenstance was at work here surely. We do know that while Luxembourg endured, for the next 200 years and more she endured without real independence, without industry, without riches, without art; so it was until the Industrial Age was well advanced. She did not invite absorption or annihilation by rebellion; she did not die of inanition; she did not surrender the individuality of language or local custom; while her flag continued to fly, still she did not flaunt it. But we do not mean to be looking so far ahead. Our concern here is the events of the 17th century. Our target date now is 1684.

The pendulum is again a useful figure of speech. It is swinging erratically. Spain is in control; the Dutch and the French have the ascendancy; Spanish power persists; France threatens more fiercely; Spanish ownership prevails even as parts of Luxembourg are lost; France wins the long fight — Luxembourg is totally hers. All the while the forceps are pinching, the knives are cutting, the sledge is hammering; the Luxembourg citizen is a personality only in his own consciousness, almost without humanity in the conciousness of the contending forces, neither of which has any reasonable right to exert control over her.

Early in the century Trier once again played a part in Luxembourg's fate, as she had done time and again for a millenium and a half. Trier, threatened by the Swedes in the 1630s, placed herself under the protection of the King of France and admitted a French garrison to her territory on the very doorstep of Luxembourg and its great fortress. So threatened did Spain feel that she sent the Governor of Luxembourg, the Count of Emden, to attack Trier. He took the city and seized the Elector as prisoner. This event occurred in 1635.

Now it was that Richelieu acted. France declared war on Spain. It signed treaties of alliance with Sweden, the protestants of Germany, and the United Provinces (the northern, protestant provinces of the Low Countries). Both the means of war and the stakes were very high. France guaranteed to put 30,000 men into the Spanish Netherlands (the southern, Catholic provinces) and undertook to stir the hitherto loyal provinces into revolt against Spain. Richelieu promised that if those provinces refused to revolt, France would annex Luxembourg, Namur, Hainaut, and a part of Flanders and that the United Netherlands (Holland) could have the rest.

Look at the map. There Luxembourg is, a bone in the midst of ravening dogs. France immediately invaded Luxembourg and undertook to master the country in conjunction with the Dutch. A year later Piccolomini with some thousands of Croats and Poles as troops of Spain invaded France by way of Luxembourg.[2] They destroyed most of the Moselle valley of Luxembourg and towns to the west of the river. They subjected the people to rapine and plunder quite as bad as the French enemy perpetrated. Plague swept the population. When Piccolomini's men were forced to retreat — Dutchmen, Poles, Hungarians, Frenchmen, Italians, Scotsmen, Irishmen and mercenaries all — they ravaged Luxembourg with the indiscipline of brigands and the morality of murderers. The suffering, compounded of brutality and starvation, was immense. A single instance provides the measure of all the cruel instances that filled this quarter of a century: when 500 citizens of the little community of Meix near Virton took refuge in the church, the Bishop of Verdun's men set it afire and burned the 500 alive.

The agony of Luxembourg made its slow way toward the total absorption by France in 1684. In 1643 the south was occupied by the French from Differdange to Echternach. In 1649 the French plundered the Moselle region. In the 1650s the crops failed again and the people starved. By 1659 Spain had no choice but to sue for peace. Supposedly peace was established by the Treaty of the Pyrenees in 1659, when Luxembourg lost to France its southern territories. But the peace was illusory in that Louis would be contented with nothing less than the whole, and despite the so-called treaty he was to continue his attacks for another 25 years, when finally the fortress and the nation would be his.

Louis XIV based his claims on Luxembourg after 1659 on an ingenious wording of the Treaty of the Pyrenees. When Thionville, Montmédy, Ivoix, Damvillers, and others came to France by the treaty, also their *appartenances*, *dépendances*, and *annexes* were to come to France. And what interpretation did Louis give to these words but practically the entirety of the Duchy! He seized on Rodemacher, Hesperange, Rollingen on the Nied and incorporated them into the French kingdom. The French encroachment was unflagging. The county of Roussy, the domain of Preisch, the district of Puttlingen; the church centers of Orchimont, Virton, and St. Mard with dozens of villages and domains; the whole County of Chiny — interpreted as dependencies of Metz or Thionville or Verdun or Bar, Louis laid claim to them and took them. He took Remich and Grevenmacher. In the early 1680s under General Bissy he took possession of the greater part of the Duchy and the County of Chiny for France. Finally, only Luxembourg City held out against him.

The efforts that Spain made during those years of usurpation and encroachment were unavailing. They do have their interest, however, in their contribution to the architectural identification of Luxembourg City and to the extension and strengthening of the fortress. Charles II of Spain (1665-1700), only four years old when he became King, was of course a weak king in a line of feckless monarchs, but some of his representatives in Luxembourg had a strength that won them a place in the Luxembourgian memory. The governor general, the Count of Monterrey (Monterey), and the military engineer Louvignies (Louvigny) applied their talents to strengthening the fortress.[3] Some hundred houses in the lower faubourgs were destroyed to make room for defenses of the upper town, their occupants removed into a new restricted quarter of the upper city. Military barracks, some of which remain today, were built in the upper town. The inner city that we now know was fixed in large part at that time.

That the final assault by France did not begin until 1682 is testimony to the desperate defenses that Spain put up. That it lasted

144

almost two years is sufficient testimony to the resistance and suffering of civilian and military alike within the fortress walls. It is little wonder that what remains in Luxembourg City from before those times is little like its original state, though the outlines may remain. And once more, in Echternach, the Abbey was devastated by invading soldiers.

When the bombardment began in December, 1683, under the direction of Marshall Créqui,[7] he followed Louis's orders to "take measures to start throwing bombs into Luxembourg and try to burn the place"; and a little later, "don't forget to do everything possible to burn all the houses of the city."

The strength of resistance and good fortune were not to sustain them long. The true and final siege began in April, 1684. Créqui had the city blocked off completely by 25,000 men. To defend the city there were 4000 men, including 400 Luxembourg citizens. General Vauban arrived in May and took over technical command of operations. He commandeered more than 7000 farmers and villagers to dig communications trenches. He succeeded in blowing up the palisades and city walls on the northwest side of the city. Closer in, the French mined the walls near today's Charlotte Bridge and blew them up. The people had gone underground and remained in the cellars for two months. The garrison shrank to fewer than 2000 men. On the day of capitulation, June 4, there were only 1300 foot soldiers and a few hundred cavalrymen remaining to desert the city under a rain of incendiary bombs and bullets. Not 10 houses out of 450 remained undamaged by cannon fire.[4] So great was the devastation, when the city fell to France, that the suffering of the people would continue for years, reconstruction (except for the fortifications) would be long delayed, and the population would need the reinforcement of French immigrants to facilitate its slow climb to practical sufficiency.

Strengthening the fortress was a major French preoccupation. The work was entrusted to General Vauban, who brought the fortress to its greatest strength and largest extent. But even after he had finished his great work, the inner city of Luxembourg City was only 880 acres; of those the habitations and streets of the citizens accounted for only 200 acres.[5] What a tiny spot to be the nucleus of a great history! Under the Spanish the extent had been even smaller, consisting of the inner ring and only three major redoubts of what Vauban would develop as the second ring of defense; of the third ring, to be developed by Austria and Prussia, nothing at all. The living conditions, which will be described later in all the inadequacies, must have been even worse than they were later.

The rule of France would last only until 1698. In that time Luxembourg lost much of the self-sufficiency that had characterized her even under the long foreign domination. The Provincial Council, put under the parliament at Metz, lost much of its administrative function. Frenchmen fixed and administered policy. Outside the capital the strength of fortified places was reduced when the nobles held out against the French as at Hollenfels, Meysembourg, Fels, Bourglinster, Pétange, Bourscheid, Schönfels, Durbuy. Their walls were demolished and the moats filled in. The fortified towns lost their walls: Diekirch, Bastogne, Echternach, Grevenmacher, Houffalize, Bitburg, St. Vith. Throughout the Duchy the type of fortification that gave the country its strength began a decline that would never be arrested.

Spain was to resume her sway, then Austria for something short of a century, then France again. Luxembourg's old privileges were abrogated or absorbed. By the time that Napoleon would come to power in 1799 what possible hope or expectation could exist that Luxembourg could ever constitute a nation again?

NOTES: Chapter XI

[1]Cardinal de Richelieu (1585-1642), chief minister to Louis XIII.

[2]"The Croats of Colloredo, the Poles of Isolani, in the country that they were ordered to defend, conducted themselves like ferocious beasts." Paul Weber, *Histoire de l'Economie luxembourgeoise* (Luxembourg, Chambre de Commerce, 1950) p. 49. Ottavio Piccolomini (1599-1656) was an Italian general in the imperial army.

[3]J.-P. Koltz, *Baugeschichte der Stadt und Festung Luxemburg* Vol. I. (Luxemburg, Sankt-Paulus-Druckerei, 1970), pp. 207-211.

[4]Weber, p. 57.

[5]J.-P. Koltz, pp. 230-264.

Chapter XII

The Distressful Years
of 1684-1714

FRANCE TOOK LUXEMBOURG CITY by conquest in 1684; France gave Luxembourg back to Spain by negotiation in 1698.

As a political entity Luxembourg took no action to make herself the property of Spain, to make herself the property of France, to make herself the property of Spain again. She was entirely at the mercy of powers other than her own. Holland feared France and wanted a buffer between the two countries. The Empire — Germany — feared France and wanted to keep the border as far removed from Germany as possible. And France wanted to push her sway as far north and east as possible to the border that she considered naturally hers. That border was the Rhine, a situation that made Luxembourg and the Rhine west bank her object.

Louis XIV's chicanery with respect to Luxembourg is a commentary on the lack of respect with which she was viewed by the neighboring powers. As a rich crook might scatter largesse with smiles and condescension, he bought a certain amount of goodwill in Luxembourg, but he was capable of any demeaning act that would ensure his having his way with the Duchy. To get his way he had to try to fight off Holland, Spain, Sweden, England, the Empire — the members of the League of Augsburg. Let us keep our eye on the map to see how he played the gambling game without any rules.

Review for a moment the provisions of the Treaty of the Pyrenees. The loyalties of the inhabitants were not a matter to be considered. By the treaty the Duchy of Luxembourg lost to France its territory that lay below the southern border of today's Grand Duchy. Louis XIV saw to it that the treaty stipulated that the towns of that area came to France along with their appurtenances, dependancies, and appendages. That provision offered to Louis all the handle that he needed to bring all the Duchy into his ownership. In the previous chapter we listed the areas one by one that his own *Chambres de Réunion* (of which one was at Metz) awarded to him and that Spain was unable to keep in her own hands. Finally, only Luxembourg City resisted falling into his grasp.

When Luxembourg City did finally capitulate to Louis, he continued the same ingenious and unprincipled political maneuverings that he had been practicing for years. In 1679 he had offered graciously to give up his claims to Ghent and Alost if he could have Luxembourg City. But the important question is this: What claims could he have to Ghent and Alost, located as they were far to the northwest in the Spanish Netherlands? Louis offered to have Charles II of England arbitrate the question. But how acceptable could the ally of France and enemy of Spain be to the Spanish king?

When Luxembourg City capitulated in 1684, the truce of Regensburg awarded it to Louis for only 20 years, but award the City to Louis the truce did, in order to thwart Louis in his claims elsewhere. It was, in a sense, an equivalent or indemnification. Louis immediately started the building of fortifications and troop accommodations to a greater extent than Spain had built them. The Church of St. Michael in the Fishmarket, the Jesuit College (now the National Library), the Congregation — all were repaired or enlarged. The forts on the Weimershof Heights were strengthened; Pfaffenthal was incorporated in the fortress by the building of towers and bridges that closed off the valley. Barracks (still there today) were built on the Rham and Holy Ghost plateaus. To accomplish these works Louis brought in workmen from France, Savoy, and the Tyrol, many of whom remained to mix further the blood of the Luxembourgers and to make still stronger the multilingual character of the country. His purpose, of course, was to extend the twenty years into permanency. Then began the wars between Louis and the coalition called the League of Augsburg. Louis was much beset. He offered concessions if he could have permanent possession of Luxembourg City. The offer was inadmissible, but then Spain ineptly inquired about what it could have in return. The situation was mercury in a glass during violent fluctuations of temperature. Louis refused to consider an exchange of property on the grounds that Luxembourg had come to him as an equivalent and, therefore, how could there be a further equivalent for an equivalent? He would have Luxembourg be his permanent possession. The Empire (Germany) wanted both Strasbourg and Luxembourg. Holland, however, wanted its protective line against France to extend to the Moselle, including Luxembourg. Louis made the barefaced pretense that such a line would not include Luxembourg.

During negotiations in 1694 Louis refused to consider giving up Luxembourg, saying that it was necessary to the safety of France; offered to give up Luxembourg in exchange for Ypres, Dinant, and Knocke (again note the absurdity of such pretense); swore that he would not return Luxembourg; again offered to negotiate.

In 1695 Louis agreed to discuss equivalents of exchange for Luxembourg. As a move in the chess game, he recognized William of Holland as King of England. He asked now to receive Condé, Maubeuge, Ypres, Knocke, Menin, Furnes.

With disagreements seeming to move toward settlement, Louis gave notice that if he gave up Luxembourg City, he would do so only if it were reduced to its condition of 1684 with all added changes, repairs, and fortifications removed. William was outraged. The best that Louis had to offer in chicanery, however, was not good enough to fix him in permanent possession. The best that he could achieve, when the Treaty of Ryswick took Luxembourg away from him in 1697, was the continued possession of the southern parts of the Duchy of Luxembourg awarded to him in 1659.

* * * * * * *

But what of Luxembourg, the people of Luxembourg, during these years of international intrigue and battle? By this time the records remaining to us are such that we can sense better the human dimensions of what happened during the years of French possession.

In the early 1680s there were some 450 dwelling places for some 4000 inhabitants within the confines of Luxembourg City. When it capitulated in 1684, 50 of them had been completely demolished, 300 were uninhabitable, and fewer than 10 were unharmed. The people generally suffered very much. During their sufferings a few of them could be grateful for employment given them in building the ramparts or in serving the armies. But alleviation is not the same as free and independent and universal industry. They were at the mercy of their conquerors, often at the mercy of the adversaries of their conquerors. If there was some advantage to French ownership, it was due only to the fact that the French were to be preferred to the Spanish.

The very first factor, apart from the French, is that Luxembourg was poor. The war served only to aggravate its poverty. The aggravation took the form of (1) limiting the crops, (2) diminishing and exhausting crop supplies, (3) ruining pasture and crop land, (4) escalating prices, (5) destroying industry, (6) wiping out trade, (7) imposing arbitrary expenses, (8) levying unreasonable taxes, (9) drafting labor, (10) driving citizens into emigration, and (11) restricting the traditional franchises. We should keep in mind, as we examine these, that the Duchy's boundaries extended well into present-day Germany from the northeast to the southeast. On the west the extent of the Duchy was perhaps three times that of the Grand Duchy. In fact, when Louis appointed a governor of Luxembourg in 1684, he described him as having authority "in all the country dependant on the Count of Chiny" — in itself an affront against the ducal dignity and a misunderstanding of the center of administrative gravity. The whole was a part of the government of Lorraine.

Looking at green and affluent Luxembourg today, we have trouble imagining the true poverty of the Duchy at the time of French ownership. When Louis was struggling in negotiations to keep Luxembourg, an official report to him said that "as for the quality of the country, there is so little for comparison that I am fully persuaded that the chatellainy of Ypres alone is worth more in revenue than the entire province of Luxembourg." What it produced did not suffice even for its own population. Witness an account of Luxembourg officials:

> Of all the provinces conquered by the glorious armies of the king, there is none of them more sterile or less productive than the country of Luxembourg and the county of Chiny. There is to be seen there nothing but wooded wasteland and gorse everywhere, which serves only for the buildings and heating of the inhabitants. The surroundings of the city of Luxembourg are abundant enough in workable lands and prairies, which furnish subsistence for many people and for garrison troops, but the rest of these countries that are commonly called the Ardennes, is filled only with woods and heath, and much of the lands is fallow, and some cultivated one time in twenty or thirty years, where it yields some wheat and oats.[1]

The Oesling in Luxembourg and the Ardennes to the west that swept south into France had seen any agriculture at all for less than 50 years, and the south might better be described as less sterile than the Oesling rather than more productive.

In such a condition of poverty, an order of Louis forbidding the sowing of crops in the lands situated on both banks of the Meuse between Verdun and Mézières — over 60 miles long, 30 miles wide — was particularly cruel. The territory affected included Virton, Chiny, the course of the Semois, and a part of what is now the Grand Duchy.[2] Louis's purpose was to prevent the enemy from drawing support from the land, but the effect was further impoverishment of the citizens. Whether by policy or not, Louis's practice imposed greater and greater hardships. During the first blockade extending into 1682, the bombardment of 1683, and the attack leading to capitulation in 1684, the French made a desert around the city.[3]

From 1688 on, when war broke out anew, Luxembourg as a frontier country had to submit to almost intolerable economic rigors. During the few years that France possessed Luxembourg there were no battles or engagements of particular importance on Luxembourg soil. But as a base of French support it had to put up with the depredations of French troops, the constant movement of troops, both French and foreign, across its soil, the billeting of soldiers, and the care of the wounded. Supply of men and animals came from the land, a land that could not support even its own population in times of peace. Food and forage on hand were used up almost immediately, so that nothing was left for the future. But worse, the presence of a moving army for only two days in a locale was voracious and destructive enough to wipe out productivity for a year or more. Pasture land and crop land were destroyed. Prices soared to levels that, even had the citizens had some money, were beyond the power of citizens to pay.

The sense of independence that Luxembourgers had nourished, despite all ravishment, since the 1200s was much endangered during this French ownership. The Provincial Council was required now to function under the parliament at Metz, being forced to surrender most of its powers to the French governor and French administrative officers.

The records of this period enable us to understand the economy of the Luxembourg region more reliably than hitherto. Over the difficult decades and centuries the Luxembourgers had developed a somewhat sophisticated, though elementary, system of economy. The main factors were crops, sheep, iron, and salt. With poverty the rule, and within the confines of the Duchy a production insufficient for self-support, the population had developed an interchange with Frenchmen on the south and the citizens of Liège on the north. The trade with Frenchmen in crops was uncomplicated, so that crop failure and limitation at this time were generally short of disastrous. But the trade with people to the north was much more delicately balanced and involved. The destruction of it was ruinous.

Iron, sheep, pasturage formed one combination of exchange. Their economic elements were horses and cattle, field crops, and cartage. The balance was delicate and precarious. Liège needed the iron products of the 33 Luxembourg forges that had developed over the centuries; Luxembourg needed the salt that Liège produced. Luxembourg sheep fattened on the local pasturage, but sickened and died if they were kept longer than their maturity. They had to be killed and preserved, and the salt of Liège was best in quality and most convenient for transportation to Luxembourg. Liège and Luxembourg both profited. The carters and the boatmen profited as well as growers and suppliers, and money-scarce Luxembourg did not have to send its currency out of the country. Since the Luxembourgers could not use their pasturage the year round, they received Liège sheep on their farms, along with a profit, which money could be expended on the leather goods, hats, etc. which the Luxembourgers did not manufacture for themselves.

When France prohibited Luxembourg trade with other nationalities, the results were disastrous. The forges were reduced from 33 to 20. The salt from France was of poor quality, so that the meat could not be preserved. Without income from Liège and Limbourg, Luxembourg had no money to buy manufactured goods and had almost no manufactories of its own. Prices went higher in Luxembourg than in Metz, Verdun, and Thionville. Suffering was severe. People fled the land, and the emigration that would mark Luxembourg history for the next two hundred years grew to threatening proportions.

Not only was the land stripped of its fruits, but villages were emptied and towns destroyed — all this without set battles or enemy engagements, but as the result of French policy. By the time that France entered Luxembourg City in January, 1685, 29 parishes and 70 hamlets in the periphery had been evacuated. Unable to find the means of subsistence the inhabitants fled into Lorraine. From then on it was to be a story of blockaded frontiers, the exaction of taxes by both France and France's enemies, marchings, pillages, and destructions.

The limits of the French area in Luxembourg shaped themselves along the Moselle, the Sure, the Our, the Attert, and the Semois, for the rivers themselves and their rugged borders offered a natural defense and delimited naturally the areas subjected to taxation. Except on the west borders we see shaping itself naturally, once again, under the pressures of attack and defense, the country that will become the Grand Duchy.

In the course of these years the French demolished Bitburg (in present-day Germany) in order to keep the enemy out; burned St. Vith, Malmédy, and Stavelot (on the north); abandoned Rochefort, Houffalize, Bastogne, Marche, and St. Hubert (to the west and northwest); razed the walls and destroyed the castles of Hollenfels, Meysembourg, Hesperange, Houffalize, Durbuy, Diekirch, Echternach, Grevenmacher, St. Vith, and Bastogne (the full extent of the Duchy east and west), effectively forestalling any revolt by the Luxembourg nobles. Certainly one would infer the imposition of martial law and martial controls, oppression and restraint, preemption and cruelty.

But the evidence argues some sympathy for the French, some degree of satisfaction on the part of Luxembourg people. French order replaced Spanish confusion. Money poured freely into the employed population of Luxembourg City. An organized police force repressed banditry preying on the country population. Better roads alleviated isolation and encouraged trade. Traditional abuses of taxation were curtailed and venality among public officials was reduced.

Such sympathy is interesting in the light of the Luxembourg predilection for the French, as compared with the Germans and Belgians, in the twentieth century. Luxembourg would be undergoing severe trials in the two centuries that lay ahead; perhaps by comparison the tribulations imposed by the French in the seventeenth century lose some of their terror. The Provincial Council and the Provincial Estates continued to exist, providing the continuity of selfhood, even though their powers were sharply reduced. The people continued the affirmation of their traditional freedoms. The immense efforts at strengthening the fortifications brought a degree of affluence that took the edge off of discontent. In 1685 more than 100 new buildings were completed. The visit of Louis and his court shed a radiance under which the citizens took on a glow of pride. He was liberal in his gifts to religious organizations and the work of education. The influx of Frenchmen, as many as 2000 of them, who settled down as citizens provided for an infiltration of French sympathy and French taste. Thus the filament of a Luxembourg-French sympathy across the centuries, though frayed and attenuated to the breaking point during the years of Louis XIV's ownership, still provided an identifiable connection between Luxembourg's past and the trying future into which it was emerging.

* * * * * * *

The histories speak of "The Second Spanish Dominion" (from January 1698 to January 1715). They might more reasonably describe the period of 1700 to 1713 as a continuation of the French domination, preceded by the Spanish hiatus of 1698-1700, coincident with the terrible War of the Spanish Succession. What happened then to Luxembourg was typically Luxembourgian — confusion, subjection, and suffering.

In summary the Luxembourg sovereignty was as follows:

1698-1700 — Spain. Ownership reverted to Spain under Charles II (the last of the Spanish Habsbourgs) following the Treaty of Ryswick.

1700-1711 — Spanish ownership under Philip V (a Bourbon, grandson of Louis XIV), but French possession and mastery.

1711-1715 — German ownership, but Dutch occupation of the fortress from 1713, determined by the treaties of Utrecht, Rastatt, and Baden, which settled the War of the Spanish Succession.

1715- — Assumption of ownership by Austria under Charles VI.

For the most part these were dreadful years for Luxembourg. The freedom of decision-making that she had lost to Louis XIV continued to be lost to her despite Spain's effort to undo all the works of Louis. The Provincial Estates had not much to do but vote subsidies to France, while France fixed the exorbitant taxes and levies. The nobles had been so weakened that no revolt by them was possible. Once again — or still — Luxembourgers were subjected to the depredations of foreign armies — French, German, English, Dutch; especially hard hit were the towns along the Moselle and the Sure.

And nature once again ravaged the Duchy.[4] The winter of 1709 was the most dreadful in the history of Europe. The cold killed most of the livestock; the very seeds were destroyed; fruit trees and vines perished. Contagious illness spread. Famine followed. Death depopulated towns and countryside, and hundreds of the more hardy fled their land in an exodus that would mark Luxembourg for the next 200 years.

The calamitous times of the Spanish were at an end. The unfeeling interregnum of France was finished. In January 1715 Austria raised its flag over Luxembourg, beginning a domination that would last until the French Revolution.

* * * * * * *

The 18th century was for the most part to be a good epoch for

Luxembourg. But as late as the first decade of the century we have referred to crop failure and famine in Luxembourg. This is a reasonable point at which to examine the ages-old practice of agriculture that barely sufficed through the centuries to keep the Duchy alive.

Except for the fortress itself, Luxembourg had been and remained an agrarian society. Apart from wars (which certainly were frequent and devastating) as the crops went so went the country. A given factor was this: the crops of any one year provided sustenance for little more than one year. It follows, then, that one crop failure brought immediate suffering; a succession of crop failures brought famine and all its attendant sufferings. We should be curious about the elements of agricultural practice that could make persistent an equilibrium of sustenance so fragile and threatening.

In the old Duchy rural dwellers accounted for 96 percent of the population. If the main town, Luxembourg, had a population of about 4000, and Clervaux 350, we have little difficulty in extrapolating the thin and rural circumstances of the country as a whole. In great measure Luxembourg was a land of peasantry. Generally, too, those citizens who practiced some kind of craft, and even those who worked in iron, came from the peasantry and combined agriculture with their hard labor. Even the parish priests produced most of their sustenance.

Unlike its neighbors, Luxembourg had few large landholders. Even as today, the land owners outnumbered the tenants by far. In such a subsistence economy, in which trade existed only on the most elementary level, in which rudimentary roads kept social as well as economic exchange at the most minimal, the tie between land and the land worker was one of the heart as much as of the stomach. Most Luxembourg peasants had neither energy nor inclination to lift their eyes to farther horizons. Such a state of affairs helps to explain the continuation of Luxembourg, at its core, as an entity; but it also helps to explain the almost automatic surrender of cohesiveness by Luxembourgers east, south, and west of the borders of the Grand Duchy when partition succeeded partition. The Grand Duchy, when separation came, lay beyond the farmers' horizons.

It took about 25 acres of workable land to support a Luxembourg family—in the Oesling, more than that. We have the facts of ownership in two communities where agriculture today is among the best that the Grand Duchy has to offer — Lenningen near the Moselle River and Echternach on the Sure. In Lenningen, of 402 proprietors 245 owned less than two and a half acres; 140 owned property of two and a half acres to 25 acres; 17 owners possessed more than 25 acres. An astonishing 96 percent of the population there had little more in good years than would keep them alive. In Echternach the numbers were about the same: 92 percent of the population were at the subsistence level or below.[5]

Other factors must be taken into account in explaining the survival of the rural population. There existed, for the peasants, collective rights that had become fixed over the centuries. All the land not enclosed constituted a common pasture under certain conditions: when lying fallow, before planting and after harvest, and in pastureland after the first cut. Thus even the landless day laborer could keep a cow or a goat, and the small proprietor had use of land beyond his ownership. The poor had the right to glean fields after harvest. All citizens of the community had rights to wood, both for fuel and building, in the forests and could graze their cattle and pigs there.

The emphasis on community is obvious. To eat, to be housed, to be clothed and kept warm, the people of a community were mutually dependent, both the well off and the poor. Not only economically but in self-government this mutuality had been exercising itself since the 1200s, when the spread of the law of Beaumont affirmed such democratic rights as ownership, movement and marrying, election of officials, use of water and pasturage to Esch-sur-Alzette, Differhange, Pétange, and Bascharage; and when other communities, such as Luxembourg City, claimed certain franchises in the choosing of officials, the determining of local laws, and the asserting of common claims.

In the twentieth century the eye discerns still an agricultural pattern that goes back to the Middle Ages. The village is and was the community center. At the outer edge of the village were enclosed, private gardens over which there were no common rights. Beyond the gardens all the land was unenclosed, divided into privately owned narrow strips, often as small as half an acre, and farmed on a system of crop rotation fixed by centuries of practice. Beyond these cultivated fields lay the wasteland of briars and gorse, open to common but generally unfruitful use.

In the Bon Pays rotation followed a three-year cycle: winter grains such as wheat, spring grains such as oats and barley, and a year of lying fallow. In the Ardennes, where rotation gave way to a much less restrictive pattern, the chief grain was rye. Bread was the main food of the population; when the grain crops failed, famine resulted. One pound of seed gave a yield in a *good* year of only three to six pounds of grain. One-third of the yield had to be set aside for next year's seed. Taxes, rent, and levies had to come out of what remained. How tragically narrow was the gap between health and hunger!

The poor crops were partly a result of the lack of manure. The cattle were poor beasts indeed. A cow might weigh 300 pounds. Horses were rare. Because much pasturing was done at the roadside and in wasteland and forest, too little manure went on the crop fields. Since there was not stabling for cattle in wintertime, there was no collected manure to spread. The Luxembourg farmer straddled the dividing line between want and bare sufficiency.

The crafts supplied needs that were not agricultural, but they were really only extensions of agriculture. Weaving, tanning, and leatherwork were of the sort of cottage industry. Most iron workers worked at the forges only in the off-season from the field work. Since Luxembourg was not a country of towns, baking and butchering and clothing making were largely the occupation of the family, with very little exchange within the community, with almost no exchange between communities.

There in the center of Europe, where elsewhere populations had found the means of taking themselves to higher and higher levels of culture, the Luxembourg population remained in a state of virtual isolation from their national neighbors. What is more, village remained isolated from village, sector from sector. We have had occasion to remark often on the forays and maraudings of armies on Luxembourg soil. But those were foot sloggers. They transported material under the drive of discipline and disdain for expense. The citizen could find neither the power nor the finance to carry on trade on the bottomless tracks that constituted the

Luxembourg roads. Except for the Moselle, water transportation was almost nonexistent. The Ardennes to north and west were often impassable. The important road running north from Luxembourg City petered out at Ettelbruck, not more than 20 miles away; pack animals, not draft horses, had to be used. Between Sandweiler and Luxembourg City, a distance of five miles, the cost of a cord of wood increased 10 times. Production and consumption, then, were almost entirely local. The great world of the European cities was held at bay. Until the 18th century its individuality was a hard core that remained impenetrable and almost unchanging.

For the Luxembourg that went to Austria in 1714-15 the change could hardly hold the threat of anything worse than she had known; perhaps it held the promise of something better.

NOTES: Chapter XII

[1]Quoted by Edouard Probst, Le Luxembourg pendant la guerre de la Ligue d'Augsburg, 1688-1697 (Luxembourg, unpublished manuscript, 1935), p. 96.

[2]Ibid, p. 105.

[3]Ibid, p. 97. The particularities of this section derive largely from Probst.

[4]A. H. Cooper-Prichard, History of the Grand Duchy of Luxemburg (Luxemburg, P. Linden, 1950), pp. 128-129.

[5]Gilbert Trausch, Le Luxembourg sous l'Ancien Régime (Luxembourg, Editions Bourg-Bourger, 1977), p. 105. This is Vol. III of Manuel d'histoire luxembourgeoise in four volumes..

Chapter XIII

The Ancien Régime —
Austria in Luxembourg
1715-1795

OR 750 YEARS OF LUXEMBOURG HISTORY one
viewing glass of a low-power magnification has served our purpose. For viewing Luxembourg in the 18th century we must —
and can — use a stronger power. The age of reason begins. The
national embryo gradually shapes itself for the parturition that
will take place only in 1839.

Our beginning date here is 1715, when Austria raised her flag
over Luxembourg. In the political, economic, and social development of the Duchy we perceive a certain unity of purpose and
action that persists until the 1790s. No particular stress of battle
or famine disrupts the steady flow of change. This period of the
18th century we shall call the Ancien Régime. Luxembourg historians use the term to cover some 300 years preceding the
French Revolution; to limit its use to the 18th century will serve
our purpose better. Our concern now will be the years 1715 to
1790. The European world will end the century in revolution;
Luxembourg will find itself playing a part.

In the Austrian Ancien Régime the sovereigns were Charles
VI to 1740, Maria Theresa to 1780, and Joseph II to 1790. Luxembourg, as a part of the Spanish Netherlands, came to Austria
by trade and barter, an artificial route that took no cognizance of
nationality. It was the largest province as it was also the poorest
and the least populated, for reasons that we have been looking at.

Politically, now, it would have 75 years of comparative steadiness. Economically it would improve without changing its character essentially. Socially it would continue to find a self-consciousness that later would see it through revolution and fluctuating sovereignties, coming out mutilated, but alive and potentially healthy.

Luxembourg had seen its last resident prince in the 14th century and would not see another until 1890. That is a period more than twice as long as the existence of the United States. Administration came from a vast distance. Once again what government Luxembourg exercised over itself came at the third level downward. Here, in a sense, the centripetal principle was operating still, for the people had to be jealous of those local powers remaining to it.

The governors, as usual, were foreigners. The private law — the law by which the citizens carried on their daily affairs — derived from the practice of custom: common law, which had not been written down until within a century of the time of which we are speaking. The Austrian sovereign was obliged, in his capacity as Duke of Luxembourg, to respect ancient custom and privilege; he was thus not an absolute sovereign, as Louis XIV had been. But that sovereign wanted to unify his jurisdiction over all his diversified possessions; to do so meant lopping, and bending, and modifying the practices of old. The sovereign as such tended to carry out the laws that he himself had had promulgated. Promulgating them, especially in the realm of taxes, was the business of the Provincial — the Luxembourg — Estates.

Society was divided into three estates, from which representatives made up the legislative body: nobles, clergy, and all the rest. The nobles were a very small body. At the time of the French Revolution there were only 13 qualified noblemen. The parish clergy were not represented at all; the abbey functionaries provided the clergy representation. The commoners who functioned as the third estate were almost entirely bourgeoisie from the towns, so that the peasant and the hand laborer for all practical purposes had no representation. True representation, then, was hedged about and severely restricted. Even so, when the sovereign asked for more money, the consent of the Estates was needed. In some municipalities the choice of local officers lay with the people; in others the Emperor made the choice, as in Luxembourg City, where he appointed the magistry members for life. What legislative duties there were were combined with their political lot. The members of the Estates held their office as large property owners with a command of money. Their vested interest was in conflict with the desires of the people who had no property at all. The proportion of nobles and clergy in relation to the unpropertied was as two to 20. The political winds that would blow revolution would send their eddies even into so subjected and isolated a country as the Duchy of Luxembourg.

We should keep in mind the tininess of the constituencies that we are examining. By the end of the 18th century Luxembourg City had grown to 8500 inhabitants living in about 875 houses. The municipality next largest in size was Echternach, with a population of 2000 in 400 houses. Outside the confines of the present Grand Duchy, there were such towns as Bitburg (in Germany) with 900 in 175 houses, Durbuy (in Belgium) with 350 in 68 houses. From such minuscule populations the self-identity of nationality developed itself. The Ardennes were a barrier to trade and social intercourse, but behind the barrier the people, few as they were, could maintain their identity. Their bilingual capacity contributed to a tension whereby any pull from the French speakers in the western and southern areas had an automatic counterforce in the use of the German language; and, above all things, the common use by all of the Letzeburgesch language within the grand-ducal area and on the periphery was a bond of sympathy among high and low alike.

Affluence for Luxembourg was to be long delayed. Still, the economic improvement in the 18th century over all that had gone before was marked and persistent. No wars tore the country apart. Despite several periods of economic stress, hunger is a better word than famine to describe them. No terrible epidemics wielded their scythes of death, though the rate of infant mortality remained high. Marriages were late — beyond the mid-twenties on the average; death often came early to the wife; the number of children that remained alive was sufficient only to carry the population forward slowly. Even so, the circumstances of life were much happier than those of the preceding century.

The social strata were fixed, though there was a sluggish upward mobility that allowed aspiration to exist and rewarded those sufficiently industrious or lucky. The nobility tended to have fewer numbers, and the old nobility resisted the addition of new. Most important for the little country that after 1800 would move steadily toward independence and democracy were the bourgeoisie or small tradesmen, who were organized in 13 guilds in Luxembourg City and in fewer than 13 elsewhere.

How restricted the economic society, how small the guilds, how unaffluent they were — all this becomes evident to anyone coming to Luxembourg after a visit to Antwerp, Brussels, Ghent. Only one guild had its own house. Since the 13 guilds represented some 1600 workmen out of a population of 8000 in the second half of the 18th century (and since the average family had four to six children), it is obvious that the guilds dominated the life of the city. Membership in 1794 was as follows:[1]

Cloth merchants	49
Bakers	73
Butchers	45
Shoemakers and tanners	125
Coopers	29
St. Eloi (blacksmiths and goldsmiths)	66
Haberdashers (small wares)	244
Tailors	56
St. Thiébaut (charcoal burners)	30
Fishmongers	59
Day laborers	132
Roasters (cook shop proprietors)	148

Officers of these corporations or guilds supplied the only representatives to the city boards and the Provincial Estates. From them developed the propertied class to which would accrete the majority of the citizens as the country made its way to modernity.

This appears to be a clear and simple picture until we face the fact that non-farmers accounted for only four percent of the population. Only four percent! Luxembourg was a country of farmers, with only enough shopkeepers and artisans to supply its basic needs. Consider the town of Clervaux, deep in the rugged Ardennes, with 350 people. Those engaged in work other than farming (most of them probably in addition to farming) were these:

Cloth workers	22
Furniture makers	2
Tailors	3
Haberdasher (small wares)	1
Tinsmith	1
Ironworker	1
Armorers	2
Tanners	4
Roofers	3
Goldsmith	1
Glove makers	7
Masons	9
Carpenter	1

Those citizens on the lowest rung of the economic and social ladder constituted most of the population. To the four percent that made up the aristocracy those citizens who added trades to farming, or who worked at clerkships in relation to the courts, would only very gradually add to their numbers.

* * * * * * *

At the beginning of the 18th century the fabric of the Duchy of Luxembourg was pretty much what it had been in the 17th, the 16th, the 15th centuries. The amount and methods of agriculture had changed almost not at all. The only crafts were still the basically essential ones. The clergy and the church played their usual role. Education was reserved for the few. Government, both local and provincial, had changed little. Life continued to be hard. The future offered no change over the present.

Until the Austrian Habsbourgs came. The age of reason arrived in Luxembourg. Changes would not be quick and dramatic, but changes there would be. Luxembourg would receive some of those changes as impositions of the Habsbourg enlightened despotism, but other changes would come as a kind of undertow sucking the reluctant Duchy into the urgent current of social change. Leadership would come from Vienna; the center of government for the Habsbourgs would be Brussels; a governor would reside in Luxembourg City.

The 18th century was a period of melioration of some of the worst weaknesses of the Duchy. But progress was slow, poverty was general, and new regulations came more by imposition from on high than as an expression of the desires of the people. Strengthening of the Luxembourg fortress was persistent for 40 years. New forts were constructed on the entire perimeter of the city. Casements were cut for miles, on three levels, in the rocks beneath the city.[2] Such work gave economic impetus to the area. Within the walls the abbeys constructed rich buildings to serve as refuges in time of war. Elsewhere within the confines of today's Grand Duchy, though, extensive building was confined to Echternach.

Rural life was not much changed in its essentials. The new highways from Namur to Trier and from Lorraine to the north, both by way of Luxembourg City, speeded up intercourse somewhat and provided a means of mail distribution. Since the local market for iron products was very much restricted, the forges needed the outlets that they found to west and north for the poor products that they produced. The forges remained small, employing on the average about six men, located usually where the ore could be found on the surface, at the side of a stream that supplied power, and in the neighborhood of a forest that provided the charcoal. A rude economic balance was functioning that would provide the potting soil for the rich industrial growth that was still more than a century away. Limited and underdeveloped as iron production was, scattered in tiny communities, it was a factor in the Luxembourg equation and would remain so in the national history until this very day.

Without manure, without lime, with minuscule holdings and very poor soil, stubbornly resistant to change, the Luxembourg farmers (the mass of the population) and the economy in general remained very poor. Emigration, when the Austrian masters needed workers elsewhere, grew to such an extent that it eventually was forbidden by law, and a disproportionately large number of young Luxembourgers joined the army. The introduction of potato cultivation in the 18th century improved the diet and reduced the threat of famine. Attempts to protect the forests by legislation hardly succeeded, but they did succeed well enough to ensure forests for the present-day Grand Duchy.[3] If we strike a balance between the 18th century and the 17th, it is very much in favor of the Habsbourg period, though much behind the rest of Europe in money, culture, and imagination.

Apart from the ruins of castles and battlements, it is chiefly constructions of the 18th century that catch the eye today and supply the architectural charm of Luxembourg. Eighteenth-century noble residences there are standing beside ruined castles, and some castles are 18th-century reconstructions. The bulbous church steeples that surprise visitors derive from Tyrolean workers brought to labor there. Today's abbey buildings in Echternach impress with their reasoned baroque dignity and give no sign of the financial burden that they imposed. The residence of the governor became today's dignified Palace of Justice. Most of the larger farms, where the residence stands on one side of a courtyard of wall and barns, date from the 18th century. There is little besides in the way of architecture in the entire Grand Duchy that impresses with its dignity and beauty. These buildings are witness to social and governmental rule by reason and conviction.

The reason and conviction of the Austrian rulers carried the day, not by the will of the people, but by overriding what the people seemed to want.

* * * * * * *

Whatever takes our attention in those periods preceding the 20th century, it interests us primarily in its bearing on the Grand Duchy that would come into being. Politically the domination and governance were the same for the entire Duchy. Economically and socially, however, there were divisions that would have a bearing on future partitions of the country.

In general, the present Oesling and almost all that then lay to the west of today's western border were a unity in surface and soil. (Excepted were the lands on the French border and the river valleys.) Agriculture was very poor. Raw materials were insufficient. Transportation and communication were difficult. Population was meager as compared with the Bon Pays. There was no room for an influx of people. There was no town that even approached Luxembourg City in population. The natives, in order to survive, had to heed the impulse to develop some income beyond crops.

Iron foundries answered some of that need; of the 33 foundries in the entire Duchy, only seven existed in the confines of today's Grand Duchy. Weaving grew modestly and steadily, with a consequent increase in the raising of sheep; workers employed in weaving grew perhaps to the number of 1500. Leather workshops spread as the resources of oak bark were utilized; there were some 20 of them in the Ardennes. Pottery, paper, glue, and glass factories sprang up. In the Bon Pays there came to be 10 potteries employing 100 workers; some 40 tanners with 40 helpers; some 100 workers in paper making, 40 in weaving, 12 in printing. The traditional guilds led the resistance to this expansion and the changing conditions of employment. In common with all of western Europe, but much behind it in scope and energy, some capitalistic spirits gave restless expression to the entrepreneurship from which one day the bourgeoisie would shape and assert itself. At the distant end of this century would come the French Revolution, in which Luxembourg would find itself caught up, and only a few decades later the Belgian Revolution, out of which Luxembourg would emerge an independent nation.

A difference in language, however, divided the Oesling from the Walloon areas to the west. Today's western border defines in an irregular way the division between the French and German languages. This difference provided for a social differentiation. But whereas the German language would find no foothold in Walloon Belgium, French would make itself at home beyond the French-speaking area in the south of the Duchy; iron workers from the west would be developing foundries farther east and would bring some usage of French with them.

While we are looking for those circumstances that more or less certainly differentiate the areas that will find themselves one day in different countries, we must note the actions of the Austrian administration that were applied without differentiation upon the whole Duchy. The Grand Duchy that will eventuate will derive some of its character from the Ancien Régime.

Habsbourg rule was a rule of discipline applied from above, not a rule given to administrators from below. Subject themselves to the discipline of hard work and subordination, they imposed order and subordination on the people, giving rise to the saying "All for the people, nothing by the people."

1. The Provincial Estates of Luxembourg were restrained by the Empire in their administrative and financial responsibilities. 2. Municipal freedoms, dating from the Middle Ages, were restricted. The people lost their right to elect their own officers. 3. The tight control of the guilds was lessened, hiring was liberalized, finances were subjected to state controls. The guilds were subjected to exact regulations over time and place of meetings, attendance and conduct, and election of officers, with a system of fines for all kinds of offenses. 4. Administration and courts were completely reorganized.

The Habsbourg goal was a reasonable one — improved economic and social conditions. But the rulers pursued it in ways counter to custom. They permitted the enclosure of common lands, encouraging private ownership; regulated the forests; reduced collective rights while encouraging the private owner; attempted to reduce the cruelty of justice, to eliminate torture and mutilation; restrained the vestiges of feudalism whereby seigneurs could put cruel demands on the tenants; spread taxes more equitably; admitted non-Catholics to residence.

Most notably Maria Theresa required in 1766 that a new and comprehensive census be taken, called the *cadastre*, resulting in a more nearly complete registry of land ownership than had ever been in existence before. It gave power, of course, to the government in levying taxes and controlling abuses by the well-to-do.

Is it surprising that no wave of enthusiasm swept across the Duchy? The very poor were deprived of their privileges in common lands and forests. The owners were restricted in their rights over the very poor. The officials who had grown accustomed to their graft and misuse of office resented the restrictions imposed on them. Those who had successfully eluded the tax collector sought to evade being placed on the tax roles. The heirs of the first franchises and rights rebelled against their loss. Catholics were offended by the leniency to non-Catholics. Austria was not an irresistible force, Luxembourg was not an immovable object; but the inertia of Luxembourg, if it may be so described, was an implacable impediment to the momentum of Austria. The great distances from Vienna and Brussels impeded and lessened the effect of decrees and ordinances. Bad roads and rugged terrain made barriers that sometimes the Habsbourgs did not cross. Isolation fed the provincialism that provided a unifying identity to the Duchy. The Duchy might be likened to a swale in which roads petered out, in which the vehicles of social change slowly sank, while it closed over all that entered it and resumed the character that it had had through the centuries. The spirit of its citizens was the very spirit that many years later would find expression in *"Mir wëlle bleiwe wat mir sin"* — We want to remain what we are.

And there was the fact of religion. Luxembourg had been, was, and would remain Catholic. Any power — in this case the Habsbourgs — that sought to move the wheels of government and social change had to reckon with Luxembourg's catholicism. For them, to reckon with it was to act; to act meant to introduce changes and to impose controls, even down to dictating the number of candles to be burned on the altar.

The Habsbourgs' interference in matters of religion was not without precedent. Some state controls had existed since the 15th century. Here we note again the important reality that Luxembourg did not have its own bishopric. Six bishoprics now divided up the spiritual direction of the Duchy: Cologne, Trier, and Metz in the German sphere; Verdun and Reims in the French sphere; Liège, a power in its own right. Any coherence in church matters had to come from the civil government, which imposed its will and authority on acts that normally were the responsibility of the church alone. The Habsbourgs moved to extend their power beyond administration to dogma itself.

Before a priest could be named to a Luxembourg parish, the bishop had to request permission — called a "placet." The church could not summon a priest for disciplinary action without the authority of the Provincial Council. The bishop could not visit his Luxembourg parishes without permission and the accompaniment of a Luxembourg official. Even pontifical pronouncements expressing dogma were subjected to civil examination.

There was reason behind all this beyond the coordination that civil authority could achieve for the disparate bishoprics. In a rude, poverty stricken, backward, illiterate society we should expect to find a secular clergy afflicted with those same shortcomings. The Luxembourg clergy were poorly educated, culturally deprived, ill paid, and, in a general sense, inadequate to the needs for spiritual guidance and help. Most priests were simply a part of the peasantry. The Habsbourgs undertook to improve that situation, a situation that had found little alleviation from the divided constituencies of the numerous bishoprics.

The regular clergy of the monasteries and the working orders such as Cistercians, Dominicans, and Clares were in better case. Their ties with the more affluent were reflected in their houses, their garb, their way of life. Their ownership of property was extensive enough, their luxuries evident enough to elicit the controls that the Habsbourgs were more than willing to impose; and such orders as the Capuchins, dedicated to poverty, working in a society where poverty was frightful, won a place in the national consciousness that could be construed as competition for civic authority. The Habsbourgs took action.

By the end of the 18th century the monasteries had disappeared. In 1773 Maria Theresa suppressed the order of the Jesuits, who had to give up their school in Luxembourg City. In 1783 an edict of Joseph II suppressed all the contemplative orders except those that ran schools and hospitals. The monarchs extended their control by putting off the taking of vows to the age of 25; requiring competitive examinations and attendance at the seminary in Louvain (later a seminary was established in Luxembourg); reorganizing divine services and coordinating parish affairs; repressing all brotherhoods and uniting them in one brotherhood; eliminating many local observances and reducing religious processions to four.

Reason shows its featureless face through all these actions of the Habsbourgs. How could anyone argue against clear thinking and good sense? Resistance to these measures was sullen and deep. Communication and enforcement were slow and attenuated. If Luxembourg swung like a pendulum between regime and regime and regime, we may say that it was the dead weight hanging at the end of that pendulum, inertia heavy within it, requiring, when the force of war was not evident, the efficient working of a complicated mechanism. The mechanism of enlightened despotism was soon to be wrecked. Revolution would break out. Occupation would sweep up Luxembourg into still another regime. New governments would impose new government. And Luxembourg, totally Catholic still, self-conscious in its social integrity, would endure all these accustomed shocks as she had borne the shocks of centuries, indestructible in her nucleus, outlasting all powers, without an iota, really, of worldly power of her own.

NOTES: Chapter XIII

[1]These figures and the figures that follow are from Gilbert Trausch, *Le Luxembourg sous l'Ancien Régime (17*ᵉ *18*ᵉ *siècles et débuts du 19*ᵉ *siècle)* (Luxembourg, Editions Bourg-Bourger, 1977) pp. 103-107. This is Vol. III of *Manuel d'histoire luxembourgeoise.*

[2]See J.-P. Koltz, *Baugeschichte der Stadt und Festung Luxemburg* Vol. I (Luxemburg, Sankt-Paulus-Druckerei, 1970), Chap. XII.

[3]See Paul Weber, *Histoire de l'Economie Luxembourgeoise* (Luxembourg, La Chambre de Commerce, 1950), section "Les Habsbourg d'Autriche (1714 à 1795)" of Chap. entitled "L'Economie d'Ancien Régime."

Chapter XIV

The French:
In Power Again
1795-1815

THE YEAR 1790 FOUND LUXEMBOURG hanging as a dead weight at the bottom of its pendulum arm. Any one of several powers would be willing to set it swinging again, had that power luck and passion and strength to work its will: Belgium (which was shaping itself from the Austrian Netherlands), of which it reasonably was a part, but from which it was always being separated, Germany, Austria, and France. The proximate loser was its present possessor, Austria. Germany would claim it as a kind of blood brother until as late as 1867. Belgium would fumble once, twice, three times before losing its power. France was the proximate winner, taking possession in 1795 and surrendering it again, this time forever, in 1815.

The thousand-year contenders for Luxembourg were caught up insensibly in the process by which they all would miss their mark, so that finally it would emerge triumphant and independent in the twentieth century, secure from all predators now until the barbarians of the future who use the atom bomb to seize — or destroy — what they covet.

Reason begat rebellion against reason. Rebellion against Austria made of Luxembourg once again a battleground. Though the rebellion won for Belgium (of which Luxembourg was one of the provinces) restoration of the old customs and institutions, it opened a way to the domination of revolutionary France and, ironically, the imposition of a reasoned order more sweepingly destructive than that of Emperor Joseph. It took five years, 1790 to 1795, for all this to take place.

Revolutionary America, revolutionary France, revolutionary Belgium — despite all its traditional inertia Luxembourg felt the tremors of its epoch. War, not of its own making, would storm its way across the land. Luxembourg City would fulfill its function as a fortress redoubt. Still a chattel, it would be claimed by another power, conquered, renamed, and redefined. The first move in this direction came with the insurrection of the Austrian Netherlands in 1789. It was labeled the Brabantine Revolution.

Joseph II's reasonable reforms had proved to be too much for the Belgian people: reorganization of the law courts, reordering of the traditional ten provinces (they can be numbered only inexactly) into nine arbitrary circles; suppression of clerical freedoms and functions; elimination of traditional religious observances. The goal of the people now was a republic, which took the name The United Belgian States.

The role that Luxembourg played was pretty much its traditional role. It supplied Austria with 4000 men to fight against the Belgian rebels. Two years later it refused to give Austria aid against France. It was not Belgian, not Austrian, not French in its sympathies. Within its grand-ducal limits, its importance to the Netherlands and to Austria lay in its fortress, which was the rallying point for the Austrian forces when they were forced to withdraw east of the Meuse. Luxembourgers felt their grievances and expressed their complaints, but we can hardly identify a Luxembourg position. In view of the grand-ducal geographical limits, the fixing of which was less than half a century in the future, Luxembourg had an amorphousness antipathetic to consistent and concerted action, either of revolt against the constituted powers or of support for them. Witness the organization of the lowest courts in the province. Those courts existed at Arlon, St. Vith, and Bitburg (all outside the grand-ducal limits), and at Diekirch. For all of the Austrian Netherlands there were two courts of appeal. One was located at Brussels, the other at Luxembourg City. But the Luxembourg court, apart from its jurisdiction beyond the limits of Luxembourg, was divided into a German-speaking court and a French-speaking court. In short, the Luxembourg court was not truly Luxembourgian. The province that belonged to the United Belgian States but did not support it; the Luxembourg that was an Austrian province but not a homogeneous unit capable of self-identification and self-consciousness apparently engendered no spirit that could be labeled patriotism or nationalism. Parochial in the extreme, even its parochialism was scattered, a matter of villages one by one by one, rather than of a province; certainly it was not the parochialism of a nation. Changes within Austria now were not such as to strengthen provincial loyalties or elicit provincial support. Joseph II died early in 1790. The United Belgian States collapsed late in 1790, and the Austrian armies retook all the Austrian Netherlands. Joseph's successor, Leopold II, lived only two years; and his successor, Francis II, only 24 years old, would have the throne only three years.

France, on Luxembourg's southern border, was now to play a mighty role again. The border between France and Luxembourg, so recently agreed on as 1769 and 1779, France would now breech again. Having yielded up those villages and lordships scattered throughout the Duchy that she had owned from the distant past, France not only seized them again but made the entire Duchy her own. Luxembourg became French in October, 1795, by decree of the French Convention. We need only the outlines of the action to know what happened.

Hundreds, thousands of French aristocratic émigrés made their way to or through Luxembourg after 1789. They hurled their defiance against the revolutionary government from their German and Austrian havens. France declared war against the Emperor in April, 1792. The old familiar sweep of troops across Luxembourg began again — from Brabant to the west, from Germany to the north and east, from France to the south; attacks, evacuations, retreats, headquartering, grouping — Luxembourg was on the route to all and from all enemy encounters. Again the people suffered. Across the south and along the Moselle the French destroyed villages, murdered citizens; they destroyed the beautiful abbeys of Orval and Clairefontaine. The blockade of Luxembourg City that began in November, 1794, became the longest in the history of the fortress. Famine subdued the 11,000 to 12,000 men who held out there; they capitulated June 12, 1795. Luxembourg again belonged to France.

* * * * * * *

Luxembourg would be a part of France for 20 years this time. Reduced to its simplest terms Luxembourg did not exist any more. "This glorious little land [a Luxembourg historian is writing] which had given emperors to Germany, kings to Bohemia and Hungary, queens and constables to France! was done away with and given over to oblivion." What had been the Duchy was given a new shape, a new name, new laws, new fiscal policies. What did all this mean for the Grand Duchy that, after 800 and more years of gestation, was soon to be? Despite the hardships and unhappiness, we can view the situation in a favorable light.

First, the new shape. By this time the southern border of Luxembourg had been definitely established by the Treaty of the Pyrenees in 1659 and agreements with Austria shortly before the French Revolution. In giving Luxembourg a French administration, France denominated the core area of Luxembourg the Department of Forests, a political unit integrated into France. But parts of the old Duchy to the north and to the west it assigned to three other French departments or states. The outer limits of Luxembourg were thus being drawn in; for 20 years now large sections that later would be German and Belgian were becoming accustomed to not being Luxembourgian. We can speculate that the fact that these sections had no language in common, and that, on the Belgian side at least, there was little Letzeburgesch to provide a bond with Luxembourg, contributed to a resignation to the separation. In any event, these divisions were throwing ahead of themselves the shadow of the small Grand Duchy that would emerge from the conflict of large nations.

Second, the administration. France imposed a totally new government without reference to the local will. All the old administrative apparatus was wiped out; all governmental activity received the new French apparatus. The jealously guarded municipal rights dating from the 1200s and surviving cataclysm, war, famine, and foreign domination disappeared by decree, as did the traditional administration of justice. There was not even a system of appeal. More strongly rooted in feudal times perhaps than any other segment of western Europe, Luxembourg had those roots cut off. By a tremendous slap of power Luxembourg was knocked into modern times. Government emanated from a central administration of five members, four of whom were Frenchmen. (On the lower level of the towns, however, the native people found a majority representation.) Justice now became more nearly equal for all citizens, high and low alike, so that impetus was given to the growth of a middle class. With Napoleon came the imposition of the Civil Code, which would determine Luxembourg practice to the present day. The government took over the registry of births, marriages, deaths. The metrical system became standard for all the country.

Third, the radically changed operation of the church. Whenever we touch on the subject of the church in Luxembourg, we deal with the very essence of the national consciousness. To some extent the Habsbourgs brought comfort and progress to Luxembourg, but their insensitivity to Luxembourg religiosity aborted their efforts and contributed to their defeat. France brought a larger and different kind of strength to its church reforms. The nation (of which Luxembourg now was a part, not a possession) confiscated the large propertied wealth of the abbeys and sold it to a new kind of buyer — the obscure local bourgeoisie — who thus developed his upward mobility into a force of economic and political strength. Required to take an oath of hatred against the nobility and royalty, some 800 priests rebelled and became either expatriots, prisoners, or fugitives. The citizens were unified in their defense, and either by sullen defiance, sequestering the hunted, or bribery protected their priests as best they could. But large properties that had belonged to the church ended up in private ownership. Practically all the important abbeys in Luxembourg disappeared, only a few of them to find a place there again later. The parishes whose priests refused the oath, and who were protected by the parishioners, often lost their property to confiscation. The strength of the church in economic life was vitiated. Beyond the economic damage was the shocking affront to religious sensibilities. Consider the Church of the Récollets turned into an army magazine; the Chapel of Notre Dame of Luxembourg, the Consoler of the Afflicted, serving as a stable; village churches where the priests were declared renegades closed, pillaged, desecrated. The affront, as we shall see shortly, was intolerable.

Fourth, the changed character of economic life. France legally pillaged Luxembourg. It immediately imposed a tremendous levy, which the country could not pay. It confiscated all funds that could be identified as public. In dividing the territory of the Duchy among four *départements* it gave away, of course, a good part of the land. The money that came from the sale of sequestered church property and that of French émigrés went into the French coffers. Forced loans, paper money, notes without collateral — these sent the value of paper money to one percent or even less. New taxes were imposed on anything that could be identified as taxable, even doors and windows. Salt, leather, tobacco, sugar, coffee were taxed at three to five times the old rate. More and more money was extorted from anyone who appeared to have any. Conscription of men between 20 and 25 years of age was labeled the "tax of blood."

Out of all this sorrow came an action, a purely Luxembourg action, that had never been seen in that country before. Luxembourgers found the affront to be intolerable. They rebelled.

When our goal is to understand Luxembourg as a social and political entity, we cannot overemphasize the importance of that rebellion, called the *Klöppelkrieg*. The war of the sticks — the name itself is an inspiration. The French referred to *l'armée des bâtons* or *la guerre des paysans*. But note: the Luxembourgers called it the army of Jesus Christ! Ardennes peasants, unorganized, with not much more than clubs and farm tools as weapons, presumed to defy the mighty power of the French. Spontaneous uprisings led to attacks on village garrisons, to death, dispersal, capture, trial, and execution. It was a national indignation that prompted the rebellion. It was a national defeat that the inadequate little forces suffered. It was a national retribution that was exacted, a national rancor that burned in the endurance that sustained the population. These may well have been the first labor pains that announced the birth of what would be truly a nation. These were the Luxembourg men who denominated themselves a Luxembourg army: "Peasants with a hard and flourishing strength, like the oaks that cling to the ruddy red rock of their mountains; in disposition stubborn and intractable, resisting all advice, literal minded [blockheads] in their conclusions, like the furrow that their plow marks out; sons of the Oesling, loving better to die in their own country, for their religion and their homes, than to go far away to shed their blood for the cause of their oppressors."

It is not too soon, recounting this event of 1798, to get into our heads a consciousness of that motto which would not yet for some decades be deliberately pronounced: "We want to remain what we are."

Even so, Luxembourg would be French for another 14 or 15 years, and the mercury in her spiritual glass would rise and fall along with that of all Frenchmen. Administration and law took on more order. Napoleon won admiration and support. But the hated conscription lost to the little area 9,000 of the 14,000 young men forced into the French army. When the continental blockades were imposed, prices rose drastically and the poor suffered. With the fall of Napoleon came one more blockade of the fortress, with capitulation following one more time after hardship and suffering. Hessians followed French, in 1815 Prussians followed Hessians; provisional government followed provisional government.

Once again something typically Luxembourgian took place that would help define the independent Luxembourg that would be a nation in the not-too-distant future. Under the Prussian government German was declared to be the official language in Luxembourg along with the French. And so it would be for all time to come.

Chapter XV

From Partition
to Revolution
1815-1839

1813 — King William is named sovereign prince of the United Provinces (Holland).

1815 (June 8) — King William becomes sovereign prince of Holland and Belgium together, the kingdom being named the Netherlands.

1815 (June 9) — Luxembourg is designated a Grand Duchy. King William of the Netherlands is styled Grand Duke and given personal possession of Luxembourg, which is "to be possessed in perpetuity and personal title by him and his legitimate successors: thus is recognized the autonomy and political individuality of the Grand Duchy."[1]

How direct, clean, and simple this statement is: there are no cobwebs, no murky depths, no tantalizing ambiguities.

But such was not the fact. Cobwebs, murkiness, and ambiguity were to plague Luxembourg still, trip up the statesmen who wanted to take forward action, befog perception on all sides, and befuddle geographic definition, government action, and political manipulation. After almost nine hundred years of national identity, Luxembourg is nowhere near out of the woods.

The Luxembourg pendulum is set swinging yet another time, but trembling erratically in the rough impulse that has set it swinging once again.

Why should what had been Duchy now be defined as Grand Duchy? Simply because the King of the Netherlands, taking his place beside the German princes, would not stoop to being called Duke of Luxembourg. He would have himself styled Grand Duke of the Grand Duchy of Luxembourg, or else — Or else what? Grand Duchy it was, for no very grand or reasonable reason.[2]

William the man and Luxembourg the country did not get themselves to this position easily or naturally. Nor can we bring into lucidity easily and naturally the confused and arbitrary and perverse circumstances of Luxembourg at this time. We can only try.

Think back. When France seized almost all of Europe in the 1790s, the Netherlands consisted of the seven northern provinces of the Low Countries, known as the United Provinces. The Habsbourg Netherlands consisted of the ten southern provinces, including Luxembourg. Came 1814, Napoleon's defeat, and freedom (hardly an appropriate word in the case of Luxembourg) of the seventeen provinces of the Low Countires. These seventeen provinces required a new political definition. A solution that could not be accepted was a return to the status of 1794. How unreasonable the situation of the Low Countries was reveals itself in the fact that no reasonable solution — that is, a solution self-evident in its reasonableness — offered itself. What was, then, the solution that was to be imposed? The common sense of hindsight argues against it.

All the provinces except one were united as a kingdom under King William I. Luxembourg was that one province, and it became a grand duchy under Grand Duke William I. King William I and Grand Duke William I were one and the same man. Did this situation come about because the people of Luxembourg willed it? Of course not. When in 900 years had the will of the Luxembourg people determined their political fate?

We begin to make our way through this political thicket by reminding ourselves to view all that part of Europe between the North Sea and the east bank of the Rhine through a wide-angle lens, for the fate of little Luxembourg, smack in the middle, is tied up with the fate of the whole. And then let us use our zoom lens to focus on William I, King-Grand Duke.

First, the overview. "Belgium free; Holland driven back on its own resources; England reformed; Ireland emancipated; the legitimate Bourbons in exile; Spain and Portugal revolutionized! How little now remains of the great work of the Congress of Aix-la-Chapelle, to bear testimony to the political wisdom *de ces braves rois*, who in their estimate of Europe only overlooked the nations which inhabit it."[3] This is the irony of the early 1830s, less than two decades after Waterloo, only a few years before Luxembourg's independence.

Who was William I? First, he was the grandson of the man who had been sovereign of the United Provinces (the northern provinces) when France seized them in 1794. There is logic, then, in William I's becoming King of the Netherlands in 1814. But King of the Habsbourg provinces, the sovereign of which had been the Austrian emperor in 1794? Well, yes. Austria was happy to receive some near-by Italian lands in exchange for the troublesome provinces in the Low Countries.

William was not only the descendant and heir of the house of Orange (Dutch); he was also descendant and heir of the house of Nassau (Germanic).[4] The lands of Nassau were at the eastern extremity of our wide-angle view of western Europe, to the east of the Rhine. The right and left banks of the Rhine — and Luxembourg — constituted a buffer area between those old enemies, Germany (Prussia) and France. Prussia took the lands of Nassau. Their duke required indemnification. The Duchy of Luxembourg, to be designated now Grand Duchy, was that indemnification. Luxembourg came to William, not as one of the Habsbourg provinces, but as a ducal entity defined as compensation for lands lost a hundred miles to the east of the Luxembourg border and held in personal ownership by him.

But all is not that simple.

The allied powers (England, Prussia, Austria, Russia) decreed that the eastern boundary of the new grand duchy should be defined from north to south by the Our, the Sure, and the Moselle Rivers.[5] In general, those lands east of those rivers can be defined as the town areas of Neuerburg, Bitburg, and St. Vith. On the boundary rivers alone, 14 right-bank localities, one of which was Echternach, were cut off from their left-bank counterparts. Luxembourgian from time immemorial, all these communities should henceforth be Prussian. Only the territory of Vianden, on both sides of the river, remained entirely Luxembourgian. Thus it was that Luxembourg, which had already lost its southern lands (410 square miles) to France, now lost its eastern lands to Germany. That consisted of 50,000 people out of a total population of almost 400,000, living on a land surface almost as large as today's Grand Duchy. Sympathetic with Luxembourg itself, we tend to forget to inquire about the shock to the heart and spirit of the people of this territory of a size equal to that of the present Grand Duchy, rent from their blood, their linguistic, brothers. But inquiring, one answer, shocking, to the twentieth century consciousness, is that perhaps the anguish of separation was minimal. After all, these people had never enjoyed the luxury of choice of sovereign or nationality. In any event, the Grand Duchy that we know today has now found its permanent definition on the eastern and southern sides. If in the future it is to be reduced still further, that reduction must come on the side toward Belgium. When that reduction does come not many years in the future, we must entertain the same doubts for Luxembourgers in the west rent from their grand-ducal ties as for those in the Germanic east. Were acceptance of a new loyalty and resignation to a new political fate more nearly a fact than the emptiness of loss and resentment against the preemptors? The actions of Luxembourgers in the next fifteen years provide reason for supposing such a conclusion to be reasonable. They were not accustomed to deciding their own fate. Adaptability was more reasonable than revolt. In view of the larger reality, that Luxembourg, however reduced, endured the crazy vagaries of the first forty years of the century, adaptability proved to be the leaven of overcoming.

William I took possession of Luxembourg in the middle of 1815. During "the regime of the Allies," which had lasted for more than a year before that date, Luxembourg was governed first as a part of the Middle Rhine administrative area, then as a part of the Lower Rhine. Prussian, Hessian, and Russian soldiers occupied it in the spirit of the enemy. German administrators took charge, with German as the official language along with French.

The nervous status of Luxembourg now becomes even more nervous. Supposedly an independent country, she is treated by her owner-king as if she were only one more province to be added to the sixteen provinces of his kingdom of the Netherlands. But in his capacity as Grand Duke, William is a member of the Germanic Confederation created by the Congress of Vienna. Thus Luxembourg is one of the federal fortresses that Germany constituted, and Germany has installed there a garrison of Prussian soldiers that will man the fortress for the next fifty years. From the Channel to the Rhine the Netherlands, Luxembourg, and Germany are an armed buffer against a possibly resurgent France. Luxembourg is leagued with the enemies of France, stretched in its loyalties between east and west, pincered and patronized by both, yet in its essential nature a part of neither. The paramount fact is, in relation to her future and though honored in the breach, that she is an independent nation.

Her independence by statute was at odds with the pragmatic circumstances in which she functioned. With callous insensitivity to Luxembourg's nature and careless indifference to his separate capacity as Grand Duke, William ruled Luxembourg as if it was a part of his kingdom in the Netherlands. It was here that William made his grand error. He was determined to make Holland (whose people were his loyal subjects), Belgium (whose people had not been and who were not now disposed to be loyal at all), and Luxembourg one unified kingdom. In this determination were the seeds of the destruction of that kingdom and the definitive freedom of the Grand Duchy from loyalty to any sovereignty but its own.

Oddly enough, the people of Luxembourg showed little concern. Having had almost nothing to say about their sovereign or their rights or their geographical definition for centuries, they apparently found in themselves now little impulse to reject, oppose, or demand. Their fate was being decided for them by powers other than their own. When William submitted a new constitution or Fundamental Law for ratification, the 73 Luxembourgers who had a right to vote were unanimous in ratification. Most of the Belgians voted against it. But the 2,000,000 Dutch had their way against the 4,500,000 Belgians (note how puny Luxembourg was in comparison). What's more, the Dutch and the Belgians had equal numbers of representatives in the Estates General. Knowing the rebellion that was to occur only fifteen years later, we recognize William's wrong-headedness in all this. "Seven hundred ninety six deputies voted against the constitution, 527 for it. It was, therefore, virtually rejected. But of the 796 opponents, 126 had, in voting, declared their opposition to have been founded on religious grounds; and about one sixth of the Belgian notables did not attend. William, accordingly, declaring the motived votes to be in reality affirmative, and the absentees to have given a silent approval, pronounced by proclamation the constitution to have been adopted."[6]

He did have some intentions in being King-Grand Duke that might be construed as good. The state of education was deplorable, a fact that in Luxembourg, where illiteracy was endemic, may have accounted in part for the almost supine acceptance by the Luxembourgers of their fate at this time. William undertook to improve education according to his lights. But his decrees discriminated against the Catholics on the lower levels, where the schools had been in Catholic hands, and the schools were discontinued. He won distrust from the Catholics on the higher levels by the requirements that he imposed for the education of priests, and education at that level was hamstrung. The anti-Catholic is never going to be popular in Luxembourg. When revolt against William finally gained force in Luxembourg, it was in great part his anti-Catholicism that accounted for the animosity.

William undertook the standardized administration of financial, military, and legal affairs in the three segments of his sovereignty. But he required the use of the Dutch language and thus effectively eliminated the French-speaking Belgians and Luxembourgers from participation. He abolished trial by jury. Against 2377 Dutch officers in the military service there were only 200 Belgians. The constitution guaranteed freedom of the press, but he restricted that freedom. He imposed taxes on such commodities as flour and meat that added to the burdens of the poor. He appropriated public domains to his own use and sold them off to amortize the Dutch debt. His financial policies drove many Luxembourgers to emigrate because their industry was unprotected and their subsistence was threatened. Though he succeeded in building a major highway leading out of Luxembourg to the west, his efforts to connect the Moselle with the Meuse by a canal failed.[7]

In August, 1830, came revolution. William's arbitrary and shortsighted policies asked for retribution. It was the Belgians who inaugurated the revolt. The phlegmatic Luxembourgers were slow in joining in. But the Walloon section — that is, the French speaking western part of Luxembourg—joined its Belgian cousins, and the rest of Luxembourg shortly followed suit. Now indeed we have a tangled web. According to the Congress of Vienna Luxembourg was an independent state, with William I its Grand Duke. A year later William indemnified his second son for the loss of the inheritance of Luxembourg; the implication was that the Grand Duchy was not really independent from the Netherlands but would pass to an heir as being incorporated in the Netherlands. Now, 1830, leaders in the Belgian provinces declared Luxembourg to be a part of Belgium.

William, too late, declared that Luxembourg would henceforth be separate and autonomous. He called on the four allied powers and France to regulate the whole situation. The powers provided for a separation of Belgium from Holland, but set Luxembourg apart in its independence. Belgium strongly opposed this decision, and the powers reversed themselves with respect to Luxembourg, making moves that would incorporate Luxembourg into Belgium.

William invaded Belgium and had some initial victories. France came to the aid of Belgium and drove the Dutch back. And now the five powers offered yet another decision. They decreed that the provinces of Limbourg and Luxembourg should be divided between Belgium and Holland.

William refused to accept this solution, offered in 1831, though Belgium accepted it; he stuck by his decision for a full eight years. In other words, from the breaking out of revolt in 1830 until final settlement in 1839 Luxembourg knew no certainty of ownership or government. All the while Prussia maintained its garrison in Luxembourg City. Within herself sympathies were split between Belgium and the Netherlands. The western areas found their sympathies lying with Belgium and its new king Leopold. Those citizens of Germanic-speaking Luxembourg who had accepted William without a quibble tended to persist in their loyalty to him. It was a situation that could not last. The Five Great Powers made a final decision.

The nine years 1830-1839 leading up to that decision are called the nine strange years. The great powers in London decided that Luxembourg should be divided between the Netherlands and Belgium. (Remember, Luxembourg's extent to the west made its territory more than two and a half times that of the present Grand Duchy.) Except for Luxembourg City itself, garrisoned by Prussian troops, the whole of the Grand Duchy was in the control of Belgium, which established a provincial capital at Arlon. For nine years, then, almost the entire area of Luxembourg was for all practical purposes Belgian. By the end of that period Belgium was unwilling to give up possession; and the inhabitants of that part of Luxembourg that was awarded to Belgium found in themselves no impulse to object to their becoming Belgians.[8]

To be the object of contending powers, to be subject to conflicting claims, took its toll on Luxembourg. Education, to which the Netherlands had given some impulse, declined still more. Industry fell behind the modernized competition of foreign states. With an uncertain judiciary, Luxembourg suffered from increased crime. Agricultural production fell.

On the other hand, there were certain advantages shaping that would make themselves felt in the new country that would eventuate. The new Belgian state had the most liberties of any European state, and Luxembourgers shared in them. The Luxembourgers had some participation in the shaping of the new Belgian constitution; later, when Luxembourg received its own constitution, the citizens would be careful to provide for their own freedoms. Freedom of the press gave impulse to the founding of newspapers. Religion was freed from political restraints. The free nation of the 1900s was finding its footing during those years of uncertainty.

Even in the state of warm friendship subsisting today between Belgium and Luxembourg, contrasting attitudes toward the Partition of 1839 prevail. In the Belgian histories we read about Belgium's loss of its easternmost territory (that of today's Grand Duchy);[9] in the Luxembourg histories we read about Luxembourg's loss of its western territories (called the Third Partition) that became the Belgian province of Luxembourg. A look at the map shows what Belgium won: 1668 square miles, as compared with the 999 square miles that constitute the Grand Duchy.[10] One hundred sixty thousand Luxembourgers became Belgian citizens, so that the new Grand Duchy had a population of 170,000. For the little country these were indeed momentous changes.

Here are the words of a Grevenmacher citizen (from the eastern border of the Grand Duchy) serving as a deputy in the Belgian government of 1839: ". . . I have to declare from this moment that in the name of my unhappy country, which recognizes neither in the Conference [of the great powers], nor in the king, nor in the government, nor in the Chambers the right to dispose of it, I protest highly against the unholy treaty which ravishes the fatherland of their choice from 400,000 Belgian citizens and which reserves to Belgium an eternal shame."

Contrast with those words of a Luxembourg citizen this speech of a citizen of Arlon, which became Belgian: ". . . the fatherland for me is not only the village where I was reared but the moral entity that is Belgian! . . . . Belgium is not at all dishonored, she has done all that she could, she has done all that she ought. As a Belgian I feel myself neither humiliated nor dishonored; as a Luxembourger, I deplore more than anyone else the fate of a province sacrificed to the implacable exigencies of European politics. Take up again the course of your momentarily interrupted prosperity, but never forget that those whom you are forced to abandon are always your old associates, that your independence is also owing to them and that Belgium remains the common fatherland!"

Such a division of opinion was to be expected. Beyond the natural human factor, however, were political realities that could not be obviated. William *owned* Luxembourg.[11] Since ethics or conscience was never a factor in political decisions, the Great Powers were quite capable of ignoring the fact of ownership and awarding Luxembourg to Belgium. But such a decision was not expedient. Luxembourg was a member of the German Confederation. German troops constituted the garrison that occupied Luxembourg City. Their presence kept Luxembourg City and its environs from participating in the Belgian hegemony with the rest of the Grand Duchy. The fortress itself and the garrison constituted a bulwark for Prussia against the ever-threatening France. All these factors, intermingled, supplied reasons for the pragmatic decision to maintain the greatly lessened Grand Duchy of Luxembourg as an independent state, with a Dutch sovereign who embodied Luxembourg's representation in the confederacy along with the other German princes.

Determining the western border was another pragmatic decision.[12] With small exceptions the people to the west of the new border were French speaking; to the east of the border they spoke their own Germanic or Frankish language. Though the use of Letzeburgesch has grown less and less frequent since World War I across the borders to west, south, and east, it still is used easily by the older people, particularly in German territory. Fundamentally the borders have been justified by the course of decades that add up, now, to centuries.

Geographically, in 1839 Luxembourg found its final definition. There would seem to be a kind of inevitability in its finding its Letzeburgesch definition, sealed in 1839. Dynastically, too, it found its definition; the Nassau roots that had been established long since were now cultivated, and the national tree that grew from them was finally strong enough to withstand all the political storms that would strike at it from 1839 to the present day. All the factors that could have been identified as weaknesses had now become strengths. Luxembourg could never escape from being assailed, but the amalgam of those factors was of such enduring strength that, however small, the world's storms could not blast it away, the rushing seas of war could not submerge it, the tidal wave of socialism could not absorb it. Geographically, socially, linguistically, dynastically it could lose its identity now only as the result of a political criminality greater even than the criminality thus far evidenced by the great powers of the Western world in the twentieth century.

NOTES: Chapter XV

[1] From Article 67 of the Final Act of the Treaties of Vienna, 1815.

[2] Albert Calmes, "Comment le Luxembourg devint 'Grand-Duché'" in Au fil de l'histoire Vol. II (Luxembourg, l'Imprimerie Saint-Paul, 1972), p. 18. The essay begins: "A pleasantry met with at school is that each territorial amputation has been accompanied by an increase in rank in the hierarchy of sovereignties."

[3]The quotation, from a novel, *The Princess*, by an Irish writer, Lady Morgan, whose spirit of liberty thrilled at the Belgian revolution of 1830. (Paris, A. and W. Galignani, 1833), p. 446.

[4]For an overview of the sovereigns and sovereign houses of Luxembourg see Robert Matagne, *Crayon généalogique illustrant depuis Sigefroid Comte de Luxembourg certains aspects des ascendances communes de la Famille Grand-Ducale de Luxembourg* (Luxembourg, Publications de la Section Historique de l'Institut grand-ducal, Vol. 81, 1966), pp. 19-41. Also, Robert Matagne, *Les soixante-quatre quartiers de son Altesse Royale le Grand-Duc Jean de Luxembourg* XIII fascicule, Vol. 7 (Luxembourg, Imprimerie Buck, 1965), pp. 5-16.

[5]Albert Calmes, "Nos frontières fluviales" in *Au fil de l'histoire* Vol. III (Luxembourg, l'Imprimerie Saint-Paul, 1971), pp. 136-156 (includes territorial arrangements at Vianden).

[6]Lady Morgan, p. 244n.

[7]Albert Calmes gives a most detailed account of all this (570 pages) in *Naissance et débuts du Grand-Duché 1814-1830* (Luxembourg, l'Imprimerie Saint-Paul, 1971). The footnotes must supply the bibliography.

[8]Albert Calmes, *Le Grand-Duché de Luxembourg dans la Révolution belge (1830-1839)* (Luxembourg, l'Imprimerie Saint-Paul, 1939).

[9]"The Grand Duchy ought by all natural laws to have formed part of Belgium, and would have done so but for the short-sightedness of the English and French ministers in 1831-9." Demetrius C. Boulger, *Belgium of the Belgians* (New York, Charles Scribner's Sons, 1911), p. 237.
". . . she was penalized by losing certain territories [including] the portion of Luxembourg which now forms the Grand Duchy." R. C. Ensor, *Belgium* (New York, Henry Holt and Co., n.d.), p. 130.

[10]Article 2 of the Treaty of London established the frontier.

[11]". . . to be possessed by him and his successors in ownership and sovereignty forever." Article 67, Congress of Vienna, 1815.

[12]For a particularized demarcation of the linguistic line see Calmes, *"La ligne de partage linguistique du Luxembourg et de la Wallonie"* in *Au fil de l'histoire* Vol. II, p. 13.

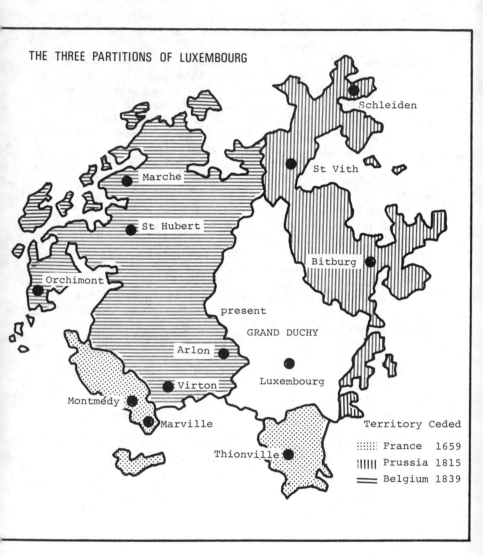

THE THREE PARTITIONS OF LUXEMBOURG

Schleiden

Marche

St Vith

St Hubert

Bitburg

Orchimont

present

GRAND DUCHY

Arlon

Luxembourg

Virton

Montmédy

Marville

Thionville

Territory Ceded

:::::: France   1659
|||||| Prussia 1815
===== Belgium 1839

Chapter XVI

Luxembourg Under the Dutch King, Grand Duke of Luxembourg
1839-1867

IN 1839, WHEN TODAY'S geographical definition of Luxembourg became a *fait accompli*, the Grand Duchy's loss was the Grand Duchy's gain. However sentimentally we might expect to find irredentism as a chronic irritation, there was no desire by the people over the borders in Germany, France, and Belgium to return to the Grand Duchy;[1] and since more people within the Grand Duchy felt impelled to be citizens of Belgium than subjects of Dutch William, there was little sense among them that their western relatives had gone astray. The 24 years since the Congress of Vienna had served as a shakedown period leading to a resolution that gave the greatest promise of a happy future for Luxembourg.

The Great Powers in 1815 had set up the Grand Duchy with three purposes: the stability of a legitimate monarchy, European balance of power, and a buffer zone between France and its suspicious neighbors. They had not been wrong, even though as late as 1839 the existence of the Grand Duchy trembled on the brink. When the Great Powers again decreed its fate, the monarchy with which Luxembourg's happiness would be firmly intertwined was fixed in place, the balance of power was reestablished for the next 30 years, and its buffer function as a fortress was reaffirmed. Strangely enough, the very fact of its being a fortress accounted for the action almost 30 years later that neutralized the country and gave it that freedom out of which its prosperity was to grow.[2] Perverse and arbitrary imposition by outside powers brought benefactions greater than sweet reason might have bestowed.

Certainly Luxembourg in 1839 stood in need of benefactions. Its territory was again reduced, this time by three-fifths; and though the Grand Duchy of Luxembourg was more fertile and more populous than the Province of Luxembourg, the Grand Duchy contained fewer iron workings than the Province.[3] After all these centuries, there were no good highways leading anywhere, so that commerce was practically impossible. Commercial relations between the two segments were completely upset, so that Luxembourg had to limit its business to the local markets. Iron production was old-fashioned and limited to a trifling amount, some 7000 to 8000 tons per year; there were eleven blast furnaces in eight places of production employing up to a few dozen workers each. Weaving was a household industry; leather gave work to perhaps 600 families; pottery employed some 500 men, paper 300; then there were beer and tobacco. There was no banking system, and there was no capital. Agriculture was still on a three-year rotation basis, production was weak. The cattle were poor, methods were outmoded; a large majority of the workers was employed on the poor land of which most of the country was constituted.

The state of teaching was as underdeveloped as industry and agriculture. Parents preferred to keep their children at home to work, and they were reluctant to pay for a teacher. The so-called normal school closed its doors, and there was no national supervision. A third of the villages had no school at all, and the rest had a school only during the winter. There was one secondary school, the Athenaeum in the capital, with 176 pupils in 1839.

Rooted to farms, most of which they did not own, these rural people were more nearly living in the medieval state from which they derived than in the energetic conditions of their neighboring countries that were well into the industrial revolution. The state of Europe being what it was, it was certain that Luxembourg would have to change.

*　　*　　*　　*　　*　　*　　*

Here we begin the historical sweep of one hundred forty years that will bring us to the proud and vital and independent Luxembourg of the 1980s. When its independence came in 1839 its Grand Duke was foreign and unpopular; a great part of its territory had been given away to strengthen one neighbor here and appease another neighbor there; it was an armed fortress fitting into a line of armed territory designed to keep great enemy nations apart. In these three conditions we see no positive attribute, no national character. Almost a century and a half later the sovereign house has rallied national loyalty and national strength through cataclysms of international struggle; the country exists, not to contribute to the balance of power, but in its own right and identity as an independent nation; it cooperates in full participation with its neighbors on all sides rather than serving as a buffer to keep them apart. The negative, unhappy characteristics that brought the nation to birth were the seeds of circumstance that flourished and flowered in contradiction to all expectation.

Fortunately Grand Duke William I in 1839 had only a year to reign and only two years to live. In the first years of his misguided reign he had impoverished the country by excessively high taxes and imposts on such necessities as flour and meat; he had hamstrung trade by oppressive duties and neglect of means of transportation; he had contributed to illiteracy by arbitrary restrictions on teaching; he had offended religious sensibilities; he had frustrated intellectuality by restricting the outlet for brains and talent in public employment; he had denied creativity and freedom of expression; he had interfered almost disastrously with the functioning of language in daily intercourse and official business. In 26 years he had not set foot on territory of today's grand-ducal area.

When Grand Duke William II paid his first visit to Luxembourg shortly after his accession, all these injuries and deprivations found expression in an official's straightforward statement to him: "The country is not happy, Sire."[4] No less straightforward was the assurance that the Grand Duke gave: "I want the welfare of the Grand Duchy, and I want it through the efforts of Luxembourgers."[5] The first requisite was met — the Grand Duke's concern for Luxembourg as a separate nation. Since William was an absolute monarch and would remain so until his death in 1849, no alleviation at all would have been possible had he not felt that concern.

He began immediately to show his sincerity by his actions. Luxembourgers replaced the unpopular Germans and Dutchmen in the chief administrative offices; a Council of Government administered the country under him. With the concurrence of a commission of eight Luxembourg noblemen he conceded a charter, a quasi constitution creating an Estates or congress that would lead to a real constitution later. He guaranteed that Luxembourgers would hold Luxembourg offices and created the framework of political life. He organized the country into districts, cantons, and communes, almost exactly the organization that is in force today. He set up an army contingent so that the country functioned appropriately in its German alliance. And he founded major changes in education.

The given factors of this new nation were almost entirely negative — economically, linguistically, culturally. Out of such a seedbed a proud nation would grow. William II began the cultivation of his new garden in the right way.

After 1870 the economic emphasis will be on iron and steel; but that will be a forty years' delay while Luxembourg's poverty is converted from a dead weight to a tolerable and even constructive way of life; from a condition in which famine stands on the threshold and lingers in the courtyard to one in which the face of downright deprivation loses its familiarity.

Agriculture provided occupation for more than 80 percent of the population of approximately 180,000 people. Income for the rest of the people was distributed in part as follows among the simple but essential occupations:

Bakers	174	Stonecutters	380
Butchers	224	Glassmakers	58
Tanners	412	Blacksmiths	683
Shoemakers	1340	Iron workers	109
Tailors	861	Nail makers	178
Carpenters	727	Tinsmiths	45
Wheelwrights	458	Carters	1163
Coopers	130	Inn keepers	1526
Turners	67		9039[6]
Masons	504		

Let us say that 10,000 workers, not counting family members employed in cottage industry, provided all of the labor and transportation which, apart from agriculture, made up the business, the economy, of an entire nation. Unable to survive above the subsistence level without economic interchange with other countries, cut off now from Belgium, distrustful of Germany, unrelated in any reliable way with France, it viewed its future with apprehension. Above all, it did not want to have to rely on Germany.

Another irony! It was with Germany that Luxembourg found its economic footing. Luxembourg could not compete with Brussels, could not find a market there or in France. Germany offered a large and certain market for many of her products. That market could be assured by her joining the Zollverein, the customs union of the German states. Against the wishes and despite the fears of a great many Luxembourgers, and against his own wishes too, William was forced to take Luxembourg into the German customs union in 1842. So successful was that relationship that the treaty was renewed time after time until it was abrogated by Germany's invasion of the Grand Duchy in World War I. The union was to account for 30 percent of the national income. Luxembourg for the first time found a free and large market for much of its goods, a matter of immense importance later in the century when it developed its iron-steel industry. The union attracted German investments that led to economic development. Railroads crisscrossed the country until there were 325 miles of them, compared with 170 miles in the 1970s. Goods moved freely within the nation, and there was a flow of goods across the borders.[7]

These years saw the preparation of Luxembourg to become an industrial nation. In only a few years 14 steel mills fired by charcoal (two by coke) gave way to 13 fired by coke (none by charcoal). All iron-steel production came to take place where it takes place today, in the southwest corner; production farther north disappeared. New production and transportation led to a lowering of prices, so that Luxembourg could compete in the international market. The rumblings of a great eruption of productivity after 1870 were making themselves felt in the decades before that date. Both a national bank and an international bank came into being. The fabric of modern Luxembourg was being set up on the weaving frames.

Even agriculture in that country of poor land and backward methods knew economic stimulation. Stock was improved; better implements were employed; the amount of fallow land decreased. Slowly, slowly the country roused itself from indigence. This improvement was bought partly by a very large emigration, which drained off many poor workers and their families. From a shocking 12.3 percent of paupers in 1847 the level fell to 3.2 percent in 1868.[8]

The main stumbling block in the way of agriculture production was the lack of fertilizer and manure. But in a few years the iron mills and agriculture would find themselves in a symbiotic relationship that would bring about a prosperity that no one could have foreseen.

* * * * * * *

In these years before 1867 we should be aware of aspects of Luxembourg that are not economic but that contribute, willy-nilly, to the vitality that would define the national self-consciousness and create prosperous reality out of economic opportunity. Those aspects show themselves in government, religion, education, and population.

If we think of the government of Luxembourg in the 1840s as a bull's-eye, then the lines that encircle it are the sovereign, the citizenry, and other countries. The sovereign is William II, a sensible, sympathetic man. The citizenry, as we have seen, consists of a large number of poor working people and a few affluent, educated men. The foreign country that concerns us most now is Germany.

We have to do with four constitutions: those of 1841, 1848, 1856, and 1868. The device of the pendulum serves us again, not, this time, as concerns who will own the country, but as concerns formalization of the means by which the country will govern itself in its independence.[9]

The constitution of 1841 made plain the autocratic power of the Grand Duke. On the national level power existed in no other hands. Still, the constitution was the nation's own, marking its independence from other nations, defining its individuality.

Knowing the governmental organization of today, we recognize the importance of the newly created *Assemblée des Etats*, an elected parliament, and of the *Conseil de Gouvernement* (Governmental Council), through which the Grand Duke acted. The members of the Estates were elected members. To be sure, only 2.9 percent of the population were eligible to vote by virtue of their property (as compared with more than 60 percent who exercise the right now), but the very act of election was an arrow pointing to the universal suffrage of the twentieth century. Only Luxembourgers now would hold Luxembourg offices. The groundwaves of independence were making themselves felt.

Those groundwaves escalated to veritable shocks in 1848. Independence had become heady wine. There was in Luxembourg in 1848, of all things, a revolution. Crowds of people came together to make their demands, following the lead of France. Progressive liberals replaced the doctrinaire liberals (misleading name) who had held leadership in their hands since 1841, given their support to the Grand Duke's dictatorship, and faced the church in opposition. Crops had been poor, people were out of work, the citizens were offended by the Grand Duke's appropriation of large sums of money for himself and his family, they objected to certain laws, particularly the one requiring the replacement of inexpensive thatch roofs by tile, the poor felt unfairly taxed in comparison with the well-to-do. Government and church had the popular sympathy. The German connection threatened the independence that the people were just beginning to feel.

The people carried the day. The Grand Duke showed more good sense than his Dutch predecessors had shown and granted the privileges that constituted the core of liberty. The press would henceforth be free. There would be a government allowing for the interplay of contending parties. Any act of the Grand Duke would require the countersigning by the appropriate member of government. Any act within the German government involving Luxembourg would require countersigning by the Grand Duke and by the Assembly (Chamber of Deputies). The Chamber, by voting the annual budget, would now be the directing power of government. The new constitution explicitly guaranteed individual liberty, freedom of expression, freedom of the press, and freedom of assembly. The Luxembourg of the 1848 constitution was like the young man on his 21st birthday, independent in his mature rights and inexperienced in using them; but in his essential character he is the man that he will be.

The pendulum swung back. Liberalism was found too liberal by the men who wielded the real power. William III in 1856 by a coup d'état took back the Grand Duke's old rights. The functioning government was removed from the control of the Chamber of Deputies, once again called the Assembly of Estates. The electorate was reduced in number. The new freedoms were to a degree put under threat. The Council of State, its members appointed by the Grand Duke, would exercise the powers of approval or veto over legislation of the Estates.

This was very bad indeed. Except . . . except. . . . There would be yet another constitution, this one in 1868. This constitution would remain the basic law up to the present day and, we may presume, will continue in force. The Luxembourgers were learning to align themselves in parties. They were learning the strong powers and tender sensibilities of cabinet government. Executive power was now affirmed to be in the hands of the sovereign, but his power was closely tied in with that of the cabinet ministry. Legislative power belonged to the sovereign and the Chamber of Deputies. All political liberties were reestablished. The requirements of suffrage were defined. The new constitution established a real equilibrium. Through its 900 years of history all that could not be compacted into the national core had spun off or been burned away. It had survived great shocks, but there had been no cataclysm. Viewing the Luxembourg of the 1980s, we can look back and identify its source.

*   *   *   *   *   *   *

The subject of the Catholic religion need not detain us long here, but we should remind ourselves that it is always a factor of great importance in the Luxembourg equation. There was a Catholic party which, following the liberal constitution of 1848, played a strong part in the reactionary changes of the 1850s. A strong apostolic vicar, Monsignor Laurent, by rallying a great many citizens around him and his religious opinions, helped cement Catholicism for the century ahead at the very time that the jockeying for power could have weakened the church so that its social force would have been less in the decades to come.

As Luxembourg was politically, economically, and socially coalescing during the 19th century, so religiously it was going through the same process. Earlier we have made much of the fact that Luxembourg territory was divided among several bishoprics, so that Luxembourgers were centrifugally distracted from a central allegiance. To that state of affairs we attributed, in part, the enduring identity of a Luxembourg that would never be entirely possessed by some greater power, as the eastern sectors became German, the southern French, the western Belgian. But now, in the 19th century, the central, essential religious identity of one social, political, and governmental whole is beginning to find itself. Napoleon put all of Luxembourg under the bishopric of Metz. After the French were defeated and Luxembourg, though now a Grand Duchy, was essentially a part of the Netherlands, Luxembourg became a part of the bishopric of Namur, a city in Belgium. When it became independent in 1839, reason dictated that it should have its own church administration, and now it took its administration directly from Rome under an apostolic vicar. The weathervane was pointing to 1870, when finally Luxembourg, in its ultimate individuality and identity, would constitute its own bishopric.

These years were full of tensions between church and state as the church found its responsibilities, its authority, and its vigor. It expressed all three as mentor, through the schools, of Luxembourg's children. Lacking teachers, the state turned to the church when it began reforms in the 1840s, and the clergy not only undertook to teach but ran a normal school to prepare teachers. By the 1850s in that country that had been largely illiterate 57 percent of the small children went to school, and 30 years later 85 percent. The state required, as one of its first educational mores, that French be taught along with German.[10]

In that quiet statement we confront an act momentous (for that tiny piece of the European continent) in its wisdom and effect. A whole people to whom formal German was a foreign language were required to use it for their formal business; and French, which was entirely outside the ken of the farmer and the working man, was given equal status. On the very eve of its industrial revolution it prepared all its people to function within the economic changes that would be taking place. What's more, tied beyond its own control to the German economic orbit, by insisting on the learning of French by its children it kept open the conduits for artistic and intellectual influence to flow into the country from France and Belgium. In the light of the economic revolution of the twentieth century we marvel at an acumen greater than reason and even foresight had a right to ask for.

* * * * * * *

The demographic characteristics of 1980 sharpen our awareness of the demographic facts of the mid-nineteenth century. Even as economic conditions improved poverty persisted. In 1847 more than 12 percent of the population were absolutely indigent, a condition that was to persist for decades, though it would be alleviated somewhat.[11] Harvests were still uncertain, and a poor harvest was still followed by near starvation. Nourishment was poor, and living conditions were primitive. There was no great wealth; even those who were rather well off were not affluent. The poor employee was subject to the grinding demands of employers who still squeezed from the worker the last ounce of energy and the last sou. Poverty impelled emigration, which grew to major proportions. Even as great waves of pestilence receded, epidemics repeated themselves.[12] The death rate was high.

But the birth rate was high too, high enough to more than counteract the population losses. The birth rate and the immigration that would come a little later would push the population higher. The drift of people — and it was still only a drift — was toward the capital and the southwest. Later that drift would become a definite shift of population.

Such was the social state of affairs when the next major political crisis came upon the country. The year was 1867. Employment, income, occupations, work methods, agriculture — all those were not much changed from what they had been for centuries. But the state of the country could be likened to that of an unstable chemical compound, ready to change its composition at the effect of pressure or temperature or shock at any moment. Once again — the first of the three great fateful moments with which Luxembourg was still to be confronted — the pendulum hesitated. Just possibly it would cease to swing altogether.

NOTES: Chapter XVI

[1]"Neither the Prussian Luxembourgers nor the Belgian Luxembourgers experienced at any time the wish to reestablish the Grand Duchy. The grand-ducal Luxembourgers developed a national feeling, but they did not clamor for the return of their separated brothers to the mother country. A Luxembourg irredentism did not exist." Gilbert Trausch, Le Luxembourg à l'époque contemporaine (Luxembourg, Editions Bourg-Bourger, 1975), p. 87. This is Vol. IV of Manuel d'histoire luxembourgeoise.
For a carefully detailed account of these years see:
   1. Albert Calmes, Le Grand-Duché de Luxembourg dans le royaume des Pays-Bas (1815-1830) (Brussels, L'Edition Universelle, 1932).
   2. Albert Calmes, Le Grand-Duché de Luxembourg dans la Révolution belge (1830-1839) (Brussels, L'Edition Universelle, 1939).
[2]See Chapter V.
[3]Paul Weber, Histoire de l'économie Luxembourgeoise (Luxembourg, Chambre de Commerce, 1950). See "Le règne de Guillaume Ier, roi des Pays-Bas (1815 à 1830)," pp. 103 to 107; "La rèvolution belge (1830 à 1839)," pp. 109-118; and "L'Accession au Zollverein (1839 à 1842)," pp. 120-135.
Albert Calmes, "Die Stadt Luxemburg im Jahre 1815," in Au fil de l'histoire Vol. II (Luxembourg, l'Imprimerie Saint-Paul, 1971), p. 141.
[4]Spoken by the mayor of Diekirch to William II. Quoted by Trausch, p. 23.
[5]Quoted by A. H. Cooper-Prichard, History of the Grand Duchy of Luxemburg (Luxemburg, P. Linden, 1950), p. 169.
[6]Weber, p. 123.
[7]Ibid., "L'Accession au Zollverein (1839 à 1842)," pp. 120-138; "Les débuts du Zollverein (1842-1860)," pp. 157-170.
[8]Ibid., "L'éclosion capitaliste," pp. 173-239.
[9]Pierre Majerus, L'Etat Luxembourgeois: Manuel de droit constitutionnel et de droit administratif luxembourgeois (Luxembourg, Imprimerie de la Cour Joseph Beffort, 1948).
[10]The law on elementary education July 26, 1843:". . . laid the foundation of our bilingual situation as we know it today." Jul Christophory, Mir Schwätze Lëtzebuergesch (Luxembourg, l'Imprimerie Saint-Paul, 1974), p. 21.
[11]Trausch, p. 114.
[12]"Epidemics in the 19th century: typhus 1813, cholera 1832, cholera 1854, typhus 1861, cholera 1861 and 1866, typhus 1879 and 1890, cholera 1893."

Edouard Feitler, *Luxemburg Deine Heimatstadt* (Luxemburg, Sankt-Paulus-Druckerei, 1967), p. 309.

Chapter XVII

Neutral and Independent Luxembourg
1867

THE FATE OF LUXEMBOURG has hung in the balance so many times through the centuries that reason does not permit declaring 1867 the most important date of all. Still, in relation to today's Grand Duchy, 1867 was the year that saw the independence and individuality of Luxembourg defined and affirmed. It had by now finished its political evolution. It could henceforth become something different from what it now was only by some power's wreaking violence upon it.

Both France and Germany in the 1860s were still ready to absorb Luxembourg by negotiation or force. Wars broke out like heat lightning, especially across the Germanic lands, which were jockeying for a relationship that would become the German Empire in one area, Austria in the other. When Prussia fought with Austria in 1866 and won after only a few weeks of fighting, the settlement included the dissolution of the German Confederation that had been in force since 1815, the domination of Prussia in the new North German Confederation, and a military alliance of northern Germany and the southern autonomous German states. All this was a state of flux, the disturbances vibrating in Luxembourg like the claps of threatening thunder.

How could Luxembourg not be involved? Seven thousand Prussian troops garrisoned Luxembourg City. (The Luxembourg armed forces of the 1980s number 630!) Luxembourg had been a member of the German Zollverein — customs union — since 1842. And though a member, she played almost no part in the decisions that the German states made for her. She was independent; her Grand Duke was the sovereign of the Netherlands; but she swung in the German orbit, and quite possibly she could be so taken for granted as to be absorbed into a confederated and consolidated Germany almost while nobody was looking.

But William III was looking. And someone else in 1867 was looking too: France, of course. The power of France had helped Prussia win against Austria. France, in the person of Emperor Napoleon III, made claims on German territory that Prussia refused to grant. France, then, bellicose and presumptuous, made claims on Luxembourg, and the Grand Duke agreed to sell, as the price he thought necessary to pay for French help against Prussia's aims against Limburg and the Netherlands. The little buffer state would become French. Prussia was ready to fly to arms. Once again the great powers intervened, and in 1867, meeting in London, they settled the fate of Luxembourg. The perpetual irony of Luxembourg again prevailed; the very threats against her integrity sprung the mechanism that made her free.[1]

Before we take more notice of that freedom, however, we should look a little more carefully at what had been happening there. Most importantly, perhaps, we should recognize the type of leadership that was shaping itself in the little country. It was the type that would continue to prevail into the very present.

First to be considered is the Grand Duke, William III, who would be sovereign not only during the period that led to the fateful year of 1867, but for 23 years afterward. His policies helped define both the threat and the advantages that Germany would offer the Grand Duchy.

Second is William's brother Henry, appointed to Luxembourg as Prince-Lieutenant to preside in the Grand Duke's name.

Third are the government and business leaders whose acumen moved their nation toward participation in the industrial world of the late nineteenth century.

The new Grand Duke of 1849, William III, was more autocratic than his father. In the stubborn imposition of his will he put in play once again the familiar irony of Luxembourg, in which unpopular and disadvantageous circumstances were instrumental in the development and independence of the nation. There were tensions between him and the local government. His will prevailed, so that the liberal provisions of the constitution of 1848 were replaced by uncomfortable restrictions. When the elected Chamber refused to confirm and countersign the new provisions, William III promulgated them by decree. He made himself more powerful at the expense of the Chamber. He introduced the Council of State, he set the property requirement for the vote at a higher figure, and, most threateningly of all, he provided that the resolutions of the German Confederation when decreed by him were to be the law of the country. This new, more restrictive constitution conformed to the will of the German Diet at Frankfurt, which was opposed to the liberal features of the 1848 constitution.

All this has a familiar ring — the imposition of the sovereign's will, restriction of the expansion of democratic participation, the threat of being subsumed by Germany. The first of these will raise itself for the last time as late as 1919, when, apart from war, Luxembourg will face its greatest crisis of modern times. The second of these will work itself out gradually, along with the other countries of western Europe, in the modern spirit. The third — the threat by Germany — will make itself felt again in the two great cataclysms of the twentieth century.

But back to the point about leadership. As compared with William II, William III was hardly a sympathetic figure. Fortunately, to the position of Prince-Lieutenant of Luxembourg he appointed his brother Henry. It was largely by the good offices of Prince Henry that the country moved through the autocratic impositions of the Grand Duke without too much trouble. Henry, temperate and conciliating, kept it on an even keel. It was Henry, of the House of Nassau, who presided over the neutrality that protected Luxembourg in the Prussia-Austria embroil. It was Henry who formulated the new status of neutrality declared by the Great Powers at the Conference of London in 1867 and the new liberal constitution of 1867. It was Henry who presided in the name of the sovereign through the years when the first railroads were laid down, the country was threatened by the Franco-Prussian War, the population grew steadily from 169,000 in 1837 to 250,000 in only 25 years, the iron-steel industry went through the changes of modernization, business found a secure footing, the country became a bishopric, and education became all but universal.[2] It cannot be said that Prince Henry accomplished all these things, but in a monarchy that was not yet really democratic he did preside with authority, persuasion, and effectiveness. In all those years William III did not once set foot in the country. What was accomplished was done in the name of the Grand Duke, but it was Henry who was the executive. Both Henry's dedication and the newly shaped spirit of patriotism in Luxembourg shine through his statement of 1875: "When I knew that danger approached, I made every effort possible to save for the country what was so dear to it, and when I was convinced that you would be saved, I understood how one could die of joy."[3] He died in 1879.

In the mid-1800s Luxembourg was now entering fully into the age of the entrepreneur. Until these years there has been little need to burden our memories with the names of Luxembourg citizens. But we should note some now who exercised the third type of leadership. There are the brothers Metz, the family de Tornaco, Prime Minister Servais, the merchant prince Pescatore — these became powerful names in Luxembourg.[4] If banking firms were to be developed, roads extended, railroads built, commerce tended to, laws passed, education strengthened, independence defended, international affairs conducted, there had to be leaders who tended to these matters. Then, as now, the tiny population produced the men who could stimulate the people to progress internally and who could earn attention and respect on the international scene.

The most dramatic development was that of transportation, particularly the railroads. Luxembourg could never have importance on the international economic scene until goods could flow into and out of the country with some ease; it could never live to a degree higher than the subsistence level until that flow of goods was established.

In 1839 Luxembourg had fewer than 125 miles of roads over which goods could be hauled. In eight years 92 miles were added, enough to connect the main places of the country. In the next 20 years, up to 1867, 310 miles were constructed. Internally now the road network was adequate. But there was one shortcoming.

Transportation by cart was too expensive. The answer to the problem would lie in the construction of railroads.

Luxembourg inaugurated railroad service in 1859. Before the century was over it had a railroad network, connecting it with all of Europe, of more than 300 miles.[5] With the construction of its railroads Luxembourg entered the modern age.

The modern age would be industrial. Industry would depend on iron and steel. Luxembourg had iron ore. Great coal fields lay only a few miles off in the Saar. The new railroads would bring the coal to Luxembourg. The new railroads would take the iron and steel out of the country to all of Europe. Luxembourg now possessed the physical requisites. Wise management, sound international relationships, and peace would enable her to take advantage of the endowment that was now naturally hers.

* * * * * * *

Let us come back to the momentous year of 1867.

Before the major burgeoning of the iron-steel industry in the last quarter of the century Luxembourg had to face one more threatening test of its independence, the test of 1867. As we have seen, Prussia and Austria had been at war; Prussia was the winner; the old German Confederacy (of which Luxembourg was a part) was dissolved; the north German states were unified in a new organization that in a few years would lead to the new German nation. What part did Luxembourg have to play in all this?

We understand a little better how reasonable it was that Luxembourg should become a part of the new Germany when we see what the component parts of that new Germany were: 25 separate states consisting of 13 duchies and principalities, five grand duchies, four kingdoms, three free cities. Some of these were smaller even than Luxembourg. In the thinking of those Germans who determined the shaping of the new Germany, why should Germany stop at the Moselle, the Sure, and the Our Rivers, when beyond them lay yet one more grand duchy that was a member of the confederation? The majority of Luxembourgers, Germanic in blood, taking economic advantage of their membership, were opposed to being nationally German, as they were to show themselves twice in the 20th century. Still, there were some who identified their financial welfare with German interests. But there were also some who leaned toward Belgium and some toward France, their Luxembourg patriotism not yet hardened into an invulnerable conviction.

Belgium still mourned the loss of the Grand Duchy of Luxembourg dating back to 1839. William III's personal ownership of the Grand Duchy, which seemed to be more Germanic than anything else, threatened him and the Netherlands with being caught up in the new German State. France still wanted Luxembourg and was willing to pay William III a large sum for it. All the circumstances of another war, this time with Luxembourg as the real cause, offered themselves; for Prussia opposed France's acquisition of Luxembourg, France was so far advanced in the acquisition that it could not retreat, and war between the ancient enemies seemed to be the only recourse.

Austria and Russia together saved the day by calling for a conference of the great powers, which came together in London in May, 1867. The result of the Congress of London was this: withdrawal of the Prussian army forces from Luxembourg and dismantlement of the fortress; the giving up of the claims to Luxembourg by France; declaration of the independence and perpetual unarmed neutrality of the Grand Duchy.[6] Nine hundred years of national evolution was complete; the Grand Duchy of Luxembourg was inviolably independent, guaranteed in its neutrality by Austria, France, Great Britain, Prussia, Russia, Italy, and the Netherlands.

We shall see the importance of that neutrality to Luxembourg, no longer a fortress, in the international crises of the next hundred years. Neutrality meant that in any international conflict Luxembourg would participate on neither side. If a national neutrality were to be maintained, the strength of sympathy among the people of that nation could not be so strong as to impel national intervention on either side. Whatever the ties of sympathy or blood, Luxembourg could not be Dutch or Belgian or German or French in its overt — and consequently, its covert — sympathies. If the citizens could not express their loyalties outside their nation's boundaries, where could those loyalties focus? Only on themselves, only on their own nation. It was now a question of Luxembourgers for Luxembourg — of *Letzeburg de*

Letzeburger — of *mir wëlle bleiwe wat mir sin* — we want to remain what we are.

Luxembourg had come of age.

NOTES: Chapter XVII

[1]Paul Weber, "La Question de Luxembourg (1866-1867)" in *Histoire du Grand-Duché de Luxembourg* (Brussels, Office de Publicité, 1949), p. 53.

[2]For detail see "La Vie Economique 1839-1870," "La Question Luxembourgeoise 1867-1872," "La Vie Politique 1839-1872," pp. 33-64 in Gilbert Trausch, *Le Luxembourg à l'époque contemporaine* (Luxembourg, Editions Bourg-Bourger, 1975). This is Vol. IV of *Manuel d'histoire Luxembourgeoise*.

[3]Spoken to the members of the Chamber of Deputies, 1875.

[4]See *Porträt-Galerie Hervorragender Persönlichkeiten aus der Geschichte des Luxemburger Landes* (Luxemburg, Verlag Edouard Kutter, 1972).

[5]Weber, "La Construction des Chemins de fer" in *Histoire de l'économie Luxembourgeoise* (Luxembourg, Chambre de Commerce, 1950), p. 173.

[6]M. Junod, "Die Neutralität des Grossherzogtums Luxemburg von 1867 bis 1948," *Publications de la Section historique de l'Institut grand-ducal* t. 72 (Luxembourg, 1951), pp. 7-103.

Chapter XVIII

Independence and Economic Development
1867-1914

LOOKING BACK OVER 900 YEARS of Luxembourg history before 1867, we cannot point to any period of a century or more as a sweep of history, as an uninterrupted march forward, as a synoptic whole in which the interplay and intersupport of the many factors are essential to the endurance of all as well as the existence of any one of them. But we can speak of all the history since 1867 in those terms. Beginning in 1867 up to the present there has been a sweep of history, threatened, yes, and interrupted, but, even so, continuous. From that date Luxembourg has marched forward in liberty, strength, wealth, and identity. Take away any one factor from its synergistic wholeness during all that time and the Grand Duchy of Luxembourg as we now know it might not now exist.

In 1867 the Great Powers, in the Treaty of London, declared Luxembourg to be separate and neutral. Although the Treaty did not stipulate the independence of Luxembourg, nevertheless in the eyes of Europe its independence was affirmed. Overweening France, still coveting Luxembourg and bidding for her with cash, had so threatened Germany that Germany threatened war. The other powers, intervening, got France to withdraw its bid and Germany to withdraw its garrison. Now that the German Confederation was disbanded, Luxembourg in no way belonged to Germany in theory or in fact; France could not have her; though her Grand Duke was also King of the Netherlands, there was no governmental union; the separation from Belgium had been so accepted as final that there was no move toward a recombination. There stood Luxembourg, stared at by all the powers of Europe, alone and, under the Dutch king, independent.

Her fate once again was a matter of irony. In 1914 and 1940 Germany, challenging the world, would try to stomp her into nonexistence; but in 1867 Germany was so leery of French power that she willingly withdrew the Prussian garrison so as to establish the little neutral state between them. The power that would later spit on the neutrality was the power that most wanted it.

The first test of that neutrality came only three or four years later.[1] Germany and France went to war despite Luxembourg's neutrality. Because some help came to France by means of Luxembourg's railroads, after the victory Germany claimed the management of those railroads and wrested it from France. Now indeed Luxembourg was in the German orbit — in the customs union, in the dependence on German coal and German markets and German transportation and German financial investments. The cultural spirit of Luxembourgers yearned toward France, but their bread and butter was a fact because of Germany.

Nevertheless, Luxembourg was free and neutral.

* * * * * * *

In the last hundred years—since 1867—Luxembourg has been above all a country of iron and steel. The major substance of its economy derived from that. Its importance on the world scene derived from that. Demographic distribution and the nationalistic composition of the population derived from that. Agriculture, even, owed its development to iron and steel.

We have had occasion to mention the iron-steel industry before, because the iron deposits figured in Luxembourg history from Roman times. But only in the last hundred years did it become the primary economic moving force to which the characteristics of modern Luxembourg are owed.

A simple fact points up the dramatic burgeoning of that basic industry. The first Luxembourg Chamber of Commerce, in 1841, consisted of 21 seats.[1] Business in general (banks, etc.) held 10 seats; tanning and leather, two; the cloth trade, pottery, spinning, iron, glove making, milling, paper making, tobacco, weaving and dyeing, one each. The iron industry's one representative came from Berg, some 20 miles above Luxembourg City, where there is no iron industry today. The canton of Bettembourg (later, of Esch-sur-Alzette), in the southwest corner of the country where the iron industry has centered for many years, had not a single representative. Until 1904, except for the period of 1857-1869, all representatives of the iron industry came from outside the southwest area of the country. The Ardennes, on the other hand, traditionally thought of as poor and unproductive, had four representatives. There has in the past century been an economic revolution indeed.

We can find other terms in which to express the amazing and fateful change that came about in the iron-steel industry, knowing what we do about that industry in the 20th century, in a matter of a few decades after the midpoint of the 19th century.

In 1857 there were blast furnaces in some 11 localities in Luxembourg, located at Berbourg, Eich, Steinfort, Berg, Lasauvage, Grundhof, Dommeldange, Septfontaines (Simmern), Fischbach, Hollerich, Bissen. Locate these on the map.[2] Only one of these is located in the area that has produced iron-steel in the 20th century. The rest of them were pretty much scattered elsewhere in the country, taking their ore from alluvial deposits.

Two striking circumstances now are apparent. The first is this: all the alluvial deposits in the country remaining after 1900 would not have sufficed to assure one day's production of iron-steel at the peak of production in the 20th century. To assure a production hundreds of times greater than that of the mid-19th century, the iron-steel entrepreneurs had to take their enterprise to the southwest corner, in the Esch-Pétange-Differdange area. They could do this because of the discovery of layers of iron ore, called minettes, that could be easily mined.[3] Vast quantities of ore lay there. Charcoal would soon be replaced by coke, which could be cheaply obtained. Membership in the German Zollverein opened up large free markets. And the quick vast extension of railroads stimulated both the use of iron products and their distribution.

In only five years, 1868 to 1873, the amount of ore mined increased by almost 90 percent; the amount of cast iron fabri-

217

cated increased by 160 percent. The new policy a little later of tariff protection gave Luxembourg, as a member of the Zollverein, an advantage over its competitors, and Germany itself took half its production. Within 40 years after 1873 production of cast iron increased 1000 percent. By the end of the century Luxembourg was producing one-seventh of the total production of the Zollverein; in terms of its population it produced 27 times the cast iron production of Belgium, 30 times that of Germany, 64 times that of France.[4] All this forecasts, as by a magic lantern, the affluence that will distinguish the state of Luxembourg in the 20th century.

In the spirit of irony that has served as a kind of matrix of Luxembourg history, a palpable hindrance and shortcoming of the iron industry in the Grand Duchy now became an economic advantage quite as large as the disadvantage had been. Up to this time agriculture had remained backward and unprofitable in relation to the rest of western Europe. Production was insufficient because the land, both in the Bon Pays and in the Oesling, lacked the necessary qualities for high production; neither fertilizer nor manure was available in sufficient quantity. Without the incentive of sufficiency the Luxembourg farmer remained bogged down in old customs, old methods, and old results.

Until the years after 1878, that is.

The iron ore in Luxembourg was overrich in phosphorus. The resulting product until about 1880 was soft and brittle, unfit for many uses, with, consequently, a limited market. In 1878 two Englishmen, Thomas and Gilchrist, invented a method for treating iron ore too rich in phosphorus.[5] To Thomas, it is said, the country owes its standard of living and its place in the world. Immediately Luxembourg acquired the rights to the process, and practically overnight Luxembourg iron and steel products could compete with those of the rest of Europe. Almost as important was the fact that the scoriae from that production method, the by-product, constituted a fertilizer exactly right for the agricultural land of Luxembourg. So important did this fertilizer become to the country that the state required of the iron-steel manufacturers a regular yearly supply of it based on the acreage in production. A revolution in agriculture accompanied the revolution in the iron-steel industry.

218

The quantity of land, the products, and their price all interest us as having a bearing on the evolution of the Grand Duchy. At the time of Luxembourg's definitive liberty and the establishment of neutrality it had about 306,400 acres under cultivation. That total diminished by 1900 to 276,700 acres. In 1970 the amount of land cultivation was only about 158,000 — just about half of the total of 100 years earlier. We find two important facts here. First, 158,000 acres is the maximum acreage in crop production, with an available fertilizer that will bring about maximum productivity, that is economically feasible. Second, that land taken out of crop production proved useful for the production of cattle. A balanced, economically sound agricultural situation was the result.

Some details of the agricultural situation take our attention. Even as the cultivated acreage was decreasing profits were increasing, so that the returns on grain crops increased by more than 50 percent in 40 years. Even as the pasture acreage was increasing the number and quality of farm animals improved strikingly. In that same 40 years the average weight of cows almost doubled. Milk production per cow increased by one-third. The number of pigs more than quadrupled.[6]

Luxembourg agriculture was not without its shortcomings. Climate, ground contour, altitude, and quality of the soil combined to put it in a less favorable situation than that of its neighbors. What's more, modern Luxembourg paid a price for conditions inherited from the Middle Ages. At the turn of the century there were 40,000 individual holdings, with an average of less than 7.4 acres for each. Of that 40,000 only 1,300 contained more than 50 acres each.[7] Picture the Luxembourg village of 10 to 20 farmhouses, surrounded at considerable distance by small fields only a dozen or so yards wide and perhaps a hundred yards long, each farmer's few fields scattered at awkward distances in all directions. Such conditions did not contribute to profitability.

The availability of markets did contribute, however. The developing iron-steel industry brought people together in larger communities that provided outlets for farm products. The new roads made hauling easier and cheaper. The Zollverein provided an outlet for agricultural products as well as manufactured products, and later a protective tariff covered Luxembourg as well as the Germanic states. After 1871 included in the Germanic protection were the lands of Lorraine, acquired from France.

The quality of life everywhere in Luxembourg improved. The farmer still was not well off, and the laborer was still not well paid. But rewards were great enough to attract the foreign worker. The circumstances of that immigration we shall deal with later, but at this point we should note that foreigners were already coming to Luxembourg in search of a better life. Farmers from Lorraine and from the Rhineland, looking for a footing in Luxembourg, brought with them better methods of cultivation and of crop rotation. The mixing of blood that had marked Luxembourg through all its history was thus continuing, in the mid-19th century by dribbles, later to increase into a stream.

The grape growers and wine makers participated in the agricultural revolution. Generally until after the mid-century their lot had been a very poor one. The quality of wine was not particularly good. But they did find a market and slowly rose on the economic ladder during the rest of the century. The small producers of eau-de-vie, however, ran into difficulty so that the little farm distilleries fell from the striking number of 1820 to fewer than half that number.[8]

In all this — industrial and agricultural — we see foreshadowed the Luxembourg of the late 20th century. Without really knowing where it was headed, it was, because of its endowment in iron ore, on its way up the main economic road with the rest of the western world. The main outlines that the iron-steel industry and agriculture provided can be filled in by some figures more or less detailed. Developing in Luxembourg was an economic interdependence more or less sophisticated. We need not pursue the details of business and industry on the local scene, but we should take note of those smaller business concerns that provided employment for 10, 20, 100, 200 families. Consider their diversity: sugar (of short duration), tobacco (long a business of considerable importance in international trade), religious statues, paving tiles, gunpowder, ready-made clothes, macaroni and other flour products, chicory, chocolate products, coaches and wagons, enamelled pottery, rose culture, beer, gas, whiskey and spirits, printing and publishing. When we add to these the little shops and services that any society needs, we recognize the diversity and interdependence of a modern society getting itself on a substantial and comfortable footing.[9]

Printing and publishing should receive special attention. We cannot conceive of a democracy without the sharing of information and stimulation of opinion by the press. There can hardly be vitality of economic endeavor without the intellectual stimulation of the printed word. Of course the publications of France and Germany and Belgium readily made their way into the Grand Duchy. But the Grand Duchy provided its own products of the printing press too. The number of printing concerns increased from seven in 1857 to 17 in 1887. In 1871 there were 12 newspapers in Luxembourg; six political, one literary, one satirical, two agricultural, one official announcements, one teaching miscellany. Publishing was reflecting the increasing complexity and variety of the daily life of the Grand Duchy as well as the results of an education that was, in the third generation of expanded teaching, becoming universal.

* * * * * * *

Expanded education, publishing enterprises, liberalization of the constitution, the tensions of an uncertain political future, jockeying for influence and affluence, cultivating favor or opposing authority — all these functioned in an interdependence that defies separation. The people had made a centuries-long accommodation to autocracy. They did not feel that the new autocracy of commercial money constituted a threat to them. If democracy was to figure in its future, though, the democratic spirit had to survive the pressures of that autocracy, that domination of the many by the few. In fact, in Western Europe, Luxembourg and the Netherlands fell far behind their neighboring countries in the democratic process.

The requirement of a money qualification for voting was to continue until 1919. The restrictions that that requirement put on the voting privilege were remarkable.

During the cloudy years from the Belgian revolution of 1830 to 1839 Luxembourg (including the present Belgian province of Luxembourg) elected only five representatives to the two houses of the new Belgium. The property requirement for the vote seems to reflect the economic condition of the country: citizens of Luxembourg City had to pay the most money, landed proprietors were next, citizens of the main towns had to pay only half as much, and those of Vianden paid even less. In the 1840s out of a population of 178,000 only 350 men had the right to vote! Of the 34 members that constituted the Luxembourg Estates in 1847, eight were landed proprietors, eight were businessmen of one kind or another, two were professional men (one lawyer and one doctor), seven were notaries, and nine were office holders in the government. Almost half of the members were directly responsible to the Grand Duke and his coterie. Immediately apparent is the opportunity for self-serving and corruption. We may be sure that both were rampant in this little country where everybody must have then (as the case is today) known everybody else's business.

The more liberal constitution coming out of the revolution of 1848 lowered the price of the vote so that 9868 citizens qualified. This number maintained itself through the more severe restrictions of the 1856-57 reorganization into the Assembly of the Estates composed of 31 members. An increase in the property requirement in 1860 lowered the number of qualified voters to 3568. When the Chamber of Deputies, with 40 members, was recreated in 1868, the Deputies were sent there by 5861 voters. The professional and financial distribution was not much changed from that of twenty-some years before.

How slow the democratic evolution was! France had already achieved universal suffrage in 1848. At the end of the century only 6.33 men out of 100 inhabitants had the vote in Luxembourg, compared with a figure of 26.3 in France.[10] Luxembourg had a long way to go to reach the 61 voters out of every 100 inhabitants in the 1980s.

But the currents of independence ran strong even though representation was very slight. When that independence was laid on the line again in 1867, there were those who favored Luxembourg's being absorbed into one or another neighboring country; there was a heavy burden of corruption, incompetence, and foreign interference, not at all separated from the Grand Duke and his party. A government elected by a very few people, made up often of representatives who served special interests rather than the citizens at large, with the voting qualification dependent on money, which could buy other votes as well as qualify the individual voter, was bound to be corrupt. An all-powerful bureaucracy, who thought of themselves as the country itself, burgeoned. Such a state of affairs constituted the governmental fabric throughout the century.

Business leaders and professional men, then, ran the political affairs of the country until the period after World War I. Political parties were slow to take shape; ideology was of less importance than dynamic personalities. The parties tended to divide, of course, between the left and right, but inexperience and flux prevented a hardening of interests into strict party disciplines.

It took money to build and run railroads, to mine ore and build larger and larger mills to smelt it, to develop international trade, to develop a capital city. The International Bank at Luxembourg was begun in 1856 and still operates. People's savings banks followed, and later there were private banks. Not all were successful. For instance, the National Bank of the Grand Duchy of Luxembourg, founded in 1873, lasted only to 1881. But over the long haul banks grew to meet governmental, social, and financial exigencies. Just as the earlier iron-steel mills foreshadowed Luxembourg's later world position in that industry, so the 19th century bank foreshadowed her major position in the world's banking operations in the late 20th century.

The beautiful, charming city that Luxembourg City was to become took shape during those years after 1867. "Luxembourg, which had been a sad city, was transformed into one of the most beautiful cities of Europe," wrote a Minister of State. The great fortifications, thick, gray, and forbidding, had made it sad.[11] Walls, looming high and rugged above the two little rivers, had cut off the central city from its suburbs. From four to seven thousand Prussian soldiers, with whom Luxembourgers found no sympathy or social intercourse, except for the inevitable marriages, were garrisoned on the plateau behind those walls. Neither commerce nor culture found a comfortable bedding ground there.

Luxembourg City, within its fortifications, consisted of only 880 acres, less than a square mile and a quarter; only about 200 acres supplied the room for dwellings and streets. Three rings of fortifications surrounded it. There were forty forts and bastions and numerous smaller fortified points; 13 miles of casemates and laid mines of explosives cut through the solid rock; manned gates of entry closed at night. The slopes between the upper city and the lower towns were stripped of the dwellings that had once been there and of the very earth itself in order to cover them with stone walls and bastions and glacis, so that the city citizens were enclosed narrowly within walls without access to fresh air and recreation. Barracks, workshops, arsenals, grain and forage storage buildings, stables, headquarters crowded the space that packed in 13,000 citizens with the soldiers. Provisions for the health of the population were few; water was insufficient and polluted; street lighting was minimal; streets were rough, dirty, and neglected; human waste was carried away in open carts.

There was enough to counterbalance these deprivations to make many citizens oppose the neutralization of the fortress and the withdrawal of the garrison. Those citizens made their living off the military. They developed societies of entertainment to provide diversion and disseminate some of the leavening effects of culture. Poets wrote, musicians sang and played. The status quo offered the security that they had known; neutrality and freedom from the military threatened the loss of livelihood.

But down the fortifications came after 1867; the ditches were filled up; the valleys were cleared; fresh air was let in and the elements of a better hygiene were introduced. The labor of centuries — the fortifications, that is — was undone in sixteen years. And in 1883 Luxembourg stood free and open to the world for the first time in 900 years. Affluence and full participation in the free world lay not many decades in the future.

The new status of the Catholic Church came concurrently with political freedom and neutrality. Neither Trier nor Cologne nor Liège nor Namur nor Metz would have anything more to say about the church in Luxembourg. In 1870 Luxembourg became a bishopric. Henceforth its church loyalties and its church squabbles would be confined within its own geographical borders.

This is a matter of no small importance. By being divided in church government among two or as many as six bishoprics Luxembourg had been armed, in a sense, against being taken over by one national power. But after 1867 religious division would no longer serve any political power. The country was almost 100 percent Catholic. It was free. And now it could have its own bishop in the person of Msgr. Adames. This national rosebush of Luxembourg was coming into blossom — politically, religiously, economically — after 1867.

When we take into account the almost unanimous Catholicism of the population, the tensions between church and state in the 19th century are surprising. The effects of 18th century liberalism, when the church surrendered a considerable part of its domination over the political and social life of the people, were still very much in force when Luxembourg got its first freedom in 1815 and had that freedom confirmed in 1839. The arrival of a new apostolic vicar, Msgr. Laurent, in 1841 inaugurated changes in that state of affairs.

Laurent's initial success lay in the passing of a law in 1843 giving extensive control of primary education and the preparation of teachers to the church. He founded a seminary for the preparation of priests. He promoted the building of churches and parish reforms. Though his aggressiveness led to his recall in 1848, he stimulated a renewal of the church that would lend it vitality up to the present day, marked by one conflict after another, yes, but animating the social services of schools and hospitals and sharpening the religious consciousness of the entire population. The establishment of the bishopric in 1870 was entirely at the instigation of the church, not the government, so that some political leaders found themselves at odds with the bishops. The church was to lose its domination in the schools, the bishop was to excommunicate deputies that voted against it, and finally the fate of the very dynasty itself would be related to the religious issue.[12] But the church became strong during these years and would remain strongly entrenched in the spiritual and social consciousness of the Luxembourg people.

*   *   *   *   *   *   *

Along with economic expansion came social developments that would find their fullest expression in the 20th century. Insurance companies, private mutual banking concerns, health and accident insurance (first within the trade or business, later through the central government) — all found a firm footing. Free and compulsory education went into effect in 1881. The first unions got their start in 1864 and developed steadily after that date, with cartels of socialist unions shaping after 1906, unions of Catholic workers forming, and agriculture associations organizing the farmers, beginning in 1875. As business flourished, agriculture flourished, as we have seen, finding new markets in the industrial centers, tendencies that would continue up to the present day.

In just 36 years — 1880 to 1916 — savings deposits multiplied by 50 times. By the time that World War I struck Luxembourg with what might have been its death blow, the once poverty-stricken country had, by means of hard work, organizational genius, and foreign capital, attained to first rank in material comfort. According to one report, in 1914, in terms of French gold francs, the individual wealth of Luxembourg and its neighbors ranked as follows:[13]

	National Wealth (in billions)	National Wealth per Citizen
Luxembourg	3	11,568
Germany	305	4,700
France	230	5,851
Belgium	57	7,247

The poor orphan, tormented by covetous and rapacious relatives, was grown into a prosperous paterfamilias with his own domicile, possessions, and income.

One particular aspect of this economic development and prosperity calls for particular note. It is the iron-steel industry, which in this period found its predominating financial role, its new equipment, its markets. Henceforth, until well after World War II, this industry would determine Luxembourg's wealth, its demographic distribution, and its place in the world. The little provincial backwater, hitherto important only for its place in military history, would be developing a financial, social, and political sophistication that would put it on a par, relatively, with the great powers of Western Europe.

Before World War I Luxembourg was largely in the orbit of Germany. The money that went into the great steel mills and the banks was German, crowding out Belgian money. In this period the combination of mills called ARBED (1911) was destined to become the third largest steel enterprise in Europe.[14] The German and Luxembourg interpenetration in these undertakings became almost total. When war broke out in 1914, Germany was supplying more than 90 percent of the fuel that fired the furnaces, 70 percent of the products found its buyers in Germany, and the half-finished steel of Luxembourg mills went to Germany for finishing.

Since 1870 Lorraine, with which Luxembourg's cultural ties had been strong throughout its history, had been German. The Saar with its coal, Lorraine with its minerals, and Luxembourg with its ore and manufacturing facilities constituted an amalgamated enterprise from which no part could be extracted.

Came August 1914. Germany invaded neutral Luxembourg. Germany's goals being what they were, how could she have done otherwise? One of the greatest commercial enterprises in Europe could not be allowed to remain neutral when Germany had need of all the tools of war that it could command.

Certainly she could not allow that iron ore and those mills to fall into the hands of France. Luxembourg now paid the price for all the prosperity that she had permitted Germany to bring to her. Her financial aider and abettor was her enemy, had always been her enemy, Germany. And thus began four years of military oppression once again, four years of self-denial and suffering, four years of shame.

Ironically, within these dire circumstances was the seed out of which its recovery and national identity would grow. Lorraine, with which German domination had established Luxembourg's intimate connection, in 1918 became French again. And Luxembourg, needing as ever close ties with a strong neighbor, would find it easy and congenial to choose the ties with France rather than with Germany.

*　　*　　*　　*　　*　　*　　*

We began this chapter by affirming that the sweep of Luxembourg's history for the past 12 decades was owing to an aggregation of characteristics and accomplishments that could sustain itself only by the lively operation of each of the factors in that aggregation, whether political, social, economic, or religious. One factor remains to take our attention. It is that of the sovereign.

In more than 900 years Luxembourg had no sovereign born on the soil that constitutes the Grand Duchy today. The first reigning Grand Duchess, the first native-born sovereign of the free and independent state, would be Marie Adelaide, born in 1894. She ascended the throne in 1912.

The greatest test of Luxembourg's freedom in 950 years would come only two years later. On the very eve of that dreadful date the nationalism of Luxembourg truly came into being. All that is truly Luxembourgian began to merge and to coalesce. Loyalties that might have tended to south, to west, to east of the grand-ducal borders reversed themselves and came together in a kind of centripetal attraction. Now the mystic meaning of *Mir wëlle bleiwe wat mir sin* sang in the hearts of all the citizens. *Letzeburg de Letzeburger* provided the focus for all endeavor. The Luxembourg spirit became an adamant from which the German steel would twice, in the years to come, strike mighty sparks; but that adamant would not shatter, would not be absorbed. The unity a thousand years ashaping would prevail.

Some mystique in the idea of a woman sovereign titillated the dour Luxembourg character. There was the mythical wife of Sigefroid, Melusine, to come to mind; Countess Ermesinde, who gave the people their first freedoms; Archduchess Isabella, whose virtues were all the greater when contrasted with the villainies and shortcomings of the male sovereigns; Empress Maria Theresa, whose greatness shed some of its light on the little Duchy.

To have no sovereign at all was unthinkable. The rolling stock of the Nassaus left the main track in 1890 when William III died without male issue. The family pact of the Nassaus provided that there would be no successor in the female line so long as there was a male successor in some branch of the Nassau family. Thus Duke Adolf of Nassau, who had lost his German lands in the Austro-Prussian War, became Grand Duke. From him descended Grand Duchess Marie Adelaide, the eldest of the six daughters of Adolf's son, William IV, Grand Duke from 1905 to 1912. William IV provided for her succession when in 1907 he promulgated a statute making her heir-presumptive. That statute was ratified by a vote of 41 to seven in the Chamber of Deputies.

When Marie Adelaide came to the throne in 1912, the full flower of Luxembourg's industrial affluence was beginning to open up. Newspapers had been proliferating. Universal education, with instruction in both French and German, was mandatory. A literature in the folk language was beginning to find more frequent expression; it had found maturity in the long satiric poem of Michel Rodange, *Renert* (1872). Good communication, both rail and road, laced the country. Banks, both local and international, served trade and industry. Agriculture flourished. Government was stable, for political parties had not yet clearly shaped themselves. The vote was extended. A liberal constitution gave rights to all. An international pact assured her independence. She was a bishopric of her own. Like a small rock around which the tides swirl without its being moved, she sat among the powers, receiving the benefits of progress and paying no penalties.

The matter-of-fact Luxembourgers, whose romanticism found expression only in religion and superstition, received the girl-sovereign's accession with rejoicing.[15] Into their conception of her they injected all their ideals of youth and beauty. Previous Grand Dukes had been protestant, but she was Catholic. They were in a very short time to allow themselves a bitter disillusionment that would drive her from the throne. But the romantic illusion prevails; her stubbornness, overweening insistence on her rights despite youth and inexperience, some sort of emotional uncertainty, and exaggerated religiosity exist in the Luxembourgian memory only as shadows. It is doubtful that confirmation of such explicit detraction would come from a Luxembourgian historian.

What cannot be denied is that she alienated the government and her people. When the Germans invaded in 1914 she kept her German advisers. During the war she visited her relatives in Germany. And after the war her country sent Marie Adelaide into exile.

Reaching the apogee of her national self-consciousness after 950 years of history, Luxembourg — almost in moments, it might be said — suffered Germany's attack, fought off destruction and starvation, discovered traitors in her bosom, and hovered on the brink of annihilation. But the national synergy, which without any one of its ingredients might not have been a nationality, remained whole.

* * * * * * *

Before turning our attention to the heartrending trials of World War I, we should brighten the colors of some parts of the Luxembourg picture of 1867 to 1914 we have been painting. Important as politics, economy, sovereignty, and religion are, the intellectual and aesthetic aspects of a nation will exert their influence, will have their due.

In the early 19th century Luxembourg had no real intellectual and aesthetic tradition of its own on which to draw. Such a situation reflected the lack of true nationalism, which was a 19th century phenomenon. Its religion tended to unify it. Its language identified it. Of literature, architecture, painting, music almost nothing beyond what was local and parochial, up to this time, can be identified. Domestic architecture added the pseudo-baroque and Victorian rococo in the towns. Churches were classical or Roman or Gothic. Other than the display that new-rich self-consciousness called for, there was little distinguished building. In its poverty, rurality, and relative isolation, it saw — if it was at all aware — the great performances of art and intellectuality pass it by. Without a resident sovereign and court, it lacked the motivation of ostentation and display that over the centuries had made the cities of Europe brilliant and beautiful.

Education, science, the arts, literature[16] — all had their rise and development together in the 19th century. Poetry in Letzeburgesch had its beginnings with the publication of a small volume by Antoine Meyer in 1829. The poetry by Michel Lentz (author of the national anthem), Dicks (Edmond de la Fontaine), and Michel Rodange (*Renert*) was to follow. *Renert* was a great work of national satire, using the animal allegory of the fox to reveal all aspects of Luxembourg life: the priests and the anti-romanists, the annexationists and opportunists, the rotten politicians, the grasping industrialists. By scourging all weaknesses of national character and practice it created a national consciousness that helped sweep the country toward a patriotism that up to that time it had not felt.

The Grand-Ducal Royal Institute came into being in 1868 by combining societies of historical research, natural science, and medical science. It added sections in linguistics, folklore, place names, arts and letters, and moral and political science. These parochial investigations led to the researches in history that provide the basis for historical research today. Some of the great names are Wurth-Paquet, Schötter, van Werveke, Neyen, and Hardt.

As the use of the local dialect grew stronger and stronger, as literary works were written, as stage plays, vaudeville turns, and songs appeared in their own tongue, Luxembourgers felt the need to know their language even better. A commission appointed in 1897 brought out a *Luxembourg Dialect Dictionary* in 1906. In 1935 a new commission was to undertake the development of a full-scale dictionary, the five volumes of which were not completed until 1977.

When a congeries of factors determines a country's fate, it could be irresponsible to name one factor as being more important than all the others. Still, there is reason in naming language as that factor. The use of both German and French in Luxembourg dates back to the 12th century. When the geographic limits shrank in 1839 to those of the present Grand Duchy, those limits surrounded people speaking basically a Germanic dialect, the *Westmoselfränkisch*. The more liberal and enlightened spoke French too, however. German became the language of newspapers, the church, and business. French became the language of the courts and cultural activities. French and German were both declared official languages in the constitution of 1868. As Luxembourg shaped itself into a democracy, the fact that all boys and girls learned French thoroughly in the schools worked to prevent a separation between the laboring classes and the most highly educated citizens on the basis of language. Looking outward, Luxembourg found intercommunication with all its neighbors easy. Looking inward, it found its unity through the medium of language.

Perhaps no other country in Europe finds itself so ready in the late 20th century to communicate internationally as Luxembourg, particularly now that English is being learned in high schools almost as thoroughly as French and German. Italians, Spanish, and Portuguese are becoming a larger segment of the population so that their languages are having a cultural impact. But, with the perversity that has seemed to characterize the

millenium-long formation of the nation, the pol
yglotism of Luxembourg has tended to strengthen and unify
rather than to weaken and disperse.

NOTES: Chapter XVIII

[1]Paul Weber, *Histoire du Grand-Duché de Luxembourg* (Brussels, Office de Publicité, 1949), pp. 141-147.

[2]Ibid., pp. 167-168.

[3]Ibid., "L'établissements de la sidéurgie sur la minette," pp. 181-186.

[4]Gilbert Trausch, *Le Luxembourg à l'époque contemporaine* (Luxembourg, Editions Bourg-Bourger, 1975), p. 69. Quoting from J.-P. Faber, *Géographie économique du Grand-Duché de Luxembourg* (Luxembourg, 1903), pp. 30-31.

[5]Weber, "L'invention de Sidney Gilchrist Thomas (1879)," pp. 200-203; "Les Progrès de l'Agriculture," pp. 209-211, in *Histoire de l'économie luxembourgeoise* (Luxembourg, Chambre de Commerce, 1950).

[6]Trausch, pp. 73-75. The acreage figures are general and should be reconciled with the figures of the official STATEC.

[7]Carlo Hemmer, *L'économie du Grand-Duché de Luxembourg* Part I (Luxembourg, Editions Joseph Beffort, 1948), p. 102.

[8]Weber, *L'économie*, p. 159. See also Albert Calmes, "Aperçu de l'histoire économique de 1839 à 1959" in *Le Luxembourg: Livre du Centenaire* (Luxembourg, l'Imprimerie Saint-Paul, 1948), pp. 147 and 148.

[9]Ibid., "L'Eclosion capitaliste," pp. 173-239.

[10]Trausch, pp. 59-60.

[11]*Luxembourg au temps de la forteresse.* Photographs, Bernard Wolff; préface, Paul Wilwertz; introduction, Paul Margue (Luxembourg, Edouard Kutter, 1967).
J.-P. Koltz, *Baugeschichte der Stadt und Festung Luxemburg*, 3 volumes (Luxembourg, V. Buch, 1944, 1946, 1951).

[12]See Chapter XIX.

[13]Weber, *L'économie*, p. 239. See Weber, pp. 161-239 for details of economic development up to 1914.

[14]Joseph Wagner, "L'Ere de l'acier Thomas," in *Livre du cinquantenaire de la ville d'Esch-sur-Alzette* (Esch, l'Imprimerie Coopérative, 1956), p. 98. The book is informative about mining and the fabrication of iron and steel in Luxembourg.

[15]Edith O'Shaughnessy, *Marie Adelaide: Grand Duchess of Luxembourg, Duchess of Nassau* (New York, Harrison Smith, 1932).

[16]Nicolas Ries, "La vie littéraire" in *Le Luxembourg: Livre du Centenaire*, pp. 285-310.
Cornel Meder, Michel Raus, Anne Berger, *Littératures du Grand-Duché de Luxembourg*, No. 89 of *Petite Dryade* (Virton, Michel Frères, 1976).

Chapter XIX

The First World War and After

1914-1922

THE FIRST THREAT TO LUXEMBOURG'S independence in the sweep of history, after the threat to that independence in 1867, came in 1914. On August 2 the German army entered Luxembourg. Then began four years of thralldom. Luxembourg as a geographical and political entity had been threatened, subsumed, defeated many times through the centuries. But the German occupation constituted more than a political threat, a geographical threat. It constituted a threat to the existence of nationhood. It threatened the loss of everything Luxembourgian.

Germany had been one of the guarantors of the Luxembourg neutrality since 1867. Now she simply ordered troops into the little nation, as much as to say, "You are ours." Resistance would have meant annihilation. Diplomatic protest meant nothing.

The politics, the economy, the way of life were now to undergo the greatest stresses. Even as we begin to examine those stresses, we should have a strong consciousness of the vital independency that was their issue when peace came again. The figure of the pendulum will serve us once again. It swings far to the left during the period with which we are dealing, but when the war ends it will swing back again and right itself. For the Luxembourg citizens after 1918 were to settle the issues of the sovereign, the franchise, international alignment, and fiscal responsibility in such a way as to establish governmental stability, international participation, and prosperity that would outlast the exigencies of the years to come.

During the war Luxembourg might have foundered on the question of the sovereign. The idealized and idolized girl-Grand Duchess failed in her job.[1] Though the rights that she claimed were given her by the constitution, her people, in the person of the Deputies, expected a more ready compliance by her with the will of the majority. Legitimacy and law were in effect, but the challenge to legitimacy and law was burgeoning in the European consciousness.

The beginnings of trouble came early in Marie Adelaide's reign. The liberal majority in 1912 voted to remove control of teacher education from the church and to free teachers from responsibility for teaching religion. Henceforth the priests only, not the secular teachers, would teach religion. The church violently opposed these changes; the bishop excommunicated those Deputies who voted for them. The Grand Duchess, almost mystically Catholic, delayed putting the laws into effect (as she had the right to do), to the almost frantic anger of the liberals. Her father and grandfather, protestants both, had tended to let the government have its way. By being obstructive, she contributed to a sharpening of the liberal opposition and pointed the way to the reforms that would follow the war. This first Catholic sovereign in a hundred years, whose faith contributed to the warmth with which she had been welcomed to the throne, won from her Catholic supporters the opposition that in a few years would remove her from it.

The war years deepened the Luxembourgers' distrust of the young Grand Duchess. Having invited unpopularity by resisting school reforms, she added to it when she gave her favor to conservative appointees to official positions over possible appointees from the political left. When the Minister of State Paul Eyschen died in 1915, she mishandled the appointment of a new government. Eyschen had been president of the Government (Prime Minister) since 1888 — a total of 27 years. In his political wisdom he might have been able to govern and direct the stubbornness of his sovereign. She appointed a government of the right even though it did not command a majority in the Chamber. When it was overthrown, she dissolved the Chamber. When the elections went in favor of the left, her opponents were now in a position to frustrate her in whatever she tried to do. The next two governments each lasted a little more than a year, with intervals that gave the opportunity for bitter words and factional fighting.[2]

The hardships that accompanied occupation by the enemy fed the flames of dissension and dissatisfaction. The workers were often unemployed and underpaid, with no possibility of redress under the Germans. They began to organize in unions. Inflation outran income. Demand exceeded supply. Town dwellers found themselves contending with farmers, who had control over the only supply of food. The black market proliferated. A great strike of the miners broke out. In every commercial field there were undersupply, loss of employment, disappearance of markets, and depletion of production. The people suffered severely.

Marie Adelaide was a visible focus for the people's anger. A young girl had the presumption to oppose her will to experienced leaders and to the elected representatives of the people. Of German ancestry, she appeared in their eyes to have German sympathies. During the years that German occupation brought suffering to the citizens, she kept the German advisers and friends who constituted her court. She received the Kaiser as her guest and was herself a guest on German soil. The 18-year-old innocent who had touched the Luxembourgers' hearts and stirred their romantic imagination in 1912 became, in a few short years, the object of their distrust and animosity. As the war came to an end, there was little doubt that she must go.

* * * * * * *

The evolution of governmental theory was at work, tardily at work, during the years of World War I. Under the Luxembourg constitution sovereignty was vested in the house of Nassau-Weilburg. Until the eve of World War I Luxembourgers had little fault to find with such a state of affairs. But the war brought to a head the infection of democracy that might have festered for a decade or more in peacetime. The state of the European world would hardly have permitted it to go on longer than that.

The formation of political parties meant the articulation and defense of policies and platforms. The political left opposed personal sovereignty; it demanded the sovereignty of the people —

democracy or socialism. The working classes demanded food and employment and salaries; these the royal sovereignty had not been able to guarantee to them.

Many citizens became convinced during the hardships of the war years that the Grand Duchess Marie Adelaide would have to go. Forced by circumstances, she consented to abdicate in January, 1919. Her successor, her sister Charlotte, was to become one of the great leaders of her country. In 1919, when Charlotte's power could not yet be known, her appointment and confirmation were the symbol of the Letzeburgesch national essence: the centripetal center, the ultimate focus of all that was national.[3]

It was entirely in keeping with Luxembourg's conservatism and common sense that she elected to be a democratic monarchy. Certainly as much as in any other nation of Europe a sovereign was integral to the self-concept of the nation, though never in her history had she chosen her own sovereign. Certainly, too, many of her sovereigns had not been objects of trust and affection, including her most recent, Marie Adelaide. But if 1919 offered her the opportunity to be free of a royal house, the citizens chose not to take it. As they sent Marie Adelaide into exile, they chose her younger sister, Charlotte, to be their Grand Duchess.

The political steps that took Luxembourg to the affirmation of Charlotte were erratic and faltering. We should follow them.

Immediately upon the fall of Germany in November, 1918, a council of Luxembourg workers and peasants, a communist-style soviet, proclaimed a republic. It did not find support and disintegrated. Less far to the left than the soviet, the liberals and socialists in the chamber called for the dismissal of the monarchy. The question came to a vote and failed by the barest margin. Thus the dynasty survived two assaults.

The attacks came not only from within the nation. French covetousness toward Luxembourg had never been dead; now French aspirations toward the Grand Duchy stirred again. French displeasure with Marie Adelaide took the form of opposition to the dynasty itself and by extension to the continuation of Luxembourg independence. When the President of the Government made a mission to Paris, the French government refused to receive him.

Belgium was equally pressing, looking to reunion with that part of the old Duchy that had been lost to it in 1839. Many Luxembourg liberals gave their sympathy to Belgium, while the socialists for the most part leaned toward France. Only the party of the right linked independence and the dynasty together as the best future for the country.

January 9, 1919, the liberals and socialists declared a republic. The focus and symbol of discontent both within the country and abroad, Marie Adelaide would have to abdicate. Immediately, on January 15, 1919, Charlotte became Grand Duchess. Luxembourg was still a nation; Luxembourg had still a sovereign. Would both — or either — survive? France and the allies were influenced against Luxembourg independence by the German Zollverein and railroad connection. They seemed to be concerned not at all with the wishes of the Luxembourgers themselves, who in a double referendum elected to retain the dynasty and to seek economic union with France. Luxembourgers were still at the helm of their national ship in the stormy seas of European politics. It would really make port in 1922 when, France having refused an economic union, Luxembourg concluded an economic union with Belgium.

The citizens of Luxembourg characterized themselves broadly in their political acts of 1919. Seventeen percent of those who went to the polls voted for a republic rather than a monarchy. Seventy-seven percent voted for Charlotte to be their Grand Duchess.[4] Sovereignty was a Luxembourg mystique; democracy was not. In a democratic and socialistic age the Luxembourgers adhered to the monarchical principle, which had been at the core of their national allegiance for 1000 years through every vicissitude. Never did any people, large or small, make a wiser choice. The expedient choice of 1919 would, in a very real sense, determine their national salvation only twenty-one years later when the German curse would maul her yet one more time. Charlotte, only twenty-three years old, was blessed with character and wisdom to match the beauty and strength with which her choice endowed the little nation.

At the same time, however, the people vested the national sovereignty in themselves. The troubling ambiguity that had supported Marie Adelaide in her opposition to the general will was removed from the constitution. Henceforth the Grand Duke should have only those powers and responsibilities that the people chose to give to him. Henceforth the Grand Duke would be the servant of the people, not the master.[5] All Luxembourg men and women, twenty-one years old or older, were empowered to vote.

In the modern world of 1919-1920 political Luxembourg came of age.

* * * * * * *

Fiscally and socially, too, Luxembourg was moving into maturity. It shared with the rest of Europe, of course, the crisis and uncertainty of the postwar years. Its economic connection with Germany, which had contributed to its prosperity from 1867 to 1914, was ended. When France refused to play the part that Germany had played, Luxembourg reluctantly turned to an economic union with Belgium in 1922. That union would prove to be not only viable but profitable; the connection that Luxembourg considered second choice would in the long run help determine the prosperity that would give the Grand Duchy a place at the international tables of decision making for all of Europe.

Of course the years immediately following World War I were not easy. After two generations of economic orientation with Germany, the Grand Duchy had to establish an untested orientation elsewhere. After three generations of relative political stability, within which the people gave support to an unaligned leadership, political parties were shaping themselves in the traditional channels of left and right. In a traditionally conservative society radical voices, those of the communists, were making themselves heard. But ancient Luxembourg was like an old but sturdy ship, at the end of a long anchor chain, wallowing in heavy ground swells and erratic cross currents. But still seaworthy and afloat.

The royal house, having invited opposition in the person of Grand Duchess Marie Adelaide, now gave stability to the nation in the person of Grand Duchess Charlotte. Not many months after acceding to the throne, she married a prince of the house of Bourbon-Parma, a descendant of Louis XIV, Felix, and proceeded to have, before long, a native-born son and heir, Prince

Jean.[6] The mystique of the sovereign house permeated all the social levels of the little country at a time of dangerous stress and tinged all the political colorations that fluctuated in the social scene.

Now, after World War I, Luxembourg needed all the strengths she could muster. The old German alignment gone, coveted by Belgium, treated cavalierly by the great powers, its old markets closed to it, its old sources of supply dried up, it faced the necessity of finding a new economic union with a larger power, shoring up its agriculture and viticulture, keeping its workers employed while finding both suppliers and buyers. Though Belgium had hardly shown itself friendly, Belgium would have to be the nation with which Luxembourg would form an economic union.

That union was agreed on in 1921; it went into force in 1922. *L'union économique belgo-luxembourgeoise* (U.E.B.L.),[7] begun with such difficulty, would grow stronger and more cordial with the passing years. Within it Luxembourg would evolve economically and socially into the nation that could survive the vicious assault of World War II.[8]

The evolution of political parties and labor unions in Luxembourg holds some interest for us. The dependence of the vote on the possession of property delayed the development of both until World War I, a very late date in regard to these matters in Europe.

Between the 1840s and the time of World War I both the office holder and the man casting his vote allied themselves to issues rather than parties. The elected man and the holder of public office supported the issues that would be beneficial to them. The citizens who had no vote — the great majority — found themselves frustrated in getting any action that would be to their benefit. Luxembourg was not a dictatorship by any means, for control of government was open to those voting citizens who could acquire and hold it. And it was not communistic, of course, with a designated few always in power and always holding everyone else at bay. But it was hardly democratic either. Always alive in the public consciousness was the desire for universal suffrage, sought by the Catholic group as early as 1848 and by the socialists beginning in 1896. The frustration in getting it led to mounting pressure; the deprivations of the time of World War I turned desire into demand; and the disorganization and freedom sprung from the sudden liberation of late 1918 blew the functioning regime to smithereens.

It is in character with all the happy ironies of Luxembourg history that within the destruction of government were the elements of construction. The dismissal of the Grand Duchess was followed by the installation of the new Grand Duchess. The demands and rebellion of socialists and communists resulted in their repudiation. From being the possession of the very few, the vote now went to all citizens twenty-one years of age or older, women as well as men. From a situation that might have been revolutionary derived balance, good sense, and direction.

The Luxembourg phoenix was again on the wing.

The new phoenix was feathered with a popular new Grand Duchess, universal suffrage, political parties, workers' unions, social benefits, and flourishing general education. In the movement toward parties, begun as early as 1848, some of the people, at least, had found rallying points.[9] The first rallying point was obvious: ownership of property and consequently the right to vote. It was associated with the name of the three Metz brothers, whose power was both economic and political. The second was Catholicism, of which a segment of people found themselves supporting this or that cause jointly. From 1848 until 1919, the Catholic group would find universal suffrage the cause that most consistently animated it. The first socialists did not appear in the Chamber until 1896, and the socialist party was organized only in 1902. The Catholics first functioned as a party in 1914, and the liberal party, so-called, would come into being only after World War I. Early attempts to form a group with the interests of the workers at heart failed. Without large industries and without an urban concentration of workers, a workers' party had little chance. Throughout the 19th century the political groupings were fluid, there was not really any party with a consistent program, and nothing like party discipline existed. Within the social atmosphere of Europe on a whole, the smallness and intimacy of Luxembourg permitted political functioning without strict party organization; that same smallness and intimacy permitted resolution of issues without desperate conflict and disintegration.

In the light of this long-lasting party amorphousness, the party aspect of the revolutionary conditions immediately after World War I attracts attention.

During the war the body politic had suffered the most severe strains. Beneath the surface the centuries-old currents of French and Belgian sympathies flowed this way and that without channel or check. The French and Belgian sympathizers were looking to a new alignment after the war. The most radical, in the sense of being most unpatriotic as regarded an independent Luxembourg, looked to a union with Belgium. These conflicting groupings found themselves agreeing in their opposition to the Grand Duchess, whom they correctly saw as personifying the Luxembourg independent identity. Those can be labeled as liberals who were Belgian in sympathy, and socialists, French in sympathy. Both France and Belgium were sympathetic to their position. Standing four-square for an independent Luxembourg, in opposition to the liberals and the socialists, was the party of the right, led by Emile Reuter. So evenly divided were the deputies between the right, on the one hand, and the others that the situation was touch and go.

The government safely sought a referendum. When by a large majority the people chose Charlotte for their Grand Duchess and France for a customs union, it was the party of the right that was in power and would stay in power, with conflicts and interruptions of course, until the eve of World War II.

Even with respect to all its cataclysms, though, the Luxembourg of 1922 was, and the Luxembourg of the 1980s is, a product of a slow evolution. We see that clearly in the labor movement and in the organization, too, of wage earners on higher economic levels.

As might be expected, the first organization had been that of businessmen in a Chamber of Commerce, which received some attention in Chapter XVIII. The date was 1841. This was not a union, but even as the owners of businesses were looking out for their welfare, they were conscious that the laborers' welfare depended to a great extent on their success in sales and profits. This was hardly enlightened, but it was realistic. An immediate favorable action, approved by Germany, was the duty-free export of Luxembourg iron ore into Belgium, a situation that assured employment to the Luxembourg miner.

"The Chamber of Commerce was the first manifestation of autonomy of a state called upon to manage its new affairs, the first legal representation of a Luxembourg newly independent, the first expression of public opinion by a legally named spokesman."[10] All branches of industry and commerce found themselves represented in the Chamber, for in those days of growing entrepreneurship many of its members combined several kinds of business, profession, and government office in each of their activities.

In the light of the international involvement of the Luxembourg of today, and the importance of foreign laborers in the work force, it is enlightening to note the foreign origin of the majority of these business and professional leaders; from Lombardy and the Tyrol, from Trier and Metz and Cologne, from Bade and Thionville, and from the part of the old Duchy that had gone to Belgium.[11] Ironically, with war and conquest over the centuries had come, apparently, a revitalization of the national blood and character. The effect of the vitalization stimulated by the Chamber of Commerce, both private and semi-official, would be felt from the inception of the Chamber to the present day: in the complications and rewards of the Zollverein system, the immense developments in iron and steel, the revolution in agriculture, the development of viticulture, the governance of customs charges, the spread of railroads, the management of bankruptcies, the development of banks, the spread of insurance, the governance of salaries, even the encouragement of tourism.

It is probably right to say that the Chamber of Commerce was the chief vehicle by which Luxembourg traveled into the industrial age and arrived at the destination of full partnership in the world of today.

But the Chamber of Commerce was not the only vehicle on the high road of economic and social development. Throughout the later 1800s the farmers were organizing themselves locally. On the local scene mutual encouragement and information made more readily possible the taking advantage of the opportunities that came from the availability of fertilizer and the modernizing of machinery. In the realm of business, artisans in the small trades were comparable to the independent farmers. Typesetters and their fellows in printing formed a union as early as 1864. Tobacco workers and hat makers soon followed; then glove makers and leather workers and brewers and carpenters. Shortly before World War I began there were formed a general association of government employees, a federation of agriculture shows, a national federation of railway workers, and Catholic organizations of employees.

These unions were not the labor unions that the western world knows and reckons with today. But they were a beginning. On the whole the Luxembourg worker did not aspire to income and services beyond what he was accustomed to. He lived and worked, to some extent, in a spirit of fatalism. A day of reckoning was coming, however. When World War I ended, a groundwork had been laid. The Luxembourg worker only flirted with Marxism and violence in 1918 and 1919 before he moved toward a constructive activism, from which derived the full and free union participation of today.

The evolution of government help and surveillance moved at the same rate as the union development. Laws removed some injustices from worker-employer relations; protected women and children; regulated the length of the workday; imposed safety measures on the mines. At first in the businesses themselves, then by the force of law, came accident and health insurance and provisions for old age.[12]

All these were first steps. From 1918 on developments could come apace because of those first steps: adoption of the eight-hour day in the very first months of peace, workers' councils in the mills for conciliating and facilitating discussion, a general federation of labor, two trade associations of Railway Workers (Socialist and Christian), and then chambers of employees in commerce, artisans, private employees, public employees, agriculture workers. The powers of the unions increased, pension funds grew, collective bargaining began. All this led to the day when all the working people of Luxembourg, employers and employees alike, were enrolled in their professional chambers or unions. The constitution guaranteed their freedom.

* * * * * * *

What follows now does not deal with the years of World War I. It has to do with emigration and immigration. It is necessary that we put this information with what we know of Luxembourg in the years following the war. It had important bearing on the nature of the Grand Duchy and its people when World War I began and on the Luxembourg that came out of the war.

In the 1980s Luxembourg stands in a position of strength. However beset it is by contemporary social, political, and economic problems, it confronts them from a position of strength. There is some excuse for the historian who emphasizes from the past every step and action that led to that strength. After all, it is the big view that we are taking; in a thousand years of history that is the view that counts. But Luxembourg had troubles enough in pre-World War I. All was not roses in the land of roses.

The main manifestation of trouble — and the symptom of other troubles — was emigration.[13] The middle years of the nineteenth century saw three waves of emigration. The chief cause was poverty. The majority of the people led meager lives, and when harvests were poor their poverty became absolute want. Between 1816 and 1854 there were five periods that can be called times of famine. In the middle of the century one-eighth of the people were indigent, unable to stay alive without help. Begging was rampant, and destitute people in bands wandered through the countryside.

It was out of conditions like these that emigrants departed for other countries and other parts of the world. After 1815 whole families, entire communities sought a better life elsewhere — the Netherlands, Belgium, France, Algeria, Guatemala, Brazil, Argentina, America. In 1846-1847 alone almost 1600 people left the country; after the Civil War in America free land there attracted many Luxembourgers; between 1881 and 1884 a total of 2533 citizens left Luxembourg; in 1890, 1600; from 1911 to 1913, 1250. In the 50-year period ending in 1891, 72,000 Luxembourgers left their native land (against a population in 1890 of 212,000).

Two circumstances tended to counterbalance this draining off of the population: a high birth rate and an influx of foreign laborers. Because in the late 20th century the birth rate (lower than 10 per 1000 citizens) could possibly be denominated Luxembourg's major problem, it is well to note that between 1900 and 1914 the rate was as high as 25, 26, and even 30 per 1000. High as the death rate was in the 19th century, the birth rate was higher.

The second circumstance was the influx of foreign workers accompanying the building up of the iron-steel industry. The Luxembourg worker found mine and blast furnace labor uncongenial. The poor laborers from other countries found employment waiting for them in Luxembourg, and they came by the thousands, overtaxing housing and putting a strain on social relations, but contributing to the economic well-being of the nation. From a production of 60,000 tons of iron in 1855, the output of the mills grew to 250,000 tons in 1873; 1,000,000 tons in 1900; 2,500,000 tons in 1913. The output of the mines was multiplied eight times in 40 years. It was the growing towns in the industrial southwest that attracted these workers, so that as the weight of national population shifted to that section, so the preponderance of foreign workers found their work and settlement there. Luxembourg City and the southwest would, by the second World War, hold more than fifty percent of the population. More than fifty percent of workers in industry would be of foreign blood.

In the birthrate and in the foreign-born population we shall find circumstances that portend change in the very essence of Luxembourg character and personality in the 1980s.

NOTES: Chapter XIX

[1]Edith O'Shaughnessy, Marie Adelaide: Grand Duchess of Luxembourg, Duchess of Nassau (New York, Harrison Smith, 1932).

[2]Paul Weber, Histoire de l'économie luxembourgeoise (Luxembourg, Chambre de Commerce, 1950). See "La première guerre mondiale et la réorientation économique (1914 à 1921)," pp. 241-247.

[3]". . . la vénérée Grande-Duchesse Charlotte, qui symbolisat notre entité nationale." Gaston Thorn (Président du Gouvernement), Bulletin de documentation (Luxembourg, Ministère d'Etat, 1978).

[4]Pierre Majerus, L'Etat Luxembourgeois (Luxembourg, Imprimerie de la Cour Joseph Beffort, 1948), pp. 30-33.

[5]Art. 32 of the Constitution:

"The Grand Duke will fulfill his office [act] conformably to the present Constitution and to the laws of the country.

"He has no other powers than those that the Constitution and the particular laws in effect by virtue of the Constitution itself formally attribute to him. . . ." Majerus, p. 270.

[6]Ernest Ludovicy, "La famille souveraine" in *Le Luxembourg: Livre du Centenaire* (Luxembourg, l'Imprimerie Saint-Paul, 1948), pp. 29-33. ". . . wedged in the crowd, I have waited among thousands the appearance of the sovereign. I have seen our people, ordinarily skeptical, scoffing, jeering, exult with spontaneous joy in manifestations which, though lacking perhaps in unity and rhythm and organization, were all the more sincere. There is no doubt. This dynasty has become ours; it seizes upon everybody's heart, everybody's will. We love our flag; its bright colors flood our streets with joy on our great national holidays, and more than the flag, it is the living reality of the dynasty that is our national symbol." P. 31. (My translation)

[7]Weber, *L'économie*, "La reorientation économique," pp. 245-247.

[8]Ibid., "L'Union Economique Belgo-Luxembourgeoise (1922 à 1940)," pp. 253-288.

[9]Gilbert Trausch, "L'apparition de partis politiques," in *Le Luxembourg à l'époque contemporaine* (Luxembourg, Editions Bourg-Bourger, 1975), pp. 80-82. This is Vol. IV of *Manuel d'histoire luxembourgoise*.

[10]Weber, p. 141.

[11]Ibid., p. 143.

[12]Trausch, p. 118; pp. 149-150.

[13]Ibid, pp. 111-112, and pp. 112-118 for what follows.

Chapter XX

Between the Wars
1922-1940

T HE YEARS 1922 TO 1940, short as they are, constitute an era in the millenium of Luxembourg history. The years
1940 to 1946 provided a sad and fearsome hiatus. After 1946 Luxembourg took up where it had left off when the Germans
invaded, and carried to fruition the political, economic, and
social initiatives that it had provided for itself between the two
great wars.

When we look at the difficulties that Luxembourg had to face
between 1922 and 1940, we may be inclined to agree with the
historian who calls those years "a period of stagnation and crisis,
of uncertainties and distress."[1] But that would seem to be an
incomplete, if not an inaccurate, summary. The miracle for Luxembourg has been its survival, even more so perhaps in the twentieth century than in the centuries that preceded it. When added
to that survival are improved living conditions, better working
conditions, some financial security despite the great depression,
and increased international participation and respect, we may
conclude that Luxembourg did more than survive. We may even
say that, in comparison with a good part of the Western World,
it fared rather well. Of no little importance is the fact that, when
World War II ended, it was ready to move ahead prosperously
with its friends and neighbors.

Of prime importance was the economic union that Luxembourg completed with Belgium in 1922.[2] It made that union reluctantly, but Belgium was its only recourse; and in the spirit of the irony that has shuttled through the events of Luxembourg history the unwanted expedient became an instrument of economic and political strength. With a common currency, with a free customs border, with reciprocal advantages that pleased both countries, Belgium and Luxembourg together entered the van of the twentieth century world.

After almost losing its independence through the indifference and callousness of the great powers in 1919, Luxembourg had its independence affirmed by the Treaty of Versailles. In that status it took its place in the League of Nations and served the apprenticeship that would prepare it to play its part in the United Nations. Without being able to field an army it had its neutrality recognized by its powerful neighbors. It found its full social and political maturity in the decades of the 1930s and 1940s.

All social and economic development took place within the political pattern of the country. That pattern, interestingly enough, was right wing and conservative. We should not expect the situation to be otherwise in a national society that had been subjected for hundreds of years, until only a decade or so earlier, to the particular mystique of its sovereign and to the domination of the sovereign's men. Russia and its satellites threw off its sovereigns by revolution, as France had done earlier. Germany lost its sovereign — and its inherent political nature temporarily — by cataclysmic defeat in war. Luxembourg by careful neutrality and the habitual admonition of common sense weathered sporadic political challenge and evolved comfortably in the modern world toward the essentially conservative democratic monarchical republic that it is today.

The names of some political leaders deserve attention. Paul Eyschen was Prime Minister from 1888 to 1915, operating above political parties, giving direction to the nation and rallying support by the strength of his personality. He took the Grand Duchy through a change of dynasty in 1890, the five-year reign of an aged Grand Duke 1890-1895, a seriously ill Grand Duke from 1905-1912, the accession of a mere girl to the throne, and the shock of total submersion under a conquering power in 1914.

Under the pressures of enemy occupation, terrible economic deprivation, and an unpopular sovereign the liberal left made conservative domination untenable for a few years. But with the end of hostilities and the accession of a sensible, beautiful, and reliable sovereign in 1919 the right wing assumed again its political domination. Emile Reuter commanded an absolute conservative government as he maneuvered the country through the difficult postwar years until 1925. In 1927 the right wing Joseph Bech — who will make himself heard from again after World War II — took some liberals into a coalition that lasted eleven years. When this predominantly conservative government passed a law against communists, a referendum threw it out by less than one percent of the vote in 1937. Then Pierre Dupong again headed a coalition including both Catholic party members and socialists. Thus it was that when the Grand Duchess and the government went into exile in 1940, it was a coalition of rightists and socialists that would see the country through this latest danger and welcome back the peace.

What we see, then, is conservative thought in power being attacked and eroded, but staying in the saddle and finding fellows to ride with from liberals, socialists, and Catholics as liberalizing thought directed national sentiment.

The exigencies of international involvement did not permit maintenance of the status quo. The Belgian economic partner boasted of an agriculture productivity that put it at the head of all Europe.[3] Luxembourg would be hard put to hold her own. Its agriculture had never been particularly rewarding, and now the farmer would be entering a market in which the natural conditions of land, climate, production, and the distance from markets would put him at a worse disadvantage. Wise management demanded two types of action. The first, by the government, was that of subsidies, which would go into operation whenever the market seriously threatened the producer. The second consisted of two parts: a redistribution of the use to which the land was put and the increased use of chemical fertilizer.

Although the total acreage of agricultural land increased slightly during the between-the-war years, the redistribution had major dimensions. Cultivated acreage was reduced by 14%; pasturage was increased by 64%. The production of wheat doubled, while that of the other grains was reduced and the production of potatoes increased by 22%.[4] Most dramatic was the production of beetroot with an increase of almost 100%, reflecting the greater use of land for pasturage.

Quite as striking is the increase in productivity per acre in that period of twenty years: 38% in wheat, 11% in rye, 31% in beet-root, and 51% in potatoes. The average milk production per cow increased by 44%; in money value the return from the milk industry increased by a striking 400%, making it the principal agricultural resource of Luxembourg.

The impulse of necessity, subsidies, the availability of fertilizer, and the canny use of hard work all together brought Luxembourg soundly through the threatening years of worldwide depression. The combination put it on a stable footing to weather the war and enter the aftermath of war with confidence in itself and the trust of its fellow nations.

The same factors were brought to bear on the vineyards and the production of wine.[5] Acreage was reduced. The old vines producing inferior grapes were ripped up. Better quality grapes were produced. Cooperatives to aid in storage and marketing were developed. Luxembourg wines could now compete with the German Moselles. Domestic consumption doubled. All this was of the utmost importance as groundwork for postwar developments.

Without reducing the credit owing to the government and its agencies for agricultural development, we recognize that the good results came primarily from the industry and good sense of the individual farmer himself and farmers generally as a class. In this area the character of the country revealed itself in its stable essence at the very grass roots. As impressive, though, and even more dramatic were the changes and developments in heavy industry — iron and steel. Here the credit must go to the acumen and zeal of management and to the clear-seeing judgment of the men who directed the government.

In the iron-steel industry organization, supply, production, and sale all underwent stringent and wide-ranging change in the years between the wars.[6] Luxembourg took second rank in Europe and seventh rank in the world; even as it suffered from the depression in the 1930s it held its place relative to the other countries. In *L'Entente Internationale d'Acier* (Luxembourg, Germany, Belgium, France, the Saar) Luxembourg's importance dictated the locating of its headquarters at Luxembourg City. ARBED, organized in 1911, consolidated and expanded, as did the combine called Hadir, and acquired foreign connections of supply and market, particularly in Brazil.

By 1927 the four mills with 18 blast furnaces at Esch-sur-Alzette, Belvaux, and Audun (in France on the border), the two steel mills, 14 laminating lines — all were united. At Dudelange the improved blast furnaces increased production by two-thirds. The mills and equipment at Differdange and Rodange were all modernized. As a result, by 1929 production of pig iron jumped by six times over the pre-war figure and steel production more than doubled. Value per ton was quadrupled; the value for total tonnage increased five times.

The problems of supply were difficult. ARBED acquired interest in foreign coal suppliers — in France, Germany, Belgium, and the Netherlands. By 1926 Germany was the chief supplier of coke. ARBED invested in steel companies in Brazil, where there were rich deposits of ore. The Brazil connection would prove to be of great importance later in the century.

Changes in equipment and changes in product went hand in hand. Whereas in 1913 the amount of iron turned into steel was 46%, by 1929 the amount was 93%. The finished product became more and more important.

The thirties were hard years of course. But at 60% of capacity early in the decade, still Luxembourg showed one of the best figures in Europe, and recovery had begun by 1935. Improvement continued as Europe drew closer to war, which closed off Luxembourg's markets, stopped the German supply of coke, and brought Luxembourg in May 1940 into total subjection to Germany.

As catastrophe time after time throughout the centuries failed to destroy the nation, so again in the twentieth century World War II failed to bring Luxembourg to its knees. The 20 years before 1940 had seen Luxembourg managerial leaders and white collar workers replace the foreign functionaries who earlier had manned the managerial posts. Now a trained native cadre was waiting in the wings to direct the nation's business affairs at the war's end. At the other end of the employment picture labor found in its circumstances certain advantages that enabled Luxembourg to weather the depression and the war.

A rural and small town people, Luxembourgers had never taken comfortably to the labor of large mines and vast mills. Luxembourg had had to make welcome large numbers of laborers, particularly from southern Europe and Germany. The peak was reached in 1913, when almost 60% of mining and steel labor consisted of foreigners.[7] In 1930 foreigners constituted 18.6% of the population and 29% to 30% of the labor force. When orders lessened and production slowed down, the country faced the inevitable problems of unemployment. Now the country found the advantages of non-native laborers, when the two-thirds of unemployed foreign laborers went back to their native countries and the government had to deal only with a one-third unemployment rate among its own citizens. The foreign laborer in Luxembourg will constitute a vexed problem later in the century and be a subject for our attention.

Despite many unhappy aspects of the depression and the pre-World War II years, certain economic facts are striking in their strength. The total of salaries paid workers rose from 171 million francs in 1920 (a year of economic anguish in much of Europe) to a high of 770 million in 1930 and 582 million in 1938. The total never fell below 436 million after 1930. On the basis of the official price index, as the cost of living rose from 100 (in 1922) to 180 (in 1939), salaries increased from 100 to 244.[8]

The worker fared well not only in salary but in the benefits derived from developments in labor organization and welfare provisions. So comprehensive did the organization of workers at all levels become, and so generous the benefits, that Luxembourg was in a position of European leadership when World War II began. That fact would prove to be of prime importance when the Grand Duchy had to pick up the pieces after the war. Unionism and social benefits had a long history in the nation.

The Chamber of Commerce, we recall, got its start as early as 1841. Throughout the later 1800s the farmers were congregating locally to look after village and local area affairs, providing the base on which the drastic changes in agriculture took place in the twentieth century, beginning with the Federation of Agriculture Shows in 1909. In 1908 came a general organization of government employees, in 1910 the National Federation of Railway Workers, and in 1922 the Professional Chamber of Railway Workers.

Nineteen eighteen saw the establishment of the eight-hour work day.

At the same time that universal suffrage was legislated in 1919, the government organized workers in the mills for purposes of conciliation and of facilitating discussion. A year later came the Federation of Luxembourg Industry (management) and a General Confederation of Labor (socialist). The mill councils were dropped for a while, but were reinstituted in 1925.

Under leadership of the political right, professional chambers for various classes of occupation were organized: commerce, the artisans, labor, private employees, agriculture. These chambers were not only consultative, but could suggest legislation and had proposed legislation submitted to them.

In the 1930s the powers of the unions increased. In 1931 the government established the pension fund. In 1936 came collective bargaining, the creation of a National Council for Labor to conduct arbitration and discussion, and the first collective contracts. All this would lead to the guarantee of union freedom in the 1948 constitution, to the creation of the Health Fund in 1951, with subgroups such as banking employees and teachers, and to the complete organization of all workers, however high or however low on the economic ladder, after the war.[9]

Apart from the governmentally sponsored organization of the employed people of the nation were the free nonprofit groups that organized themselves around specialized employment. Ramifications into the civil and economic life by these groups were complete. Where interests overlapped or merged there was cooperation among the appropriate associations. The entire nation became an amalgamation of the divisions of employment and social services. Without being a socialist state, the Grand Duchy so organized itself that self-interest and national interest flowed together in one stream of work and management.

The day when to name the sovereign power was to define the nation was past. Thus in this examination of the Luxembourg of the 1920s and 1930s we have dealt in dates and details much more minutely than in the treatment of earlier eras. The sovereign power after 1919 was the people — each individual person that made up with 349,999 other individual persons the national state that was Luxembourg. Ultimately our goal is to know the Luxembourg of the 1980s. What happened in these years was fundamental to shaping the role that it would play in the roiled international life that would be the aftermath of World War II.

NOTES: Chapter XX

[1]Gilbert Trausch, Le Luxembourg à l'époque contemporaine (Luxembourg, Editions Bourg-Bourger, 1975), p. 139. This is Vol. IV of Manuel d'histoire luxembourgeoise.

[2]Paul Weber, "L'Union Economique Belgo-Luxembourgeoise" in Histoire de l'économie Luxembourgeoise (Luxembourg, Chambre de Commerce, 1950), pp. 253-284.

[3]For comparative figures see Weber, p. 260.

[4]Ibid., p. 261.

[5]Ibid., p. 263.

[6]Ibid., pp. 264-267.

[7]Ibid., pp. 206-207; 273-275.

[8]Ibid., p. 275.

[9]Trausch, "Le Monde du Travail," pp. 207-212.

Chapter XXI

The Second World War
1939-1945

THE WORDS OF THE IRISH POET Yeats catch the situation of Luxembourg during World War II: "The Horses of Disaster plunge in the heavy clay."

On September 1, 1939, the great war began. Germany invaded Poland; now she was at war with the other great nations. Luxembourg snuggled up to Germany's borders on the east and to the borders of Germany's enemy France on the south. Luxembourg's enemy Germany and her friend France were the jaws of the nutcracker in which the little neutral nation, for all practical purposes cut off from the rest of the world, waited to be crushed.

May 10, 1940	— The German army invaded Luxembourg.
July 29	— The German civil administration took over control from the army.
August 14	— Luxembourg ceased to exist (according to Germany) as a nation.
April 30, 1941	— Germany conscripted Luxembourg's young men for labor.
October 10	— The Luxembourg people defied Germany at the polls.
August 1-5, 1942	— The people showed open revolt.
August 30	— Germany imposed military conscription.
September 15	— Germany organized deportation of Luxembourg citizens.
September 9-13, 1944	— The liberation.

255

December 16 — The Germans launched the offensive that became the Battle of the Bulge.
March 2, 1945 — The final liberation.
May 7 — Peace.

Those bare bones carried a burden of agonized flesh. The events in which Luxembourg had suffered from war and foreign domination many times in the course of 1000 years appear in cold type in the impersonal pages of history. But World War II occurred in our day. The fear, the depredation, the suffering, the bereavement were experienced by people who still live; the death, by men and women who otherwise might be alive today. The nearness of that terror to our hearts and minds gives reality to it still.

The venial sins of Luxembourgers were the venial sins of Germans and Frenchmen. The mortal sins in relation to Luxembourg were almost entirely the sins of Germans alone. Luxembourgers had observed what the Nazis were doing. Between September 1939 and May 1940 they lived on the edge of a precipice that they knew must crumble beneath them. Neutrality, they sensed in their hearts, was a feeble and yielding prop.

They had been preparing, though, for the realization of their worst fears. Nervous waves of apprehension, like the twitching of a person's skin, had been rippling through Luxembourg for a decade before the war began. As early as 1930 the little militarily powerless nations of Western Europe formed the Oslo Group — Norway, Sweden, Denmark, Finland, the Netherlands, Belgium, and Luxembourg— to build up economic cooperation and to formulate common political action to counteract the threatening rivalries of the great powers. The German threat drew closer to the Luxembourg doorstep when Germany reoccupied and militarized the Rhineland in 1936. In 1938 the German army occupied Austria and in 1939 seized the Sudetenland of Czechoslovakia. Could not those rapes on the German eastern border be repeated on the western? General war threatened in 1938 and 1939. So palpable was the threat that Belgium made ready to receive the entire Luxembourg population in retreat from the expected invasion. The people made runs on the banks, cleaned out the stores, and in general prepared for economic siege. At the same time they gaily celebrated the 100th year of their freedom and made a jaunty representation of their independence at special events abroad.

While the common man made prudent provisions for himself and his family, the government made prudent provisions for the political continuity. It most carefully reconstituted its unarmed neutrality. It interned certain foreign nationals and provided against spies. Against the German juggernaut gathered on the eastern frontier, with installations of the Siegfried Line within yards of the Luxembourg border, the feeble little country installed feeble little roadblocks along the roads leading from the three rivers that constitute the eastern barriers. In a gesture of neutrality it placed the same barricades along the French border. It whistled in the dark. Most importantly, and secretly, it carefully planned safeguards for the government in case of dire emergency.

These were the general conditions when war broke out in September 1939; and these conditions, aggravated by actual want, unemployment, closing of businesses, and deprivation, prevailed during the eight months of "the phony war."

* * * * * * *

In the blackness of early morning on May 10, 1940, the German guns fired, the trucks rolled, the soldiers marched, the parachutists dropped. For Luxembourg the real horrors of war were beginning.[1]

From the industrial southwest 47,000 Luxembourgers streamed into France, entangled with multitudes of Frenchmen fleeing to the south. Above the temporary line between the French and the Germans another 50,000 were moved into the Ardennes to find what refuge they could among their shocked countrymen. One-third of the nation was on the move. Imagine the frustrations and confusions and apprehensions of the displaced multitude.

Immediately some secret provisions of the government went into effect. Ahead of the German invaders the Grand Duchess and her family, the Prime Minister and other members of the government between three and five o'clock on May 10 crossed into France, their automobiles mingled with 1000 others getting behind the Maginot Line and pushing south. Having traversed France, near the Mediterranean they succeeded in entering Spain, then Portugal, and finally England, which was reeling under the blitz. Because the plans for the Grand Duchess and government leaders to leave the country were secret, a temporary antagonism labeled their action as a flight rather than a defiance. But the citizens soon realized that a sovereign free to rally the support of the allies was of more help to them than a sovereign held hostage and subject to the pressures of a cruel and oppressive foe.

Practically alone, while German parachutists were falling around her automobile moving in blackout toward the French border, she made her way through the black night, succeeded in getting the French roadblocks raised, and began the treacherous pilgrimage that would eventually take her to the United States. Her young son Jean, the heir to the throne, flew at more than a hundred miles an hour ahead of the invader to evade capture and find asylum in France with his mother.[2]

The experience of Marie Adelaide in World War I was an unhappy memory. That experience repeated might have led to the annihilation of the nation. Her sister took a wiser course. Charlotte would, from the moment of her flight ahead of the Germans, be winning the sympathies of the Allied world. She would be the symbol of Luxembourg spirit and independence. Her picture in dwellings of the homeland would win the kind of reverence once given by the Russian peasant to the picture of the Czar. Her government, working with her, could keep Luxembourg identity in the minds of Luxembourg's distracted friends. When liberation came, she and her husband and son, along with officials of the government, would be on the doorstep to assume leadership and give inspiration.

* * * * * * *

It is well in our blurred memory of the events of 1939 and 1940 to bring the unhappy experience of the little Grand Duchy into sharp focus. That, now, is history, which, if we value the continuity of the free world's liberty, will not bear forgetting.

German villainy had been slithering within the borders of the nation for two decades.[3] Already in 1920, through its chargé d'affaires, it was assembling information about Luxembourg and Lorraine. Before long it had reestablished offices and branches of the great German industries, bringing with them German workers.

German, anti-French propaganda found a voice in a newspaper called *Soziale Republik*. German immigrants came and settled down, particularly in the industrial area of Differdange and the border area of Echternach. German orchestras and troupes of players and publications made their way into Luxembourg, and German-trained doctors sent their Luxembourg patients into Germany for the cure. Germans succeeded more readily than the French and Belgians in making friends, infiltrating the Luxembourg economy, winning administrative positions, as well as filling ranks of labor.

Some alert Luxembourgers were alarmed. As early as 1924 more than 3000 Germans were seeking naturalization. They organized themselves in clubs. There was considerable intermarriage. They were indeed a fifth column. As the years moved inexorably toward the open warfare of 1939, some Luxembourgers were won over to the Nazi ideal, and the infiltration of Germans who were actually spies instead of workers grew apace. During the eight months of the phony war the Germans and the German sympathizers among Luxembourgers increased their activities, particularly along the barrier rivers. German agents and officers disguised as tourists pervaded the country, listed and mapped every resource and physical detail, preparatory to the armored terror that would sweep through the country on May 10 and swiftly bring France to her knees.

* * * * * * *

On the German side of the three rivers that constitute its border with Luxembourg the land rises quickly — in some places immediately — to heights of hill and escarpment that grow wilder and more precipitous toward the north. Generally they are covered by thick forests. Villages dot the edge of the streams and occasional bridges cross them. Converging on the bridges are direct routes from Aachen, Cologne, and Coblenz to the north and northeast, from Mainz, Frankfurt, and Mannheim to the east, Saarbrucken and Strasbourg to the southeast. Communicating roads on the east banks of the rivers go from village to village. Along those roads and on the tops of the ridges the Germans dug in gun emplacements protected by concrete of immense thickness from which they could command the entire landscape of

Luxembourg, give fire cover to an invasion, and repel attack. Their snarling remains, as indestructible as primeval rock, testify to the awful threat that Luxembourgers observed in the making during the months before the invasion.

The testimony of *La Résistance du Peuple Luxembourgeois* catches the nervous inevitability of that dire night:[4]

"The night of May 9, 1940, about 11:45 P.M., the first messages arrived from the frontier. 'Important troop movements can be seen on the German-Luxembourg frontier, especially at Palzem [in the extreme southeast].' At a distance could be seen files of trucks which descended from the heights to group on the right bank of the Moselle in order to get to the embarkation points. The situation became more and more threatening; invasion was imminent.

"As if by chance, one began to see groups of armed men wearing armbands with swastikas on them. They were members of the fifth column who had finally come out in the open and were waiting for their masters. At the German legation all the windows were lighted up, as if an important meeting was taking place. Everything indicated that the Germans were on the road to war, ready to go into action. The messages from the frontier bore out the events in the capital.

"About three-quarters of an hour after midnight the radio post in the St. Esprit barracks at Luxembourg received word: 'Our patrols observe many troop movements along the left bank of the Sure, principally between Echternach and Weilerbach.' About 2:30 A.M. patrols saw troops and trucks grouped on the opposite bank. They were waiting for the moment that A. Goebbels had set to break the agreements signed at Berlin with the Secretary of the Government, Albert Wehrer, according to which the Germans pledged themselves to respect the neutrality of Luxembourg in case of conflict with France.

"The message at 3:51 A.M. said: 'Incidents at the German-Luxembourg frontier. A Luxembourg policeman killed and a police sergeant badly wounded at Grevenmacher, a policeman killed at Bous by Germans living in Luxembourg, telephone communications interrupted between Echternach and Luxembourg, and between Grevenmacher and the capital.'

* * * * * * *

"Identical news came from other frontier posts: 'Commando groups have crossed the frontier and seized policemen and customs officers.'. . . Operators of the PPT . . . confirmed that parachutists had landed in the south and that many other troops had invaded the Grand Duchy. The fifth column . . . started to attack. About 70 members had assembled at Felsmühle [above Grevenmacher]. Surprised in their hiding-place, by a patrol of control, they attempted to resist. In the skirmish that followed a policeman was killed and a police sergeant gravely wounded.

* * * * * * *

"The last message from the frontier at 5:15 A.M. announced: 'Invasion of the Grand Duchy of Luxembourg by German troops.' It was the beginning of a long calvary that was to last almost five years."

* * * * * * *

The first months of the occupation were as much a respite as an oppression, in that the first occupation was the disciplined imposition of the German army. After August 1, when control of the country went into the civil administration of the German government itself, imposition and unreasonableness and fear turned into cruelty and torture under the direction of the German *Gauleiter* or district chief. The words of Hitler became an actuality in Luxembourg: "We can go to the limit of humanity if we restore its happiness to the German people." Now the Germans were to go to the limits of humanity and beyond.

Within two weeks Luxembourg ceased to exist as a nation. The Council of State, the Chamber of Deputies, the political parties, the Constitution, Luxembourg laws — all were suppressed. German immigrants and a few Luxembourg sympathizers with Germany, as members of *Die Volksdeutsche Bewegung* (the German People's Movement), formed gangs to beat up citizens wearing patriotic insignia or otherwise manifesting patriotism. Some Luxembourgers swallowed their pride and hatred and joined the VDB in the hope of saving their jobs and even their lives.

Without humor or restraint, the Germans went to ridiculous lengths.[5] They forbade the men to wear the Basque beret, which was practically a national uniform. When they undertook to out-law the use of the French language, they were taking a much more drastic step. They went so far as to forbid the use of "Mon-sieur" and "bonjour" and "merci," all the French terms that had found a place in daily Letzeburgesch usage. Then they forbade the use of French Christian names, so that François had to become Franz, Camille, Kamil; and French family names, so that Jacques became Johan or Jacob and Dupont became Brückner. In such losses of identity, and in the search to refind it, people's spir-its hardened, and acceptance metamorphosed into resistance.

Then came attacks on the Jews;[6] the seizure of property; a con-certed campaign of Nazi propaganda; intimidation of holders of public office, who were deprived of job and income on the slight-est pretext; impressment into the labor force and transportation to Germany; destruction of the monument to the 3000 Luxem-bourg soldiers who had died as volunteers in the Allied armies in World War I. At the end of the first year the men in control seemed to observe enough success that they could pull off the coup that would take Luxembourg into the Reich without further delay. They called for a vote on three questions: the nationality of the voter, his ethnic roots, and his mother's language. To answer "Luxembourg" was supposed to be impossible.[7]

The affair was, for the Germans, a fiasco. The slogan "Three times Letzeburgesch" swept through the population. The author-ities had to cancel the referendum. The victory for the people helped harden their will and coalesce them into a national citizenry.

Pressure and brutality grew into terror.[8] Lawyers, teachers, judges, doctors were dismissed from their work to labor on the autobahns in Germany. The Gestapo raided bars, took and pun-ished hostages, and thousands of citizens were deported to live in hutments at German factories. The convents were turned over to Nazi schools. The goods of the Jews, the emigrants, and the deportees were confiscated. In three days in November 1941, the German police seized 1200 citizens and shipped half of them off to concentration camps. It was Himmler's plan to seize and absorb 30 percent of the Luxembourgers because they had become "racially degenerated by their ancient contact with Belgium."

Required labor for Germany was imposed on the young people in the spring of 1941. In late summer of 1942 the Germans introduced conscription to the army on a five-year age group of young men, later adding two more years. In the wake of Luxembourg resistance came executions, the seizing of young children to be sent to Nazi education camps, deportation of entire families to camps in Polish Silesia and Bohemia. Himmler projected the maniacal plan of transporting two-thirds of the population to the Ukraine so that "the sheep at the frontier would be replaced by wolf-dogs."

The entire population of a neutral, essentially powerless nation was caught up in a paroxysm of terror, anger, suppression, and rebellion.

* * * * * * *

The Luxembourg resistance was a tribute to nation and nationality.

The act of leaving Luxembourg by the Grand Duchess and the Government when the Germans invaded was an act of resistance rather than a sign of defeat. In exile they would continue to remind the Allies of the Luxembourg cause, rally the citizens who escaped from the Germans, and prepare for the day of liberation.

At home the citizens displayed their acts of resistance from the moment of invasion, fumblingly at first, wearing the red-lion sign of resistance, testing the indistinct line between what was possible of acceptance and what was outright defiance. Almost immediately the first clandestine resistance movement organized itself, to be followed by another and another, to the total of at least five. Often one did not know what the others were doing. They published underground newspapers. They forged papers. They smuggled draft resisters and Allied escapees into France. They spread symbols, draped flags, painted slogans. They sabotaged production. They led boycotts against collaborators. They spied and gathered information that they passed on to the Allies.

When the Germans instituted the draft into military service, the entire nation rallied its resistance in a general strike.[9] It began in Wiltz, where 700 employees left their work. Offices closed, stores locked up, school children stayed home. The strike spread through the mills in the south, the railroad workers joined in, the printers, the postal workers.

Resistance was strong among the young men to be drafted. From a population of 300,000, there were 12,031 called up for service. Of these, 3,510 never reported. Later, many Luxembourg soldiers who had leave failed to report back, but hid in the forests or made their way across the borders to liberty. All the country rallied to resist the oppressor and protect their young men.

The fate of the people during the remaining two and a half years of the war was dire indeed.

We have seen what the Luxembourg people did to oppose the enemy and affirm their independence. A summary of what the Germans did in retaliation will suffice.

The Germans threatened, arrested, interrogated, shot. They took hostages and killed many of them. They shipped off individuals and then whole families to work camps and concentration camps, where many of them died. They closed down businesses, dismissed employees from their posts. Wherever men congregated, however small the group, they might be seized and hauled off to intimidation and incarceration. The Germans even threatened the deportation of the entire citizenry. Such were the conditions that prevailed until the liberation of the country in September 1944.

These are the gross figures.[10] Of the 15,409 young men summoned, 10,211 were drafted by the Germans, 2848 died or disappeared, and 3,510 failed to report or deserted. In other words, only about one-third of the draftees were in a position to give effective service.

Of the 3963 men and women sent to prisons and concentration camps, 791 died.

Of the 4186 men and women deported, 154 died.

Of the 584 men who joined the underground or the Allied armies, 57 died.

In all, 5259 Luxembourg citizens died as a result of the war.

The brutal German policy of absorbing Luxembourg into the German state cost the Luxembourg citizenry the highest proportion of people sent to concentration camps, people imprisoned, and people deported of all the countries of Europe. Fear, misery, and death laid their wounds on the nation from 1940 to 1945.

* * * * * * *

September 10, 1944 — a day of bright sunlight, after heavy fog, that matched the joy of the citizens — was the day of liberation. Prince Felix, husband of the Grand Duchess, and Crown Prince Jean entered Luxembourg City as soldiers with the liberating American forces.[11]

That day had been preceded by the two-weeks spectacle of the German conquerors trying to save their own necks and fill their pocketbooks with as much as they could stuff into them. Gauleiter Simon fled to Trier on September 1, but was forced to return three days later in shame by a German general. He and his cohorts sought to commandeer butter, tobacco, shoes, leather, and textiles for shipment into the Reich. They issued orders, which were not obeyed, for blowing up factories and railroads and the Luxembourg City viaducts. They sought to seize securities and savings for transfer to Germany. As the Luxembourgers marked time waiting for the Allies' arrival, they saw in the fleeing German troops and the collapsing enemy government the recapitulation of numerous moments in their history when a hated enemy got out of their country as best it could.

Because this history is written for English-speaking readers, we can make available here a description of the American soldier that would be otherwise almost lost in an obscure Luxembourg book:

> We shall add at the most that with the general spirit of overflowing joy was mixed a bit of astonishment. Our liberating friends differed so much by their bearing, their conduct, from the conventional image of the soldiers that we had formed for ourselves, and to which four years of occupation had accustomed us, that they seemed to us to come from another world! Dumbfounded, we would look in vain on their uniforms for everything that belongs to the traditional military person: metal buttons, appliqued pockets, insignia of grades in colors. It was thanks to that great simplicity, not only in their clothing, but above all in their hearts, that the G.I.'s were able to make themselves liked immediately. The entire city was infatuated in a blink of the eye with those big awkward boys, with a tough and nonchalant appeal, in their trucks and vehicles, resembling more mechanics than warriors in the field.[12]

Those big awkward boys with their tanks and cannons and machine guns would liberate almost all of Luxembourg in a few days after a massive attack from the south and the west. The liberation was concluded on September 13. The attack stalled at the river boundaries, bordered on the east by the Siegfried Line, where the Germans continued to occupy some riverfront communities. Except for German shellings of Luxembourg territory and a breaching of the wall that took Americans into German territory in a narrow spearhead for a period of days, the battle situation subsided to a quiet stalemate. The wild welcome that the Luxembourgers gave the American forces in those beautiful September days settled down into a quiet and nervous waiting. The active fighting shifted to fronts elsewhere, and the Americans distributed themselves lightly through Luxembourg, confidently secure and making of Luxembourg a place for rest and recuperation of troops worn out in battle. Physically the country had been only lightly touched in the five years of war, for very little fighting had taken place there.

On December 16 the peaceful front erupted.

* * * * * * *

Some two miles to the east of the center of Luxembourg City 10,000 American soldiers lie buried in the village of Hamm. Innumerable rows of white crosses stretch away in the green cemetery from the monuments that depict the battles that gave rebirth to the Grand Duchy. The Battle of the Ardennes from December 16, 1944, to March 2, 1945 — the Battle of the Bulge — the final breaching of the Siegfried Line, this American-German battle, largely fought on Luxembourg soil, was one of the great battles of history. Whatever the fateful wars and campaigns of 1000 years that had caught up and trampled Luxembourg, the Battle of the Bulge was for Luxembourg the most fateful of all. Thousands of Americans died to decide that fate.

Beginning in September, the history of Luxembourg was now to be, for a few months, integral with the history of the thousands of American citizens who constituted the First and Third Armies.

Apparently the Germans offered no great threat in the autumn of 1944 on the eastern borders, where the rugged terrain was inimical to the maneuvering of soldier and machine. To the north and south the threat apparently was greater. The Ardennes sector was hardly interesting. America stretched its forces thin on the riverine borders of Luxembourg: two thinly spread divisions marked time on a front of more than 50 miles. Three and a third American divisions covered 100 miles.

The normal maximum for a divisional front is eight to ten miles. The Germans knew, of course, how feeble the defenses were on the Luxembourg border. However steep the hills, however deep and confined the valleys, however narrow the roads and few the bridges, this territory had the advantage of familiarity to them. Almost as soon as the stalemate developed they were planning the offensive meant to take them to the Meuse River and the sea. They chose their route through the inhospitable Ardennes. They counted on American inattention. A major part of their armament would be surprise.

Against the eight American divisions on the entire front Hitler readied 25 divisions. He had 800 to 1000 planes at his disposal (though he would generally be denied the opportunity to use them). On December 16, at five-thirty in the morning, he unleashed the greatest German offensive since the battles of Normandy. Cannon fire blasted not only the communities and camps of the borderland but also targets halfway across the country.

Observe the map closely. Above Vianden, German units crossed the river and penetrated Luxembourg. This was the Luxembourg Oesling, the northern Ardennes, that merged with the locale called the Luxembourg and Belgian Siberia.[13] This is a wild and threatening terrain, difficult under the suns of summer, an icy hell in winter. The Germans were well started for Clervaux, Wiltz, and Bastogne. Surprise and overwhelming strength gave the attack momentum that would carry the bulge clear across the northern half of the country, the entire river area, and along a southeast-northwest line from a point below the confluence of the Sure and Moselle rivers. Luxembourg City was less than fifteen miles away. After almost five years of conflict without an appreciable amount of physical destruction the dwellings and business places of more than half of the country were turned into debris. Bridges and forests were destroyed. In a territory subjected to freezing weather, icy blasts, sleet and snow, mysterious and hampering fog, while contending soldiers fought, thousands of

Luxembourgers had to flee their homes, take shelter where they could find it, suffer bombardment and deprivation, to return weeks later to rubble and the blankness of unemployment and want. There were major towns in this area of destruction: Echternach, Vianden, Clervaux, Wiltz, Diekirch; and hundreds of farms and villages. No medieval armies had wrought such terrible devastation. In Luxembourg and the contiguous area of Belgium in the first 30 days 120,000 German soldiers and 77,000 American soldiers were casualties. Eight thousand American men lay dead; 45,000 were wounded; 21,000 were missing or captured. Altogether more than 1300 tanks and armored vehicles, as many as 12,000 vehicles, 1600 German planes littered the landscape.

This terrible battle — terrible for the combatants, terrible for the Luxembourg civilians — ended officially March 2, 1945, with the liberation of the Moselle valley and the breaching of the German West Wall on the riverine borders. The fascination of the Battle of the Bulge is in a way that of Napoleon's battle of Moscow and the French retreat. From an Ardennes height, denuded of all but ice and snow, the prospect across the crests was that of an empty plain. But those plains were cut across by valleys, some of them steep and narrow. Forests lay on the white surface like gray clouds. The winds were icy. Sometimes — often — fog blanketed the ground and precluded air reconnaissance and attack. Tracked vehicles, such as tanks, slithered on the hillsides and plunged down declivities. The feet of infantrymen carried on trucks into battle froze; men in foxholes perished of cold if they escaped death by bullets. Skirmishes over villages or farmhouses lengthened into hours and days of attrition. Soldiers covered with sheets made ghostlike progress across the snow, blending into the frozen landscape. Day and night merged 24 hours until fatigue became another enemy. Convoys of trucks carrying reinforcements, gasoline, food, and ammunition were defeated as much by the weather as by enemy fire.

But the German attack wavered, stalled, and was flung back. From March 2, when the Battle of the Bulge ended officially, until May Luxembourg was a place for headquarters, a staging area, a pathway for troops and supplies, even a place for soldiers' rest and relaxation. The citizens could mark time while the war worked its way to its conclusion, wait the return of their loved ones, contemplate the wreckage of their buildings and economy, make their first plans for recovery from the trials that they had endured, make friends with the friendly Americans.

Their twentieth-century nightmare would soon be over.

NOTES: Chapter XXI

[1]*Luxembourg and the German Invasion: Before and After.* Preface by M. Joseph Bech, Foreign Minister (London, Hutchinson & Co., 1942).

[2]Gino Candidi, *La Résistance du Peuple luxembourgeois* (Luxembourg, Editions du "RAPPEL," 1977), pp. 31-32, 205-211. Translated into French by Georgette Bisdorff.

[3]Ibid., "L'entre-deux-guerres," pp. 11-19.

[4]Ibid., pp. 31-32.

[5]Ibid., p. 37.

[6]"Of the 3,500 Jews living in the Grand Duchy 71 percent perished as victims of criminal racism." Gilbert Trausch, *Le Luxembourg à l'époque contemporaine* (Luxembourg, Editions Bourg-Bourger, 1975), p. 159. This is Vol. IV of *Manuel d'histoire contemporaine luxembourgeoise.*

[7]Candidi, pp. 53-54.

[8]Ibid., pp. 50-53.

[9]Ibid., "La grève de 1942," pp. 59-92.

[10]Trausch, pp. 159-160.

[11]E. T. Melchers, *Les deux libérations du Luxembourg 1944-1945* (Luxembourg, Editions du Centre, 1959). This book of 264 pages gives the military aspects of the two liberations in detail.

[12]Ibid., p. 29.

[13]Albert and Christian Calmes, *Au fil de l'histoire* Vol. III (Luxembourg, l'Imprimerie Saint-Paul, 1972), pp. 86-87.

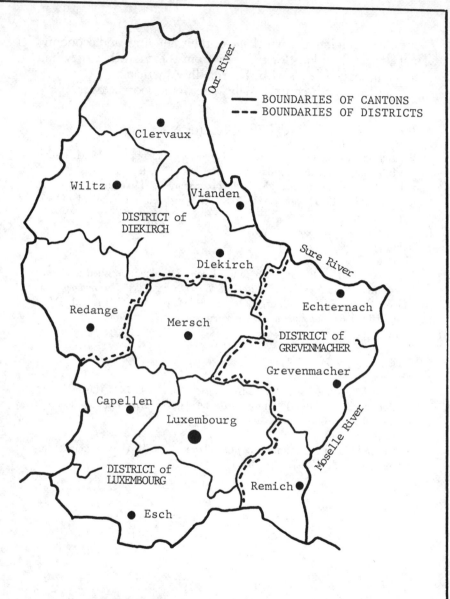

Clervaux

Wiltz

Vianden

DISTRICT of
DIEKIRCH

Our River

BOUNDARIES OF CANTONS
BOUNDARIES OF DISTRICTS

Diekirch

Sure River

Redange

Mersch

Echternach

DISTRICT of
GREVENMACHER

Grevenmacher

Capellen

Luxembourg

Moselle River

DISTRICT of
LUXEMBOURG

Remich

Esch

ADMINISTRATIVE MAP OF LUXEMBOURG

Chapter XXII

From World War II to the Present

ALUXEMBOURG HISTORIAN WROTE shortly after World War II: "Slowly the country is recovering from the effects of the occupation and of the Runstedt Offensive, as from a mortal illness."[1] The illness had not been mortal, but it had been a near call. It gave way to a national health more vital, more rich, more exuberant, more comprehensive than Luxembourg ever before had experienced. Up until 1939 she was still keeping one foot in the past. With the coming of peace she stepped off into the future, excited and alert, imaginative and self-assertive. The past was still there, but as an inspiration, not an impediment. The future bent its finger by way of invitation, seductive rather than threatening, with promises of unexperienced rewards.

The familiar pendulum figure serves us once again. In World War II the pendulum swung far to one side, stopping just short of annihilation. In the years following the war it swung back again in an arc of self-confidence and affluence. Most importantly, Luxembourg played an up-to-date role in her own way. Of equal importance with other nations in organizations of international cooperation, she in large part determined her own destiny.

Her starting point in 1945 was discouraging enough. Her wounds were both mental (as we have seen) and material, and they were great. Three thousand of her vital young men had died.

Almost half of her cultivated lands was ravaged beyond the possibility of immediate productivity. Of her 60,000 dwelling places, 4,000 were totally destroyed and 14,000 were badly damaged — almost one-third in total.[2] Heavy industry sat there almost idle, and provisions were hard to come by. All of the northern half and most of the eastern border were "a pile of ruins, which formed an eloquent appeal to national solidarity." The enemy's brutality had forged a national consensus. The first move was to house the dispossessed, at whatever expense to the nation. Other steps, economic, political, and social, would follow swiftly. Whatever desire for revenge the people may have cherished, the putting to death of five of their own traitors and the imprisonment of some Germans who allowed themselves to be caught sufficed.[3] The state "got ready to move mountains."

Because of the physical destruction one is tempted to use the word "shambles" for the Luxembourg of the late 1940s. Such would be an error. Certain vital signs identified the social organization of Luxembourg. The thread of life, which determined the personality of the nation, persisted. The factors are easily identifiable; the problem is to give order to them, to fix a priority. Any order, however, would have an inherent falsity in that the interplay among all, which determined the after-war continuity of the Grand Duchy, would be weakened, or even destroyed, by the removal of any one factor however large or small, however relatively important or unimportant in itself.

Consider the sovereign. On the world scene the matter of the Grand Duke or Grand Duchess as the chief of state is no doubt a matter of indifference; but in the Grand Duchy during and after the war it made all the difference in the world. At the time of the liberation the ubiquity of Grand Duchess Charlotte's picture, of the red lion and the gold crown, was sharp evidence of that same ubiquity underground for almost five years. As one man the totality of the citizenry chose her for their symbol of hope and victory. When the Allied world identified Luxembourg, they identified the nation in the person of her sovereign. Luxembourg in the eye of the man in the street in England and America was a noble, regal woman. Her husband and her son were military figures who personified the nation's military opposition to the enemy, both within the nation and without. Not as in the old days when the

Grand Duke reigned by ownership and possession, but in the right of character and the acceptance of obligation the Luxembourg sovereign reigned in practicality and in the spirit.[4] When the Grand Duchess in 1964 surrendered her responsibilities to her son Jean, who succeeded her as Grand Duke, the institution of the grand-ducal sovereign faltered not for an instant. He proceeded in the performance of his duties to justify the people's trust.

Except for the iron-steel industry, until World War II Luxembourg played an exceedingly minor role on the world's economic stage. After World War II she was one of the leading players; she now was not only in the world but of the world. After consideration of the sovereign as the very kernel of her national existence, her international role takes first place among the factors of her nationality.

By 1965 Luxembourg, with the population of a modest American city, was participating in 66 international organizations, 15 of those within the framework of the United Nations; Great Britain participated in 93, the United States in 67.[5] Here is a summary of her major involvements:

1942 — The United Nations. Luxembourg was a founding member in 1945.

1948 — The Brussels Pact. She joined Great Britain, the Netherlands, and Belgium in economic cooperation. She changed her constitution to give up her neutrality and provide an army.

1948 — The Western Union Defense Organization (within the Brussels Pact) provided for mutual defense.

1948 — The European Organization for Economic Cooperation (O.E.C.E.). It provided for Luxembourg's participation along with 15 other nations in the Marshall Plan (ERP — European Recovery Program), a means of aid to reconstruction provided by the United States.

1948 — Atlantic Treaty Organization (O.T.A.N.).

1949 — The Union of Europe (U.E.O.) with a consultative assembly. The Federal Republic of Germany was admitted.

1948-49 — Economic Union of Belgium and Luxembourg (U.E.B.L.). Basically in existence since 1922, it led to Benelux.

1950-52 — European Community of Coal and Iron (C.E.C.A.). It began with France and Germany united under a high authority; joined by Benelux and Italy. Luxembourg became its seat, thus the first "capital" of Europe.

1957 — European Economic Community (C.E.E.) and Community of Nuclear Energy (Euratom) by the Treaty of Rome. Organized in a European parliament; Luxembourg has six delegates out of 434.

This last figure — one in 72 — flaunts the minuscule aspect of Luxembourg as regards population and economic strength. How could such a tiny nation bring its influence to bear on international decisions, make its voice heard without being shrill, keep in the social and economic forefront of Europe even as the powerful nations sought as usual to have their own way? In a sense the world — that is, public opinion in the world — was ready to let the small and the weak nations have their day. Luxembourg was not, of course, a part of the third world of nations. But in size and power she was akin to many of them. In education, aptitude, and moral unanimity she occupied a unique position of superiority. She had not known that destiny would bring her to this day, but from 1867 onwards each step — political, social, economic — had been a step forward toward the realization of a national ego and a national force.

At the end of World War II of first importance economically was the reconstitution of Luxembourg's connection with Belgium, "the first country to recover its economic equilibrium" on that chaotic continent. On her own Luxembourg had cultivated aid from Switzerland even while the battles were going on, so that Swiss-Luxembourg economic agreements, relating particularly to steel, leather, and food, went into effect early in the peace. She immediately entered into agreements with the French to supply wood and services in bridge building and road repair. The Belgium-Luxembourg economic union (U.E.B.L.) developed trade agreements with the Scandinavian countries, Czechoslovakia, Poland, Hungary, and countries overseas. Gradually a balance of exchange was worked out that led eventually to sale for money among the nations involved as opposed to exchange of product for product, and eventually to inclusion of Germany again as a trade partner in a surprisingly short time.[6]

Without a solid base of firm and common currency the European countries, however self-reliant and industrious they were, could not reestablish themselves economically. It was now that the United States came to their aid by means of the Marshall

Plan,[7] which facilitated inter-European payments by direct dollar gifts, by long-term loans, and by a system whereby creditor nations established dollar drawing rights for the debtor nations.

The Marshall Plan has been characterized as the most comprehensive and most generous experience of mutual aid in history. However large or small the part it played, the after-war prosperity of Europe, including Luxembourg, became the evidence of its efficacy. In Luxembourg the mindfulness of her participation in America's generosity is possibly stronger than in any other European nation.

If the economic unification of Europe could be considered to be the goal of the Marshall Plan, Benelux[8]—the economic union of Belgium, the Netherlands, and Luxembourg—constituted the first step toward that unification. The possibility of such a union had probably existed below the level of consciousness for a century or more, for from 1815 to 1830 one king-grand duke, the Dutch William I, ruled over all three; and although Luxembourg was separate from the other two, William was incapable of thinking of her as a country apart. In the most dire straits during World War II the three small nations saw their future in terms of mutual effort and help.

Their first move was toward standardization of tariffs on imports from other countries, the elimination of tariffs on goods moving among the three countries themselves, and the free circulation of money and people. But such was only the beginning. There were questions of subsidies to be solved, salaries to be equalized, monetary and commercial policies to be established, agricultural inequities to be evened out; social policies to be shared or emulated, questions of fiscal affairs and investments, of waterways and harbors (Luxembourg has a port on the Moselle River), the participation of the vocational sectors. The simplicity of overriding principle led inexorably to demanding complexities of practice.

Since exports were the beating heart for all the lifeblood of Luxembourg, some details become of vital importance in defining the country. Overall, her exports at the end of the 1940s were four to five times as great as those of the late 1930s — sufficient witness to her rapid industrial recovery. To Belgium alone she

275

supplied ten times her prewar delivery. To other countries she was delivering seven times as much.[9]

Before the war Germany received about one-quarter of Luxembourg's exports; in the first post-war years only about one-twentieth. But the share of Belgium was now almost eight-twentieths, and the Netherlands, Switzerland, and other European countries (omitting France) were all taking Luxembourg products in increasing amounts. This was not a stable situation, of course, in the shifting economic currents of the post-war years; there would be increased exports here (France, for example) and decreased exports there (Belgium, for example). When we note that 98% of the iron-steel production, 92% of materials extracted from the earth, 85% of the leather, and 83% of chemicals and fertilizer were exported, we put our finger on the importance of exports. The general situation prefigures the prosperity and international involvement that will mark Luxembourg now for almost three decades.[10]

We need not give the details of production and export in Luxembourg industry other than iron-steel except to note the general and growing prosperity. We should, though, make passing note of certain aspects of agriculture, the products of which, except for wine, were largely consumed at home. The acreage devoted to grain and potatoes was sharply reduced; to pasturage, sharply increased. The value of crops, however, was now twice that of 1939. The production of milk almost quadrupled; of cattle and swine slaughter and of eggs, the same.[11] Agriculture production, whether in crops or cattle or wine, would be in flux from that time until this day. The number of owner-operated farms decreased, and the average size of a single farming operation was increased to more than 50 acres. A union called the Peasant Central (*Centrale paysanne*) drew its membership from 95% of the farmers. It operated silos, feed mills, dried milk factories, slaughterhouses, and refrigeration plants for its members. Its technological operations became as advanced as any others in Europe.

All the citizens of Luxembourg ate well, improved the quality of their living, acquired more and more consumer goods, and found themselves close to the top of the privileged people of Europe in terms of income, security, and comfort.

* * * * * * *

Reconstruction, manufacturing, trade, exports and imports — such activities successfully carried on required financial organization and administration equal to those demands. If in the 1980s Luxembourg is one of the leading banking centers in the world, we can assume that a groundwork for such a financial structure was laid down early enough and strong enough to support the superstructure of today's operations. Such was the case.

Luxembourg took its first modern step in the very depths of World War I, 1915, when she subjected the formation and administration of private business to explicit and liberal law. Freed from arbitrary administrative interference, business enterprise took a leap forward. What happened between 1918 and 1930, and again in the first years after World War II, could be likened to the ground shocks preliminary to an earthquake; small undertakings would presage major financial developments. The figure of speech fails us here in respect to the prosperity and vitalization that trace their beginnings to the prosperous twenties and the exigencies of the late forties.

The ten years following World War I saw 829 new firms started up in that small country, mostly involved in food and clothing. Business enterprise needed credit; the need for credit called for banks; the invitation to public stock subscription required a financial exchange. The Luxembourg stock exchange got its start in 1928. The number of banks in a very short while doubled to 24. The International Bank now represented Belgian, French, and German banking interests as well as Luxembourgian. Concurrent with banking expansion was the development of insurance companies, four of them. The depression of the 1930s, devaluation of the Belgian and Luxembourg francs, reduced possibilities for investments, the diminution of national resources, and the canceling of large public works — the new Luxembourg weathered them all.[12]

Two aspects of Luxembourg economic life shape themselves as foci of attention to which all other aspects are subordinated: entrepreneurship and labor. Starting with the recognition that Luxembourg was always an agricultural country, we recognize also that its agriculture was so poor that it could not sustain the nation economically. Necessary, then, was the development of nonagricultural business — manufactories, distribution, and sales. But the little country could not possibly absorb the products that it was capable of producing. Necessary, then, was a foreign market. If the state was not to be paternalistic or communistic, its citizens would have to find the ingenuity to organize its affairs and the talent to manage them. Which brings us again to the two foci of entrepreneurship and labor. We must understand them if we are to understand the viability of the modern Grand Duchy.

As we have seen, the Luxembourg Chamber of Commerce got its start as early as 1841, on the very morrow of the country's independence. Its members were the entrepreneurs who owned and managed the businesses — 21 of them. They were the same men who held posts in government. In other words, all the interests of the new nation were concentrated in the hands of the employer.

In the next hundred years this social monolith would become only a nucleus. Agglutinating around it, from the point of view of occupation, would be the laborer, the farmer, the employee, the bureaucrat, and the salaried and self-employed.[13] It would take a century to complete this conglomerate. From the point of view of services it would include all kinds of insurance — health, unemployment, pregnancy, retirement, etc., the provisions for which would involve the members of the Chamber in all kinds of government representation and influence. In addition to such government involvement would come the evolution of work regulations involving hours, pay rates, unemployment, vacations; such manufacturing, wholesaling, and retailing activities as domestic and foreign conditions of sale and exchange, laws of bankruptcies, and of course subsidies and taxes. In relation to all these would be development and regulation of all phases of banking.

What began as the paternalism of self-interest in financial and social matters developed into the total involvement of the citizenry in every form of safeguard and regulation. The orderly subjection of freedom to social and official control was essentially the guarantee of that freedom against its arbitrary misuse or abrogation. It all occurred in a century of orderly progress, by way of the deepening integration of every aspect of national life — progress that overrode the several threats against national sovereignty, economic vagaries of a world order, and even annihilation twice at the hands of a self-seeking Germany.

Economic and social progress was paralleled by the development of compulsory and universal education. Education made participation and leadership possible and extended them more generally. The enlightened self-interest of the leadership of the 1940s spread by a kind of osmosis through the body politic; so that in the twentieth century an enlightened national self-interest enabled the state to be one of the important building stones in the international structure without which, small as the nation is, the structure would be weakened.

* * * * * * *

The body politic — let that term comprehend the wholeness of the Luxembourg state in all its parts. We may use the adjective of that expression now to point to the political aspect — the politics — of the process of self-government by the social body called Luxembourg.

From the time of independence until many decades later the political pendulum was nervous and erratic. Native historians made much of the political differences and the public demonstrations of the disaffected. But to Americans and Englishmen, for whom the memory of civil wars, rebellion, and demonstration is very real, the political course that Luxembourg followed after 1839 appears to be reasonably direct and relatively peaceful. Had the dissentions within Luxembourg been the dissentions of one state within a large body such as the German empire, they would find few pages in the larger recorded history. But when the spotlight is brought into focus on 1000 square miles and 189,000 people, the dimensions of those fracases loom large.

Let us remind ourselves here that the emphasis of this chapter is on the free, democratic, prospering Luxembourg of post-World War II; and that our concern is to pace off the steps which — as we see them in retrospect — led inevitably to that Luxembourg that received the fruits of victory after 1945. On stage, with the spotlight on them in the 1980s, the characters come out of those years of history off stage; and the vicissitudes of the shadows become blurred and obscured in the awareness of the bright circumstances of the present.

To begin, then, our political progress toward the postwar years.[14]

The Grand Duke is a given factor, the personal and symbolic focus of nationhood from the year one of independence to this very day.

A first issue of the new order of things was the *Constitution d'Etats*, granted by the Grand Duke in 1841, beginning an orderly succession of constitutions. The title translates with difficulty — civil constitution? government constitution? constitution of representatives? It located national sovereignty in the Grand Duke, from whom issued all rights, levies, and responsibilities. The actual function of government resided in a council of the governor and four members named by the Grand Duke, of which the governor was designated president. The assembly was elected by citizens who paid appropriate taxes.

1847-1848 was a period of civil protest for a good part of Europe, France and Germany particularly, in which the Luxembourg people shared. Now came demonstrations, originating as usual in the north and spreading through the country. The result was the constitution of 1848, drawn up by representatives of the people themselves, not received by decree from the sovereign. By this constitution the grip of the Grand Duke was loosened; his powers were now defined; that is, they were no longer automatic and limitless. It required the government — which meant the Chamber and its officers — to ratify any grand-ducal decree before it could become effective. The government came under the control of the Chamber, which voted a budget annually. It spelled out individual freedom, freedom of opinion, freedom of the press, and freedom of assembly. Here it adumbrated the free democracy of eighty years later.

But it was an adumbration only. Luxembourg felt the encumbrances of its membership in the German Confederation, which came out of the revolutionary activities of 1848 still reactionary and restrictive in its governance. The great majority of Luxembourgers not only were denied the vote because of paying no taxes or too little tax, but also they were largely illiterate. The oligarchy of 1839 was, after 1848, an oligarchy still, as regards political practice, just as the economic life of the nation was controlled by the few enterprising and prosperous entrepreneurs; in actuality, political powers and economic leaders were the same people.

All these circumstances were far enough removed from actual democracy to make possible the new Grand Duke's (William III) reclaiming the powers that his father had relinquished. He did so by decree, illegally (as far as the old constitution was concerned), proclaiming the new constitution. In its capacity (or the Grand Duchy's capacity) as a member of the German Confederation, it was incumbent on Luxembourg to surrender back to the sovereign the powers that the constitution of 1848 gave to the people. "The sovereign power," it was now expressly proclaimed, "resides in the person of the King-Grand Duke. The King-Grand Duke will exercise it conformably with the statutes of the German Confederation, to the present constitution [1856] and to the laws of the country." The German Diet demanded such action. Once again it was required that the press surrender its freedom, along with suppression of freedom of assembly. The legislative Assembly of Estates, harking back to times of less free and responsible representation, was reestablished, and the tax requirement for voting was increased.

All this recessive action was, illogically enough, by way of progress toward the liberal constitution of 1868, which in all its grand outlines and with the various amendments that would follow through the decades would be the constitution of the liberal and democratic state of the late twentieth century. From 1868 onward Luxembourg was free from political connections with Germany. Most importantly of all, sovereignty was now invested in the people.

1841, 1848, 1856, 1868 — these constitutions marked the last throes of ownership, paternalism, and subjection as also they marked the grand steps toward the grand end of independent nationalism. For 30 years the political pendulum was in constant, nervous, erratic sway before it settled into its sturdy, regular, energy-giving swing.

We have been looking at the bare bones of history here. The purpose has not been to spread out the bones for view, but to provide a skeleton that we can flesh out with the political realities of a twentieth-century democracy.

Politically, the major factors were the Grand Duke, the Catholic Church, and the spirit of liberalism. There were the adherents of each and the opponents of each. Issues included the vote, the organization of law making, taxes (of course), the press, education. The English-speaking countries through all their modern history have been nations of political parties, each with its platforms, its leaders, its henchmen, and its devices. But in Luxembourg, parties as such — in action rather than as labels — were slow to develop.[15] The labels were the usual European ones — liberals who were in reality conservative; progressive liberals who stopped their progress short of reasonable goals; Catholics, some of whom were unsympathetic toward the church, etc. Under those circumstances it is quite reasonable that party loyalties were slow to develop. It was reasonable that reasonable goals could hardly be the prerogative of one party as opposed to another. Thus universal suffrage — which included the vote for women! — came into being in 1919, along with the disappearance of the required tax qualification for the vote. And thus it was that government by coalition came to be the standard practice, so that the government in modern years is manned pretty much by the same people though this party is in power now while some years back another party was in power, and tomorrow the power may shift again without any real loss of party influence.

The explanation of this pragmatic unity may derive — we may assume that it does derive — from the fact that the greatest issues of its history have been settled. It is inconceivable that the sovereign power should again be put to the vote, assuming that the Grand Duke does not invite opposition and that economic threats do not push the people into communism. It is inconceivable that there should again be a Belgian party or a French party or a German party. It is inconceivable, after Hitler, that to have or not have a dictator should ever come to the vote.

The issues of the 1980s are different from the great political issues of Luxembourg history. The national future will be decided by the decisions that the people take on those issues, which, to our consternation, could be as fateful as the issues of sovereignty, international alliance, and government by democracy.

And suddenly we look at the gorgonlike specter, figured perhaps in a nuclear cloud or in a mountain of computer figures or in a demography different from previous demographies, a specter of challenges and threats that a tiny people will have to oppose itself to in wisdom and strength enough to find survival in today's world.

NOTES: Chapter XXII

[1] Albert Northumb, "Avant-propos" in *Le Luxembourg: Livre du Centenaire* (Luxembourg, l'Imprimerie Saint-Paul, 1948), p. 5.

[2] Paul Weber, *Histoire de l'économie luxembourgeoise* (Luxembourg, Chambre de Commerce, 1950), pp. 334-335.

[3] Gilbert Trausch, *Le Luxembourg à l'époque contemporaine* (Luxembourg, Editions Bourg-Bourger, 1975), pp. 164. This is Vol. IV of *Manuel d'histoire contemporaine luxembourgeoise.*

[4] "The love of their Grand Duchess is deeply rooted in the heart of each Luxembourger, and all venerate her as a true benefactress. During the blackest hours Charlotte of Orange-Nassau had continued to be the symbol of their native land. Now the new life was reorganized around the well beloved sovereign whose voice had known how to touch so many hearts in distress." Gino Candidi, *La Résistance du Peuple luxembourgeois* (Luxembourg, Editions du "RAPPEL," 1977), p. 215.

[5] Trausch, pp. 167-172.

[6] Weber, pp. 355-356.

[7] Ibid., "Le plan Marshall (ERP)," pp. 358-361.

[8] Ibid., "Les problèmes Benelux," pp. 362-364.

[9] Ibid., p. 366.

[10] Ibid., "Les échanges internationaux," pp. 365-368.

[11] Ibid., "La production agricole," pp. 369-370.

[12] Ibid., pp. 276-277.

[13] For details of industrial and agricultural activity, banking, employment, social welfare, etc. see these official publications of the Luxembourg government in English:

George Als, Luxembourg: *Historical, Geographical and Economic Profile* (Luxembourg, Ministry of State, Information and Press Service, 1980). Translated from the French.

Investment in Luxembourg (Luxembourg, Ministry of National Economy, n.d.).

Raymond Kirsch, *La Société Nationale de Crédit et d'Investissement (S.N.C.I.)* (Luxembourg, Imprimerie de la Cour Joseph Beffort, 1978).

[14] For what follows see Pierre Majerus, *L'Etat luxembourgeois: Manuel de droit constitutionnel et de droit administratif luxembourgeois* (Luxembourg, Imprimerie de la Cour Joseph Beffort, 1948).

[15]Trausch, "La Vie Politique," pp. 193-206.

Chapter XXIII

The Eve of the Future
The 1980s

NY GIVEN MOMENT is the test of whatever worth and strength the past has built into a nation. For us in this study—for Luxembourg—the 1980s are a time of reckoning.

We have just been looking at the Luxembourg that rose out of the wreckage of World War II. We have seen her take her destiny in hand, surrender her neutrality, embark on every kind of international cooperation that the Western World offered, develop her industry and trade, extend her social services, unionize and organize almost every kind of paying endeavor, raise her standard of living remarkably, and carry her head high among the highest in the nations of this world.

In 1975 the Luxembourg supertrain came close to being derailed. "The year 1975 was that of the most severe economic recession that Luxembourg had known in 40 years."[1] That of 1976 was even worse. In the wake of this recession comes an unfavorable trade balance, a budget operating in the red, and the inevitable attendant social and economic ills.

Here are the major factors that would prevail from 1975 into the 1980s.[2] It was evident now that her iron ore was all but exhausted. Foreign competition was overtaking her exports. The balance of trade turned against her. Unemployment was threatening. The oil exporting nations were steadily increasing the price of oil. Machinery and methods were becoming outmoded.

Inflation was taking its head. Agriculture was inadequate. Population was shifting away from the farms. The number of foreigners in the population was growing. The birthrate was sinking lower and lower, the age of death was growing higher, the number of retirees was increasing.

We shall set aside for the moment the question of birthrate, which has ethical, spiritual, and religious dimensions, and consider the matters that preoccupy the Luxembourger most: employment, finances, and security. Perhaps he is right in giving economic considerations his priority. The older people are not far removed from poverty; they do not want to revert to that. Hard labor rather than blue collar and white collar comforts is clear in their memory. The insecurity of illness, unemployment, and old-age dependency has given way to the security of a comprehensive state paternalism; there is nothing about the good old days that invites nostalgia or return. The social weaknesses that have given way to social strengths were associated in the past with the danger of the country's being wiped out by other people's nationalism; ergo, their social strengths are the hallmarks of their independency.

All these good things are being challenged in the last quarter of the twentieth century. The weapons against the challenge are ingenuity, intellectual acuity, industry, and adaptability. Add to these a granite-hard sense of independence, which is in curious contrast to the nation's perception of its welfare as deriving from internationalism.[3]

A nation fundamentally agricultural has become a nation fundamentally industrial. The industrial economy that took over from agriculture was based largely on iron and steel, which has been weakening steadily now for some years.[4] The farmer has had to find industrial employment. The unemployed worker in iron and steel has to find work in other industry. Fortunately, while affluence was growing, the Luxembourg people through their government were looking ahead. The new agricultural distribution and methods would not permit keeping the young people on the farms, but the location of industry in rural areas and small towns could keep those areas populated. Thus the location of a Goodyear factory at Colmar-Berg (the largest Goodyear factory in Europe), Dupont de Nemours at Contern, Monsanto and

Texas Refinery (Monsanto has recently closed) at Echternach, a half-dozen smaller firms at Wiltz. In fact, since 1951 more than 60 new firms, employing 12,000 people, have found a footing in Luxembourg. The government provided for tax allowances, made loans at reduced rates, and gave subsidies. In 1980 some 18 new firms were employing more than 500 people and looking to an eventual employment of 2600. Since employment in iron-steel is inevitably falling, the new diversified, scattered industries take up some of the slack. And with the iron-steel share of the national product falling from 60% in 1970 to 40% in 1975 and to 20% in 1980, the necessity for new products became imperative.[5]

In 1980 the government identified the three major problems of the Grand Duchy as follows:

1. the increased cost of social security
2. weakness in the machinery of production and its adaptability
3. a demographic evolution.

One solution to unemployment in iron-steel was to force retirement on the employee at the age of 57. While such action relieved the industry and assured employment to the younger wage earner, the burden on the state became much greater. The average age of death is growing higher, so that an increase in social security payments becomes greater every year. These increases are occurring at a time when the balance of payments is unfavorable, and industry needs to be retooled and adapted to new uses, new industry needs to be subsidized (as we have seen), and a standard of living among the highest in the world must at all hazards be maintained.

The times are nervous indeed.

Positive and encouraging aspects exist to ease what is difficult and inspire optimism about the Grand Duchy's economic health. In a world that is beset by economic woes, a world in which some nations will fare less well than others, the possibilities are that Luxembourg will weather the financial and social gales better than most.

Labor and political peace is mightily reassuring to the capitalist investor. In no other Western country is the history of that peace more reassuring and the existence of that peace more palpable than in Luxembourg. Until April 1982, no industrial strikes had occurred since 1921, in fact. While the country has been in the process of almost universal unionizing, the unions have kept peace among themselves as memberships have settled into the various labor organizations that prevail. As labor (and here the term takes into account all types of work, including high levels of the white-collar worker) has found and felt its powers, the employer, including the state, has found a modus vivendi with labor that satisfies both. As this employer-employee relationship has become established, government has made its way through social legislation governing hours, wages, vacations, insurance, and retirement to the satisfaction of all citizens.[6]

Not all economic adaptations are a matter of law. Many have come about through the willing cooperation of employer, employee, and government. Instead of laying off workers no longer needed because of reduced sales and improved methods, iron-steel has continued employment or made jobs in highway construction and maintenance, building, utilities, etc. Government has provided the necessary subsidies, and labor has given its cooperation.

What's more, the radical citizenry has almost disappeared. The divisions of political difference have been subsumed into two major parties and two parties of somewhat fewer numbers and powers. As national loyalties as to party have shifted from left to right and right to left (to use terms, which, in Luxembourg, tend almost to be inappropriate), coalitions have come about so easily as to command national support without the violence of party contention and the unsettling effects of major or violent change of power.

In contrast to France and Germany and England, Luxembourg until 1982 enjoyed labor peace and political peace ever since World War II. As it faces the economic problems that derive from world conditions in the 1980s, it has the confidence for the time being that comes from having satisfied its people for 60 years in terms of employment, income, and security. It has the experience of arriving at consensus through the confrontation of all aspects of its society and resolution of conflict by an ordered process.

Luxembourg has shown a confident face to the rest of the world. The world has recognized the dimensions of its shrewd

conduct and orderly processes. And the world has brought to it a new means of money making and employment just in time to soften the shocks that are vibrating in the structures of all of Western society.[7]
That means takes the form of banking.

* * * * * * *

Some figures here will put the banking situation in clear relief. In 1947 Luxembourg counted 13 banks; in 1965, 20; in 1973, 70; in 1977, 90. In 1981 there were 113 foreign banks alone, involving 40 foreign countries. The total assets of Luxembourg banks were $110,000,000,000.[8]
How big is $110,000,000,000? Well, the assets of all the foreign banks in London amount to $280,000,000,000. The 1980 budget of the United States of America was $645,000,000,000. The United States budget deficit for 1979 was $80,000,000,000.
Such tremendous dollar figures are in no way a threat to the internal economy of the country. In terms of cash their chief effect is to offer a base for appropriate taxation on transactions of deposit and loan. Luxembourg is becoming more and more an attractive place where bonds can be issued and where currency risks are reduced by combining several currencies in a common funding unit. Belgian nationals are easing their home tax burdens by Luxembourg deposits. Swiss banks are escaping withholding taxes on anonymous accounts by placing them in Luxembourg. The Arabs consider Luxembourg to be a safer place for their money than Germany, say, whose strength could make anti-Arab sentiment a threat to their investments. Proximity in a small city simplifies interbank transactions.
Of particular note is the presence in Luxembourg of the European Investment Bank, the main lending arm of the European Economic Community. This nonprofit bank has as its chief responsibility the financing of projects for underdeveloped areas, projects for modernizing and retooling plants, and coordinating projects involving several member nations. The bank is becoming more involved in investments outside the Community — countries in Africa, the Caribbean, the Pacific. Where the world banking highway diverges to London, Switzerland, and Luxembourg, more and more traffic is taking the fork that leads to the

little city that time and again in history has, for other reasons, been called the crossroads of Europe.

As to the local economy, all those banking operations have to be housed in buildings that have to be built on property that has to be bought and sold, using furnishings and services supplied by other businesses that employ Luxembourg citizens, who draw salaries that are subjected to taxes that supply money for the operation of government and the furnishing of all forms of public service.

The impact of these banks on employment is anything but negligible. In a work force of 155,000, banking accounted in 1981 for 7726 jobs — roughly one in 20 or 5%. That figure alone takes up almost all the slack in the job figures for iron-steel, though the job reductions in that industry will continue to grow.[9] In a society that develops more and more jobs that require intellectual qualifications, banking is offering opportunities to both men and women. The workers whom the foreign banks bring to Luxembourg from their own countries can be an enriching force in a land of such small dimensions as Luxembourg.

Of prime importance in the spirit of cooperation among the three interested parties is a provision by law dating from 1965: wages must automatically be adjusted to a consumer price index. Thus, as prices of goods and services have increased to one of the highest levels in Europe, the man in the street has not felt the stresses of inflation in his paycheck. His relative buying power has remained steady.

In both England and the United States inflation has been, and in the early 1980s continued to be, rampant. Buying power did not keep pace with prices. Strikes, extending even into such public services as fire and police protection and public school teaching, flash like heat lightning presaging perhaps greater extent and greater violence. By comparison tiny Luxembourg would appear to be in much better shape. Unemployment is at one percent or less. The Luxembourg citizen, hearing a foreigner's concern about high prices in the Grand Duchy, especially for food, can hardly comprehend the foreign point of view. He is employed. His pension is assured. He has the money in his pocket to pay for what he wants. His national leaders share quotes and pictures with the leaders of the great powers. His little capital of 79,000 persons burgeons prodigiously. Public services are complete and of the highest quality.

What is the cause for concern? And yet — and yet — there is the heat lightning, there are the ground tremors. On the base of 100 set in 1965, the price index had increased by 65% in 1975, in that last year alone by 10.77%. The greatest increases occurred in food, dwelling costs, and goods and services. In 1979 the price index reached 207.49. In February, 1982, Belgium unilaterally devaluated the franc with apparently no concern for the effect on Luxembourg. The budget is running at a deficit. The details of demography, as we shall see soon, are disturbing. Ready energy is insufficient. However complacent the average Luxembourger had grown only six or seven years ago, he cannot now remain complacent before the threat of loss of comfort and affluence. Less readily excitable, perhaps, than his neighbors, less ready to shift political allegiances and adopt liberal measures, there is little doubt that severe economic stress would stimulate more liberal political action. Luxembourg is an active participant in the interplay of the political and economic world; she would not remain on the sidelines if her citizens saw their interests seriously threatened.

* * * * * * *

Only a few city blocks above the remains of Sigefroid's castle a stark red bridge spans the deep valley of the Alzette, connecting the Avenue Schuman on the west with the Avenue J. F. Kennedy on the east. Robert Schuman, a Frenchman born in Luxembourg, is called the Father of Modern Europe, and John F. Kennedy lent his name to the new autoroute as a symbol of hope and youth when a new kind of future was being shaped out of the international animosities and conflicts of the past. The nononsense straight trajectory of the bridge carries the representatives of all Western Europe to the great modern buildings of the Kirchberg Plateau, where they perform much of the work of the European Community. The bridge and the buildings make it possible for Luxembourg City, tiny as it is as a world capital, to share with Brussels and Strasbourg the administrative activities of the Western World's most powerful coalition.

The bridge and the buildings leave no room for doubt as to the Luxembourgers' will to be a part of a united Europe. For a good part of a thousand years their country had been a possession or a pawn or a passive victim of aggression. When they found themselves surviving the cataclysm of World War II, they cast their vote for the internationalization of European government and economies. Should any foreign power threaten it again, it wanted to be a component of an international conglomerate that would resist aggression. Independent, but too small to participate alone in the economic conflicts of Europe and the world, it foresaw its economic welfare in cooperative planning and action. An adequate summary of this appears in the address of the Minister of Foreign Affairs to the Chamber of Deputies in the 1980 budget:

"You are acquainted with the guidelines of our foreign policy that have not varied for a good number of years. It consists of being a part of the larger groups of nations, such as the Belgo-Luxembourg Economic Union, Benelux, the European Community, the Council of Europe, which alone are able to assure us of the necessary support in maintaining our political and economic independence. It consists of belonging to the Atlantic Alliance [NATO], the guarantee of our security. It consists of maintaining correct relations — if possible, friendly ones — with the other nations of the world, in the framework of the United Nations and on a bilateral level. These choices have not changed and will not change in the foreseeable future."[10]

Overtones of insecurity sound in the statements of position and the reports of action that issued from Luxembourg in the first years of the 1980s. She is seeking to open new markets in Asia, Africa, the Near East, and Central and South America. She is retooling her industries and seeking to vary her products. With the rest of Europe she aims to reduce her energy needs while increasing her productivity. Her leaders announce the need for self-sacrifice even as her citizens acquire more possessions and raise their level of living. She worries about the need for protection by means of short-range missiles, which still are lacking. "About 1983," the Minister announced, ". . . will be the most critical moment when the nuclear advantages of the Warsaw-Pact nations will be most probable."[11] Having recently built a new meeting hall for the Parliament of Europe, she is suspicious that her partner nations will take the Parliament and other European Community activities away from her. As she announces her intention to protect her vested interests, she looks askance at the efforts of each of her fellow-ten to cultivate its own self-interests. In the economic world a nation's smallness is not an advantage. Luxembourg knows that "the hard daily realities demonstrate a little more every day that the economy determines policy." It must increase its strength through international cooperation. It needs the strength of its partnership in Benelux, which constitutes the fourth largest export bloc in the world. It would like to find closer economic cooperation with the great nations and tries to resist their tendency to concentrate all initiative in their own hands. While speaking proudly, Luxembourgers worry about the evidence that there is less and less effort to achieve a truly united Europe, in which Luxembourg sees its only hope for continuing self-identity and prosperity. It reminds all Europe time and again of the great unhappiness and misfortune that the glorification of absolute sovereignty and the incantation of national egoism have brought to Europe in the past.

*   *   *   *   *   *   *

The President of the Government reported thus to the nation: "The present problems with our labor market ought not to make us forget that our demographic situation, characterized by a drop — without precedent in Europe — of the birthrate, conceals serious dangers in the long run for financing our social security system, for our economic growth, and even for the survival of our national society."[12] The statement of another official in 1980 is even more portentous, for he speaks of "the catastrophic evolution of our demographic situation."[13]

A threat to the survival of social Luxembourg itself — those are grave words indeed. In another context the President of the Government stated the situation thus: if the rate of reproduction does not rise to maintain the population, "the choice is very clear, leaving only recourse to a massive and structural immigration, which would signify in time the end of our national identity and the advent of a different Luxembourg; the alternative will be acceptance of a progressive reduction in our main strengths with the consequences that are tied up with them in the lowering of the quality of life of the population!"

That was in 1978. In 1983 there is no promise yet that fateful changes in Luxembourg will not derive from the refusal of Luxembourg couples to have children.

The problem is not an old one, having made itself ostensible only in 1966, when the deaths of native Luxembourgers first exceeded the births. But the rate at which the imbalance has grown is threatening. In 1967 deaths exceeded births by 116; in 1976, by 1830; in 1979, by 1,076. For only a short while the birth-rate of resident foreigners kept the total population steady; if birth and death rates stay unchanged, only an influx of foreigners could keep the population at 364,000 or above.

The President of the Government is persistent in his warnings: ". . . if the present trend continues, and if immigration is stopped, the number of employed people will be no more than 130,000 by the end of the century; by the end of the next century it will have fallen to 73,000 which represents a diminution of almost half."[14] But if there is a foreign influx to be added to the children of foreign parents who grow to maturity and have children of their own, Luxembourg will become something of a Mediterranean nation. The offspring of the inevitable miscegenation will constitute a national type so distinct from the Letzeburger that it will bear the name only as a matter of convenience of identification, as foreign to exactness of designation as the foreignness of the blood that will flow in their veins.

The sturdy, handsome flower that grew only after World War II and, like the century plant, came into blossom only in the 1970s, suddenly (even as the Luxembourg people seem to be unaware) takes on a fascinating exoticism. Will it fade and fall as quickly as it bloomed? Is there a sudden odor of decay? As the national leaders speak repeatedly of their plans for industrial development and diversification, full employment, complete social compensations, a raised standard of living, international cooperation, diversified education, enlarged gross national product, one seems to detect a growing shrillness, a suggestion of apprehension, a doubt that shelters itself in bold planning and affirmation.

We have, through the long course of this history, found the Luxembourg people admirably adaptable and enduring. Their enemies have always been *the* enemy — the outsider who has crossed the border swinging his battle ax, shooting his guns, driving his tanks over the rubble that he had created. But who is the immediate enemy now? Even if we identify him as Russia, it is hard to suppose that he fixes his eye on Luxembourg in the way that Spain or France or Germany has fixed it in the past. But it is not hard for the Luxembourger to suppose that. He knows very well that Russia has pushed westward over 900 miles in the last 300 years; he has a lively fear that Luxembourg may lie on the route toward Russia's goal, the sea. The deficiency in medium range nuclear missiles in Europe as a deterrent to Russia's use of such missiles makes him nervous indeed. The thought of neutrality in the 1980s never enters his head.

Russia aside, is there a chance that the enemy lurks in Luxembourg's own psyche? By refusing to have children is she subconsciously seeking her own destruction? It is not at all impossible that that self-destruction will come about. Or is a social force at work — a social force that, by mixing Italian and Spanish and Portuguese blood in the veins of Luxembourg citizens, will guarantee renewed strength to blood that has grown old? There is probably no more a pure Luxembourg blood, anyway, than there is a pure American blood. Roman blood has flowed there for 2000 years. A new Mediterranean infusion, come about peacefully this time, could be the best guarantee of a Letzeburgish future. Speculation or no speculation, the birthrate of the moment augurs retrenchment below the point of no return.

For the English-speaking world — as for the large nations of all languages — Luxembourg could be an instructive cynosure, had those nations the good sense and the power to be instructed by what they see there. The small size and the evident factors make analysis possible. If we want an understanding of socialistic democracy at work in a capitalistic context, Luxembourg offers us a clear opportunity to reach that understanding.

Luxembourg, by its free will working within its constituted political structure, aims at employment for every employable citizen. It offers a high level of education to every citizen. It guarantees health care, unemployment compensation, and high income in retirement to every citizen. Very likely, any government that opposed cradle-to-the-grave security — indeed, comfort — would be voted out. Signs seem to point to the conclusion that were the Grand Duke himself to evince sympathy with any act that would reduce the citizens' security and comfort, the Grand Dukes would be eliminated in short order. Not only will the Luxembourg citizenry control the pragmatic affairs of daily living; it will also control its symbols. It is doubtful that the citizenry has asked itself how a change in symbols would change the pragmatic affairs of daily living.

It may be that in its prosperity Luxembourg finds itself as seriously threatened as at any other time in its long and painful history.

Like a prize animal, in the running for the best of its breed, it can be and should be viewed from all sides.

An unemployment rate of one percent[15] ought to be the envy of the Western World. However was it managed? In the first place, the total of jobs available has been, up to very recent years, greater than the available native manpower. Foreigners were needed to take those jobs. Two main developments, other than those already mentioned, ensued. When the world market for Luxembourg goods declined, the number of jobs fell below the number of people available to man them. That would seem to mean unemployment. But Luxembourg gave to the face of unemployment two new physiognomies. The one physiognomy is that of retirement. At the age of 57 a displaced steel worker receives 80% of his regular pay for the rest of his life, the expense to be borne by the social security system. As the retirement age is lowered, the burden of payments to retirees increases alarmingly in relation to the total of salaries and the income of the state.

Early retirement, though, is not sufficient to compensate for the reduced number of jobs. The steel companies have made jobs within their organizations, thus increasing their losses; and the nation has made jobs in the way of public works, putting a burden on the budget that will put the budget in the red.

The Luxembourg rate of unemployment, then, requires a definition quite different from that used in England and the United States. One wonders if the end results, though somewhat delayed, will not contain threats to the social and economic equilibrium quite as serious as those in countries whose main answer to unemployment is the dole or unemployment compensation. Statistics concerning the cost of living call for a second look also. The costs of goods and services in Luxembourg have kept pace with, or even outrun, those costs in other countries. But unlike the great powers, Luxembourg paychecks until 1982 kept pace with the increased costs, so that the Luxembourg worker in these years of inflation felt no stress or strain. The price index system worked admirably, if the citizens' satisfaction is the test. But yet to be determined is the system's strength against all possible economic stresses and strains. Certainly the great powers have not seen enough advantages in it to warrant adoption of it. Neither Republican nor Democratic politicians in America see their welfare in the sop to the voting public that such a system would provide. Inordinately large increases in pay to match inordinately large increases in commodity prices carry the threat of economic collapse. Couple those threats with the prospect of bankruptcy of the social security system if identifiable trends continue: the possibility is that conditions attractive at the moment are the seedbed of troubles that could quickly ripen.

In the confident words that Luxembourg's leaders speak about their level of living and their controlled economy is a sharp edge of worry. The controls of the automated vehicle that they are driving are quite as difficult to manage as the 20-mule team of the American West. Production, machinery and equipment, employment, education, social services, income and prices — all have to be kept in hand and maneuvered so that a pull on one rein will not put all the others into a tangle that could wreck the vehicle.

There are many references in the official reports of the 1980s to selfishness. It hardly becomes a foreigner to make the judgment of selfishness for himself, but he can identify the factors that induce the reproaches of some Luxembourg leaders. The Luxembourger has never taken comfortably to the manual labor of the mines and the mills, though the hard work of the farms he would do with pride. Thus the foreigner came, continued to come, and by doing the jobs the native refused to do helped the nation to arrive at the affluence that it has been enjoying. The citizen is not only unwilling to do manual work but is unwilling to have children with whom he will share his income. Along with the lack of children grows a striking increase in the statistics of divorce. While the native guards his income and his welfare, he witnesses a slow and steady rise in crime, so that a small, intimate national community that not long ago was almost crime free finds itself dealing with the same criminality, including drug traffic, that plagues its powerful neighbors. A religious nation almost totally Catholic, in which the observation of religious forms was an obligation, now becomes a nation of stay-at-homes from religious services, a people insistent on making their own decisions about their lives in opposition to the dictates of the church. These factors must be figured in with the economic and demographic factors in setting up the national equation. The number of automobiles and telephones and television sets; the elevated levels of cash savings; the rich and copious goods in the stores; the hustle and bustle on the streets of Luxembourg City — in the 1980s all these place the Luxembourg citizen among the best served citizens in the world.

The heat lightning of trouble may dissipate as economic strains subside and the osmosis of peace brings the competing nations of the world together in a unified effort to attain the comfort and happiness of their people. But suppose the heat lightning presages a real storm. Suppose inflation breaks through all restraints, national selfishness overrides all international concert, the bottom falls out of credit, the individual citizen sets the state at defiance. If these become the straits of the Western World, there will be no need for the Russians' missile to bring their Christian opponents to their knees.

Let's not play Cassandra. The Luxembourg people are educated to know the thousand years of enduring that has brought them to this day. The national characteristic of enduring should have been built into their subconscious too. They are being educated to be managers and salesmen and negotiators. They are practiced in the art of cooperative endeavor. They are steeled to require from their fellow nations the concessions absolutely necessary to their national welfare.

If cataclysm engulfs the Western World, of course it will engulf Luxembourg too. But if the breath of life remains in the men of that world, some of them will be Luxembourgers, enduring the calamities of the moment and emerging from those calamities into a new and characteristic self-affirmation as the Luxembourg nation.

NOTES: Chapter XXIII

[1]"Note Documentaire" (Luxembourg, Service Information et Presse, May, 1976), p. 2.

[2]For the end developments in 1981 see "Déclaration sur l'état de la nation" (Luxembourg, Service Information et Presse, April, 1981). An address to the Chamber of Deputies by Pierre Werner, President of the Government and Minister of State.

See also "L'économie luxembourgeoise au début des années 80," "Le Luxembourg n'est pas un paradis fiscal," and "Le Luxembourg dans la presse étrangère" in Bulletin de documentation (Luxembourg, Service Information et Presse, March, 1980).

[3]". . . The process of European unification has not been pursued as vigorously or as rapidly as we had hoped." Speech by Gaston Thorn, then Foreign Minister, November, 1979. Pub. in Bulletin de documentation. Annexe.

"But our two countries [Luxembourg and Lichtenstein] have learned the bitter lessons of history. The hearts and the minds of our citizens are fully open to a Europe at last united, a Europe that has conquered its old demons and forgotten its old antagonisms. According to our means we have contributed and we shall continue to contribute to the building of that Europe." Speech by Lydie Polfer in Bulletin de documentation (Luxembourg, Service Information et Presse, April 8, 1982), p. 1. Polfer, Mayor of Luxembourg City, was speaking at the wedding ceremony of Princess Margaretha to Prince Nicolas of Lichtenstein.

[4]"The recession has left its mark in the form of heavy accumulated losses, an increased burden of debt and a sharply reduced workforce. . . . Arbed is still a long way from the prosperity that it enjoyed up to the onset of the recession at the end of 1974." Ibid., p. 26.

[5]"Note Documentaire" (May, 1980). This "Note" is labeled "The Luxembourg Model of Anti-Crisis Management."

[6]Ibid. The strike of April, 1982, derived from new austerity measures of government, especially a ban on wage increases.

[7]". . . we are today at the point of passing from an economy of production to an economy of services." Statement by Echo de l'industrie in an interview with Pierre Werner, President of the Government, March, 1981. Reported in a "Note Documentaire" (n.d.).

[8]"Evolution du nombre et de la structure des banques" in "Note Documentaire" (Nov., 1980).

Nicholas Colchester, "Banking and Finance in Luxembourg," *The Financial Times*, London, September 20, 1979.

[9]In 1974 the steel industry employed 29,000 persons; in 1979, 20,000 persons; projected for 1983, 16,500 persons. "Note Documentaire," May, 1980. In addition "The *three partners* [industry, state, trade unions] engage themselves to create 7500 jobs until 1983."

[10]*Bulletin de documentation* (n.d.), p. 2. The speech was given Nov. 6, 1979.

[11]Ibid., p. 3.

[12]*Bulletin de documentation* (No. 1, 1978), p. 6.

[13]"Note Documentaire" (April, 1980), p. 2.

[14]*Bulletin de documentation* (No. 4, 1979), p. 7.

[15]In 1981 unemployment grew by 7.5% to a level of 1.2%. Overall unemployment in the European Economic Community (excluding Greece) at the end of 1981 was 9%. Some rates of increase of unemployment in western Europe in 1981 are as follows: Netherlands 49.4; Luxembourg 44.4; France 25. Unemployment in Belgium stood at 12%. The figures are from Eurostat, statistics agency of the EEC.

Luxembourg Statistics

1. Territory

Geographic location

Northernmost point	50°10'58"N
Southernmost point	49°26'52"N
Easternmost point	6°31'53"E
Westernmost point	5°44'10"E

Land Surface

Total extent of the Grand Duchy	999 sq. mis.	100%
Surface of the two natural regions		
— In the north: Oesling	320 sq. mis.	32%
— In the south: Bon Pays	680 sq. mis.	68%

Dimensions

Length north to south	51 miles
Largest width east to west	35.4 miles

Length of the frontiers

Total length	221.3 miles
— With France	45.4 miles
— With Germany	84.0 miles
— With Belgium	91.9 miles

Altitude

Highest point	1533 ft.
Lowest point	795 ft.
Luxembourg City	823 ft.

Acreage of Agricultural Land

	1960	1970	1978	1980
		Unit: Acres		
Total	349,224	336,938	320,827	321,380
— Grains: Percentage	52.3	47.7	44.5	43.9
— Meadow and pasture: Percentage	45.6	51.2	54.3	54.8
— Vineyards: Acres	2,931	2,913	3,093	3,121

Forests

	1960	1970	1978	1980
Acreage	212,348	204,938	202,718	202,718
Production (cubic feet)	6,436,000	8,808,400	11,335,700	

Climate (average for 1970-1979)

	Bon Pays	Ardennes
Mean annual temperature (°Centigrade)	9.1	8.0
— Maximum (June 1976)	34.5	32.2
— Minimum (January 1979)	−17.5	−18.9
Average atmospheric pressure	733.1	721.6
Hours of sunshine	1443	1436
Rainfall (inches)	29.6	32.7

2. Population

	1947	1960	1970	1978	1980*
Total population	291,000	314,900	339,800	366,300	365,100
Luxembourger	261,900	273,400	277,300	271,300	271,100
Foreign	29,100	41,500	62,500	95,000	94,100
Foreign (in %)	10.	13.	18.	25.	26.
German	7.5	7.9	7.8	7.6	8.0+
Belgian	3.6	5.2	6.5	8.0	—
Spanish	—	—	2.2	2.2	—
French	3.7	5.0	8.5	11.0	—
Italian	7.6	15.7	23.4	23.5	—
Portuguese	—	—	5.8	27.0	—
*Estimations					

Population according to age

	1947	1960	1970	1978	1979
Of working age (15 to 64)	205,700	213,700	221,800	243,300	245,400
— Men	102,900	106,200	110,300	121,700	—
— Women	102,800	107,500	111,500	121,600	—
Children (0 to 14)	57,700	67,200	75,200	20,700	69,200
Over 65	27,600	34,000	42,800	48,300	49,100

Population over the long term

	1821	1871	1922	1970
Total population (x1000)	134.1	197.5	260.8	339.8
— Men	—	98.2	132.0	166.5
— Women	—	99.3	128.8	173.3

— Luxembourgers	—	—	191.6	227.3	277.4
— Foreigners	—	—	5.9	33.5	62.5
Density (inhabitants per sq. mi.)		134.2	198.	261.	340.
		1841-1922	1923-30	1931-44	1945-78
Balance of migration		−85,403	+22,727	−28,556	+50,680
Employment (yearly average)	1960	1970	1975	1978	1980
Total (x1000)	132.0	139.8	157.4	157.8	160.9
Activity (x1000)	1960	1970	1975	1978	1979
— Agriculture	21.9	11.7	9.3	10.0	9.5
— Industry	59.1	61.3	70.0	69.5	69.5
— Services	51.0	64.3	74.2	75.5	76.5
Status					
— Salaried	94.2	110.7	129.6	135.0	136.5
— Employers, self-employed, family members	37.8	26.6	24.6	23.0	22.6
From across the frontier					
— From France	—	2.1	4.4	4.4	4.5
— From Belgium	—	3.8	5.7	5.8	5.7
— From Germany	—	1.5	1.3	1.4	1.5

3. Changes in Population

	1947	1960	1970	1978	1980
Living births	4,178	5,019	4,411	4,072	4,169
— Luxembourgers	—	—	3,143	2,496	2,611
— Foreigners	—	—	1,268	1,576	1,558
Births per 1000 inhabitants	14.4	15.9	13.0	11.2	11.4
— Luxembourgers	—	—	11.3	9.2	9.7
— Foreigners	—	—	20.3	17.3	16.8
Deaths	3,548	3,716	4,154	4,187	4,113
— Rate per living births	6.0	3.1	2.5	1.1	1.3
Surplus of births	630	1,303	257	93	56
— Luxembourgers	—	—	−632	−1,076	−1,138
— Foreign	—	—	889	1,169	1,194
Marriages	2,616	2,236	2,156	2,086	2,149
Divorces	146	153	217	443	582
Naturalizations	—	123	173	162	213
Deaths according to causes					
— Circulatory ailment	1,054	1,413	2,091	1,993	1,978
— Tumors	456	671	848	905	937
— Auto accident	47	79	132	105	111
— Suicides	32	32	48	76	47

4. *Origin by branch of activity of the gross interior product at the market price*

	1970	1974	1978	1979
		Percentage		
Agriculture	3.9	2.8	2.5	2.4
Industries	51.1	45.1	30.8	31.5
Of which: Iron/steel	27.6	22.7	10.2	10.5
Chemical	4.9	4.4	3.0	3.0
Construction	6.2	7.5	6.3	6.4
Banking services	33.1	37.8	49.7	49.3
Commerce and transport	14.1	14.2	14.8	14.4
Public administration	7.9	8.1	10.2	10.3

Rates of Increase (gross added value at the market price by branch activity): at price of 1970)

	1975	1976	1977	1978	1979
			Percentage		
Agriculture	−6.5	−12.8	+9.3	+12.3	0.0
Energy	−10.9	12.8	0.6	5.1	−2.2
Industry: total	−17.0	−0.4	0.0	+3.9	+5.0
Iron/Steel	−29.3	+3.5	−1.3	+7.5	+2.9
Other Industries	−9.9	+2.4	+2.2	+2.2	+5.7
Construction	−7.4	−12.0	−3.2	+1.7	+7.0
Banking (mercantile)	+8.5	+10.0	+3.7	+1.2	+2.9
Gross national product	−2.3	+4.3	+2.1	+3.2	+3.6

5. Agriculture

Overview

	1960	1970	1978	1980
Farms of 4.88 acres or more	9,148	6,433	4,651	4,366
Average acreage	36.64	50.9	67.63	70.03
Cattle (in thousands)	150.1	192.8	215.9	224.8
Horses (in thousands)	5.5	1.2	1.5	1.6
Farm acreage: total	344,843	329,749	316,801	318,213
— Cultivated land (in %)	52.3	47.5	44.5	43.9
— Meadows and pasture (in %)	45.6	51.2	54.3	54.8

Machines

	1960	1970	1978	1980
Farm tractors	6,633	8,475	9,234	9,579
Combines	611	1,974	1,893	1,848
Rake balers	1,358	3,820	3,496	3,347
Manure spreaders	757	3,753	3,575	3,442

Crop production
Total production of principal crops

Unit = 1,000 short tons

	1960	1970	1978	1980
Bread cereals	31,884.0	17,146.3	20,438.6	34,005.9
Secondary cereals	34,242.9	42,907.0	58,631.3	81,922.9
Vegetables from seed	936.9	391.3	33.1	35.3
Root plants	165,841.6	55,627.6	29,409.4	28,461.4

Fodder	37,042.8	31,421.1	29,321.2	28,461.4
Maize	—	—	128,274.6	115,080.1
Hay	65,603.4	68,403.2	115,752.5	86,464.4
Animal production		*Unit: 1,000 tons*		
Meat	19.6	21.1	19.5	20.2
Milk	190.7	216.9	256.0	269.6
Butter	5.3	6.9	8.2	8.2
Cheese	1.1	1.3	2.6	2.1
Viticulture				
Acreage of vines in production	2,782	2,772	2,867	2,908
Agricultural Indices	1950	1972	1979	1980
Cultivation of 4.88 acres or more		*Base of 100 in 1970*		
— Number	177.9	92.2	72.3	67.9
— Average size	57.9	107.0	137.6	142.1
Cattle	61.9	99.5	116.2	116.6
Horses	1274.2	97.6	151.4	133.0
Tractors	0.4	97.1	96.8	93.6
6. Industry	1970	1974	1978	1980
Mineral production		*Unit = 1,000 tons*		
Iron mines	5,722	2,686	835	560
— Iron exported	81	110	36	—
— Iron imported	9,422	11,674	8,125	7,873

Cast iron	4,814	5,468	3,721	3,568
Rolled products	4,252	4,977	3,800	3,746
Steel	5,462	6,448	4,790	4,619

Unit = tons

Production per inhabitant	16.2	19.0	13.2	12.7

Steel Production

Unit = 1,000 tons

Sheet steel				
Finished sheets	3,926	4,506	3,425	3,530
Of which: Beams, etc.	852	926	809	877
Bars, etc.	1,114	1,210	828	800
Plates and coils	485	535	407	438
Hot sheet metal	814	984	660	755
Cold sheet metal	39	43	61	33
Semi-finished products	326	471	375	216

Employment in steel production

1977

Number employed

	%	
Of the industrial employed	32.5	21,600 out of 66,400 workers
Of total working population	14.3	21,600 out of 151,000 workers

Relative importance of steel industry in industry in general employing 20 or more workers	1952/53	1960	1970	1974	1977
			Percentage		
— Gross value of production	65.9	64.7	51.7	53.7	42.1
— Value of exports	87.7	86.1	69.0	65.9	51.8
— Persons employed	41.7	48.4	44.2	49.4	48.7
— Wages and salaries (including withholding assessments)	55.7	57.1	52.8	56.6	52.8

New Industries (created 1960 or after)	1965	1970	1974	1977	1978
Net added value in % of steel	17.7	29.6	27.7	57.1	48.6
Employment in units	2,996	5,434	8,717	9,002	8,721
Employment in % of steel	12.0	23.0	36.1	41.2	43.

Investments in % of steel	102.3	72.7	105.2	75.3	16.2

Energy	1970	1974	1979	1980
		Unit = millions of kilowatts		
Production of electric energy				
Rough figure	2,148	2,078	1,338	1,115
— Thermal energy	1,261	1,159	1,007	828
— From steel industry	1,164	1,025	866	709
— Hydroelectric energy	887	919	331	287
Imported energy	2,349	3,270	2,934	3,050
Exported energy	804	846	251	205
Total available energy	3,693	4,502	4,021	3,959

Services

Figures are 1975

	Number of Enterprises	Number of People Employed	1977 Turnover outside of TVA (Mis. of Lfrancs)
Wholesale	876	8,407	56,733
Retail	3,704	16,802	41,271
Restaurant and lodging	2,375	8,371	5,665
Maintenance and repairs	276	1,057	1,688
Total	7,231	34,637	105,357

Banks (as of Dec. 31)

	1960	1970	1978	1980
Number of banks	19	37	97	111
No. of people employed	1,321	3,756	6,707	7,600

Liabilities *(Unit = billions of francs)*

	1960	1970	1978	1979
Deposits in loan societies and banks	23.0	235.8	2,508.7	3,917.4
— Bank deposits	16.9	87.2	426.3	758.0
— Savings deposits	10.2	70.7	376.2	706.0
Volume of banking credit in the private sector	6.7	16.5	50.1	52.0
	8.8	86.1	831.7	1,374.2

Insurance (as of Dec. 31)

	1972	1975	1978	1979
No. of contracts in force (in thousands)	632	771	937	960
— Life	45	59	78	86
— Accidents; civil responsibility	269	320	355	358

— Fire	183	205	188	181
— Legal protection	78	112	158	171
		Unit = millions of francs		
Value of premiums issued	*1960*	*1970*	*1978*	*1980*
— Life	1,350	2,106	3,224	3,649
— Fire	302	447	674	799
— Accidents; civil responsibility	251	385	519	71
— Legal protection	676	1,045	1,589	1,679
	23	48	78	88
Postal Service and Telephones	*1960*	*1970*	*1978*	*1980*
No. of C. C. P.	29,661	40,472	56,546	61,572
No. of telephones	36,486	81,645	121,770	131,660
Roads	*1960*	*1970*	*1978*	*1980*
Total Mileage	2,987	3,075	3,156	3,164
Merchandise truckers		*1970*	*1978*	*1979*
— National companies		141	259	278
— International companies		228	535	548
Number of automobiles	*1960*	*1970*	*1979*	*1981*
Total	58,986	113,735	183,738	206,584
Motor scooters	10,078	3,992	3,279	3,908
Private and commercial vehicles	33,446	84,816	153,051	173,061
Buses	355	560	718	770

	1970	1975	1980	1981
Road working and construction vehicles	645	3,147	3,121	11,409
Farm tractors and vehicles	6,824	9,844	13,175	13,715

Private and commercial vehicles according to country of origin

Percentage

	1960	1970	1975	1980	1981
Germany	36.7	43.3	39.8	37.5	37.1
France	20.2	24.3	30.2	32.4	32.1
Great Britain	19.6	17.5	11.0	6.3	5.8
Italy	4.2	7.0	8.3	7.9	7.8
Japan	—	0.7	4.2	8.3	9.6
U.S.A.	18.1	4.8	2.5	1.8	1.9
Other	1.2	2.4	4.0	5.8	5.7

Railroads

	1960	1970	1978	1980
Mileage	244	168	168	168
U.S. ton-miles (in millions)	438	523	445	456

Luxembourg Airport

	1960	1970	1978	1980
Total passengers (in thousands)	55.6	476.9	791.8	670.
In transit	15.9	5.5	29.1	42.
Freight (in American tons)	342.8	2,740.1	47,721	60,852
In transit	167.3	95.8	509.4	655

The Moselle Barge Port

		Unit = 1000 American tons		
Loading	—	574.4	1285.5	1031
Steel products	—	486.1	726.5	516
Unloading	—	895.2	725.4	676

Prices

Average index of consumer prices (1965 = 100)

Year	General Index	Food	Drinks	Housing	Clothing	Hygiene & Health	Other Goods & Services
1970	115.97	119.10	119.08	111.61	109.42	121.42	115.66
1975	164.31	170.94	152.04	159.12	153.94	194.92	161.27
1978	198.47	202.49	207.04	183.94	190.41	233.53	194.67
1979	207.49	207.83	210.41	201.20	202.32	246.36	204.48
1980	220.6	215.3	215.9	227.0	219.9	260.7	219.3

Salaries and Wages

	Autumn 1980	Autumn 1981
Gross minimum hourly wage (adult)	113.37LF	127.10LF
Gross minimum monthly salary	19,614LF	21,990LF
Gross average hourly wage in industry	233.6	—
Gross average monthly salary in industry	58,728	—
Average remuneration of the salaried (1979)	642,000	—

Standard of living
Consumption
Teaching
Standard of living

International Comparison

| Country | Consumption of Energy per Inhabitant | | | Motor Vehicles in Circulation as of Dec. 31, 1978 | | |
| | Energy 1978 | Electric Energy 1978 | | Private and Commercial Vehicles | | Buses, Trucks, etc. |
	Total Kgep*	Industrial Use KWH	Other Use	Total (x1000)	Per 1000 Inhabitants	(x1000)
Luxembourg	12,497	6,748	2,718	153	428	14
Germany	4,369	2,572	2,668	21,212	346	1,581
Belgium	4,709	2,526	1,807	2,973	302	268
France	3,459	1,845	1,998	17,400	333	2,494
Italy	2,392	1,613	1,060	16,371	291	1,648
Netherlands	4,594	2,123	1,933	4,100	295	326
Denmark	3,840	1,185	2,954	1,408	276	277
Ireland	2,267	942	1,509	643	195	132
United Kingdom	3,723	1,828	2,564	14,417	258	2,373

* gasoline kg equivalent

Country	Radio Receiver & Television Sets (as of 1978)		Telephones (as of 1979)	Doctors 1977	Pharmacists 1977	Hospital Beds 1977
	(x1000)	(per 1000)	(per 1000)	(per 100,000 Inhabitants)		
Luxembourg	105	293	539	128	54	1,236
Germany	19,019	311	404	204	44	1,178
Belgium	2,811	286	332	225	93	893
France	17,500	372	372	163	61	1,055
Italy	13,024	220	301	225	69	1,036
Netherlands	4,033	290	453	172	10	1,009
Denmark	1,637	327	569	195	26	872
Ireland	655	207	172	120	62	1,050
Great Britain	17,729	317	447	153	35	766

Consumption per inhabitants

	1960	1970	1975	1978	1980
			In pounds		
Whole milk	245	206	188	181	181
Butter	25.2	17.9	16.6	14.8	15.0
Cheese	15.0	16.8	23.4	19.2	20.8
Beef	49.7	55.5	64.5	57.9	57.9
Veal	15.7	14.9	13.3	—	15.5
Pork	63.6	72.9	93.9	97.5	95.6

	1970/71	1975/76	*In litres* 1978/79	1979/80	1980/81
Beer	118	128	128	—	114
Wine	—	37.0	41.3	42.7	48.2
Teaching	*1970/71*	*1975/76*	*1978/79*	*1979/80*	*1980/81*
Total no. of students	63,895	68,498	66,183	65,026	—
Preschool	7,814	8,625	6,928	7,610	7,625
Primary	35,497	34,980	32,436	30,315	28,813
Secondary, technical	9,657	13,769	15,159	15,172	15,096
Secondary	8,924	8,086	8,558	8,809	9,039
Higher inst. of technology	247	445	538	597	587
Teaching institute	140	232	115	135	128
University course (2 semesters)	157	195	241	213	337
Luxembourg students at foreign universities	1,459	2,077	2,208	2,183	—
— In Belgium	395	644	657	636	—
— In France	516	608	682	706	—

Composition of the Chamber of Deputies

	1954	1959	1964	1969	1974	1979
			Unit = number of seats			
All the parties	52	52	56	56	59	59
Christian-Social	26	21	22	21	18	24
Socialist-Worker	17	17	21	18 (12)	17	14
Democratic	6	11	6	11	14	15
Communist	3	3	5	6	5	2
Popular independent movement	—	—	2	—	—	—
Social-Democrat	—	—	—	— (6)	5	2
Independent Socialists	—	—	—	—	—	1

Bibliographic Essay

Available to the English-language reader are books and pamphlets in four basic categories: history, statistical information, government publications, and popular accounts for the reader with only a casual interest in Luxembourg.

Most important is A. H. Cooper-Prichard, *History of the Grand Duchy of Luxemburg* (Luxemburg, P. Linden, 1950). This is a translation of Arthur Herchen, *Manuel d'histoire nationale*, with additions by N. Margue and J. Meyers. It takes the history to the end of World War II. Its value lies in its balance, comprehensiveness, and general reliability. The multiplicity of names, dates, and facts, not always clearly or idiomatically stated, makes for difficulties that I hope to have avoided in this new history. The addenda — "Genealogy of the Sovereigns of Luxembourg," a historical chart fixing Luxembourg in relation to other countries, excerpts from general histories, a chronology of Luxembourg history — are useful. The bibliography is fairly full, divided into periods from prehistoric times to the 1940s. All items listed are in German or French.

A valuable study beginning with the Romans and ending in the fifteenth century is John Allyne Gade, *Luxemburg in the Middle Ages* (Leiden, E. J. Brill, 1951). Gade is a reliable student who went to sound sources listed in his bibliography.

Of less importance, because anecdotal and chatty, but nevertheless pleasant reading, is George Renwick, *Luxembourg: The Grand Duchy and Its People* (London, T. Fisher Unwin, n.d.). It is organized according to natural features and municipalities, with history, legend, and encounters woven together. Richer in detail, but outdated and obfuscating in its rhetoric, is T. H. Passmore, *In Further Ardenne: A Study of the Grand Duchy of Luxembourg* (New York, E. P. Dutton and Co., 1905(?)). A book of similar weight, meant to entertain as much as inform, is Robert J. Casey, *The Land of Haunted Castles* (New York, The Century Co., 1921). This is pleasant journalism. More matter of fact, informative in a summary way, is Joseph Petit, *Luxembourg Yesterday and Today* (Luxembourg, P. Linden, 1964). Luxembourg issued the book because English readers "may find it difficult to unearth a suitable English book giving them the desired information" — justification, perhaps, of the appearance of my study. The government, through its Information and Press Service, frequently issues English-language versions of informative publicity. Among them are George Als, *Luxembourg: Historical, Geographical and Economic Profile*, 1980; Jean Dargent, *Luxembourg: An International Finance Center* (translated from the French by Fernand Rau), 1972; Pierre Majerus, *The Institutions of the Grand Duchy*, 1970. For Luxembourg in the first years of World War II see *Luxembourg and the German Invasion, Before and After* (London, Hutchinson & Co., 1942); based on official documents with a preface by Joseph Bech and published by authority of the Luxembourg government.

The Information and Press Service issues yearly a small, detailed statistical document called "Grand Duchy of Luxembourg in Figures." It deals with geography, population, employment, budget, agriculture, etc. Statistics on Luxembourg appear in English in publications of NATO, the European Economic Community, etc. One example is *NATO: Facts and Figures* (Brussels, NATO Information Service, 1978), regularly updated. And, of course, Luxembourg figures in histories of Belgium and the Netherlands.

* * * * * * *

The American or English scholar in whose scholarship Luxembourg plays a part will have acquired his knowledge in the bibliography compiled for the four volumes of the *Manuel d'histoire luxembourgeoise* [the *Handbuch der Luxemburger Geschichte*] (Luxembourg, Editions Bourg-Bourger, 1973, 1974, 1977, and 1975). The author and volume titles are as follows:

I. Gerard Thill, *Vor- und Frühgeschichte Luxemburgs*. Mr. Thill is Director of the National Museum (Staatsmuseum).

II. Paul Margue, *Luxemburg in Mittelalter und Neuzeit (10. bis 18. Jahrhundert)*.

III. Gilbert Trausch, *Le Luxembourg sous l'Ancien Régime (17e, 18e siècles et débuts du 19e siècle)*. Mr. Trausch, a historian, is Director of the National Library.

IV. Gilbert Trausch, *Le Luxembourg à l'époque contemporaine (du partage de 1839 à nos jours)*.

After the Cooper-Prichard history in English, the student of Luxembourg will do best to begin with these four volumes in German and French. The bibliographies will direct him to the specialized — or more comprehensive — studies that will illuminate any aspect of the Grand Duchy that he chooses to pursue. The bibliographies of Trausch are subdivided by topic — international law and foreign policy, for example, political life, political parties, unions, the dynasty, the language, etc. — in the most useful way to facilitate research.

Mr. Trausch's bibliographic guide — "Orientation bibliographique" — appears at the end of volume IV of the *Manuel d'histoire luxembourgeoise*, in four volumes. With two exceptions, all the volumes and essays listed there are written in German or French. Since no other comprehensive bibliography exists, the student who reads only English will have to make do with Mr. Trausch's compilation. The negative aspect of such a statement is balanced by the clarity of organization and the detailed compartmentalization that he has employed.

Probably only in Luxembourg will the student have access to all the items that Mr. Trausch lists. Whether he can put his hands on many or few items, Mr. Trausch's guide will facilitate the search. He organized his listings under the following heads: general bibliographies, history bibliographies, history journals, general works about the country, international status and foreign policy, institutions (law and government), the various constitutions, political life in the 19th century, personalities of the 20th century, political parties, professional associations (unions), the crisis of 1867-1872, the crisis of 1914-1922, the second World War, the Luxembourg army, the Prussian garrison, the dynasty, the press, economic life, economic unions (with foreign countries), general works on the economy in the 20th century, the economy by industry and employment, agriculture (including viticulture), financial problems, certain establishments such as banks and railroads, industrial diversification, demographic problems, emigration, daily life in the past, societal problems, foreign laborers, religious life, particular aspects such as the church, intellectual life, literary classics, the arts, the Letzeburgesch language, nationalistic feeling, and the Luxembourg people.

I make special mention of the history reviews *Ons Hémecht, Organ des Vereins für Luxemburger Geschichte, Literatur und Kunst* (1895 to 1939) and *Hémecht, Revue d'histoire luxembourgeoise* (1948 to present).

The four bibliographies list 700 titles (with very few repeats) — evidence of the hurdle over which the English-language reader will have to get himself.

The Grand Duchy of Luxembourg: The Evolution of Nationhood touches on every subject that the bibliography mentions. Certain of the listings have proved to be especially useful to me.

Of prime importance is *La Formation Territorial du Pays de Luxembourg depuis les origines jusqu'au milieu du XVe siècle.* The editor and author of the historical text is Joseph Goedert, Conservator of the National Archives. To celebrate the thousandth anniversary of its founding, Luxembourg assembled some 367 documents dating from 762 A.D. to 1451, held by 26 archives and libraries in six countries. Collecting them and presenting them was the work of Antoine May, Archivist of the National Archives. Because the text is related to the documents and substantiated by them, *La Formation* takes precedence over all other sources for the period with which it deals.

A French-text general history that is helpful in organization and clarification is Paul Weber, *Histoire du Grand-Duché de Luxembourg* (Brussels, Office de Publicité, 1961).

Useful and authoritative is a general overview of Luxembourg, *Le Luxembourg: Livre du Centenaire* (chairman of the editorial committee, Albert Nothumb; Luxembourg, Grand-ducal Government, 1948). After an introductory overview, the various sections are devoted to limited aspects of Luxembourg life: the sovereign family, the constitution, literature, the people, emigration, etc. Specialists of knowledge and repute deal with their fields of study. The air of pride and enthusiasm does not dilute their authority.

A different type of book spans the history of the nation, but does so in terms of a special interest — economics, the castles, art, and the capital city, for example. Indispensable to this study was Paul Weber, *Histoire de l'économie luxembourgeoise* (Luxembourg, Chambre de Commerce, 1950). Three-quarters of the book deals with economic matters since 1839: roads, business, agriculture, steel, labor unions, demography, railroads, banks, etc. Unfortunately, no similar study for the years 1950 to the present exists. Another book dealing with the economy is Carlo Hemmer, *L'économie du Grand-Duché de Luxembourg* (Luxembourg, Editions Joseph Beffort, 1948). It lays a groundwork of climate, geology, soil, population, etc., then deals with minerals, agriculture, and viticulture in Vol. I. Vol. II, 1953, deals particularly with the steel industry.

Les chateaux historiques du Luxembourg [photographs by Tony Krier, historical essay by Jean Pierre Kolz] (Luxembourg, Imprimerie Saint-Paul, 1975) by picture and commentary puts the extraordinary castle riches of the country into their historical setting.

L'Art au Luxembourg (Luxembourg, Imprimerie Saint-Paul, 1966), its various sections by one authority or another, is a book of extraordinary riches in relation to the art of so small a country. It begins with the Romans and traverses the various periods up to the Renaissance. Its information about architecture (church, castle, and otherwise) is particularly useful, as is the section by Joseph-Emile Muller, "Les miniatures d'Echternach." Related to *L'Art* are two volumes by Joseph Hirsch, *Vièrges de pitié luxembourgeoises* (Luxembourg, Hémecht, 1967 and 1968). The ubiquitous pietàs of Luxembourg vibrate to the chords of piety and suffering in the Luxembourg nature.

Though Luxembourg City is small as world capitals go, its function as a fortress was important from the day of its founding up to 1867. The three volumes of J.-P. Koltz, *Baugeschichte der Stadt und Festung Luxemburg* (Luxemburg, Sankt-Paulus-Druckerei, 1970) present that history in minute detail and rich illustration. A book of 869 pages, Francois Lascombes, *Chronik der Stadt Luxemburg* (Luxemburg, Sankt-Paulus-Druckerei, 1976), deals with the city and the fortress from 1444 to 1684 in great detail.

Local pride has resulted in a good many books devoted to individual municipalities. The narrow focus permits the use of details for which there is no room in the general histories of the country. A good example is Edouard Feitler, *Luxemburg Deine Heimatstadt* (Luxembourg, Sankt-Paulus-Druckerei, 1967). A handsome example, which begins with prehistory and moves through

Roman times, etc., up to the present is *Echternach Notre Ville* (Echternach, Imprimerie Burg, 1977), a project of the Société d'Embellissement et de Tourisme. The Syndicat d'Initiative was responsible for *Aperçu historique et touristique illustré de la commune et de la ville de Differdange* (Differdange, Josy Wagner-Hentges, 1937). *Chronik der Stadt Vianden* (Vianden, Veiner Geschichtsfrënn, 1976) chronicles a mere 25 years of a small town's history in minute detail. One of the most interesting of these municipal accounts is *Livre du cinquentenaire de la ville d'Esch-sur-Alzette* (Esch-sur-Alzette, L'Imprimerie Coopérative, 1956), produced by an editorial committee and written by a variety of authors. It catches the excitement, pride, and even beauty of a raw industrial city.

The Information and Press Service is generous in distribution of its weekly "Note Documentaire" and the monthly *Bulletin de documentation,* usually in French, sometimes in German.

* * * * * *

The student of Luxembourg cannot afford to ignore the volumes that come under these two general titles, both by Albert Calmes: *Histoire contemporaine du Grand-Duché du Luxembourg* and *Au fil de l'histoire.*

The *Histoire* covers the years from 1814 to 1848 as follows, each of them published in Luxembourg by the Imprimerie Saint-Paul:

Naissance et débuts du Grand-Duché 1814-1830, 1971.

Le Grand-Duché de Luxembourg dans la Revolution belge (1830-1839), 1939.

La Restauration de Guillaume Ier, 1947.

La création d'un Etat (1841-1847), 1954.

La Revolution de 1848 au Luxembourg, 1957.

Calmes is a historian to be reckoned with, a man of relentless scholarship. He collected some 150 or so essays in the three volumes of *Au fil de l'histoire.* They are all rather short studies, but each is like a flash of light in the sometimes murky history of Luxembourg. "La 'Partie cédée,' " for example, though only a few hundred words in length, clarifies the partition of 1839. "Le centenaire de notre première loi contre d'alcoolisme" contributes to our understanding of the Luxembourg character. "Le bilinguisme, atout international", amplifies the importance of the language factor. "1872: Une fresque historique: Le 'Renert' de Michel Rodange," a contribution of Christian Calmes to Vol. II, is a welcome comment on some aspects of the national epic.

* * * * * * *

The mention of *Renert* brings us to consideration of Luxembourg language and literature. Michel Rodange, *Renert* (Luxembourg, Edi-Centre, 1968) is a readily available text with introduction, textual aids, and commentary. It makes the 1872 poem in the Letzeburgesch language available to the student with a knowledge of German and a facility with language. What pieces of the poem have been translated into English are not very helpful, though better than no translation at all.

No definitive dictionary of the Letzeburgesch language appeared until after World War II. The final form of the *Luxemburger Wörterbuch* appeared between 1950-1975 in four volumes. The specialist in language can make use of Robert Bruch, *Précis populaire de Grammaire luxembourgeoise*, 3rd ed. *[Luxemburger Grammatik in Volkstumlichem Abriss]* (Luxembourg, Section de Linguistique de l'Institut gr. -d., 1973).

Robert Bruch, *Critères linguistiques de la nationalité luxembourgeoise* (Luxembourg, *Bulletin de Documentation*, 1957) is a keen analysis of (1) the way in which language reflects national character and (2) the effect of bilingualism or trilingualism on the Luxembourg character. The importance of the theory that the language situation may be the greatest single force in determining the singularity of Luxembourg appears in Bruch: "But if it [Letzeburgesch] continues modestly to be for all of us speakers our most intimate speech, while permitting us, while forcing us to open our windows wide to the great wind from two world languages it will make true Europeans of us: and it will not die out — nor will those above all who speak it" (p. 16).

Some scholars besides Bruch whose studies deal with literature in the Luxembourg language are Nicolaus Welter, Fernand Hoffmann, Albert Hoefler, Alphonse Arend, Claude Contes, and Marcel Gérard. Of particular importance is Fernand Hoffmann's *Geschichte der Luxemburger Mundartdichtung* (Luxembourg, Publications Nationales du Ministère des Arts et des Sciences, two volumes, 1964, 1965). Besides dealing with the history of Letzeburgesch writing from the beginnings to the 1960s, Mr. Hoffmann presents an anthology of Letzeburgesch prose and poetry. Carol Hury's *Luxembourgensia. Eine Bibliographie des Bibliographien* (Luxembourg, Publications Nationales du Ministère des Arts et des Sciences, 1964) lists the bibliographies and anthologies dealing with Luxembourg literature in Letzeburgesch, French, and German.

Two popular publications by Jul Christophory on the national language appear in every bookstore: *Sot et op lëtzebuergesch* (Luxembourg, Imprimerie Saint-Paul, 1973) and *Mir schwätze lëtzebuergesch* (Luxembourg, Imprimerie Saint-Paul, 1974). Both are informative and well organized for instructing in grammar, vocabulary, and idiomatic usage. The second book contains a most useful section that brings together examples of Letzeburgesch literature with translation and commentary, notes on orthography and spelling, songs, and bibliography.

A small book that can serve as a starting point or guide in becoming informed on Luxembourg writing is *Littératures du Grand-Duché de Luxembourg* (Virton, 1976). It contains three essays: Cornel Meder, "Notre littérature dialectale"; Michel Raus, "La littérature d'expression allemande"; Anne Berger, "La poésie luxembourgeoise d'expression française." The reader may have reservations about accepting the strong opinions of the three authors.

* * * * * * *

Whoever wants to know about Luxembourg in World War II will find the subject well covered in Gino Candidi, *La Résistance du Peuple luxembourgeois* [translated into French by Georgette Bisdorff] (Luxembourg, Editions du RAPPEL, 1977). Its lists of documents consulted and its bibliography can guide the reader more deeply into the subject. Americans will be especially interested in E. T. Melchers, *Les deux Libérations du Luxembourg 1944-1945* (Luxembourg, Editions du Centre, 1959). It is minutely detailed about army units and actions, along with many maps and illustrations.

On the subject of the various constitutions Trausch has a listing including J. Goedert, P. Weber, and A. Bonn. I would add to those Pierre Majerus, *L'Etat luxembourgeois* (Luxembourg, Imprimerie Joseph Beffort, 1948). It is an explanatory handbook on all phases of Luxembourg law and contains the text of the constitution with revisions up to 1948.

It is almost incredible that a population as small as that of Luxembourg, without a long tradition of scholarship, should have produced a body of writing of such scope and depth available to the casual or to the serious student. The National Library is under the direction of Gilbert Trausch, who made available to me everything that I could possibly use. Antoine May (now deceased) at the National Archives gave his encouragement and help to me. I owe much to Emilie Hoffmann, daughter of Mr. and Mrs. Théophile Hoffmann of Obercorn, an old friend from the days of World War II, who sent me books and pictures over the years. André Claude, Director of the Information and Press Service, kept me up to date almost weekly with releases from his office; and I took heart from his encouragement to complete this up-to-date history of the Grand Duchy in English. Louise and Camille Hoffman - Ziger; Louis, Milly, and Jacques Meyer of Obercorn gave me information and encouragement, as did Frank Meyer of Texas Refinery Corporation in Echternach. I am indebted to Edouard Probst, a scholar, particularly of the seventeenth century, now retired from the Ministry of Culture. He was relentless in pursuing error in my manuscript and open always to discussion of ideas and interpretations.

I have cited Carlo Hemmer's *L'Economie du Grand-Duché de Luxembourg*. In his foreword he writes: "The national economy of a small country like the Grand Duchy of Luxembourg is a complex organism which presents under a form perhaps simplified the sum of the problems of a large country."

Exactly so!

— James Newcomer

N. B. Laura Braddy and Ruth VerDuin were meticulous in preparation of the manuscript. Judith Oelfke Smith designed the book. William Ray gave help with the maps. Frank Reuter's counsel and encouragement were always welcome. I am grateful to them.

J. N.

INDEX

Bruno, Archbishop of Cologne, 50
Brussels, 25, 103, 122, 124, 125, 167; court of Wenceslas at, 110
Brussels Pact, 273
Burgundy, 34, 109, 111-113, 119-120; Upper, 119
Business, post World War I, 277-278; post World War II, 276, 279
Bübingen, 99
Byzantine Empire, 26

Caerosi, 24
Calmes, Albert, 324-325
Calmes, Christian, 325
Candido, Gino, 326
Capetians, 50
Capitulare de villis, 32
Capuchins, 139, 173
Cardinale, Mgr. Eugène, 18
Carinthia, 89
Carlovingians, 28-31, 33, 34
Carmelites, 87
Casey, Robert, 319
Castile, 123
Castles, 6-8, 97-100
Casualties, Battle of the Bulge, 268; World War II, 264
Catholic Church, 5, 11
Catholicism 5, 129-131, 134-135, 138-140, 171-173, 202-203, 210, 234, 240, 282, 298; church services, 11
Celtic art, 9
Celts, 9, 24
Chamber of Deputies, 16, 201, 202
Chambres de Réunion, 150
Champagne, Count of, 73

Character of Luxembourgers, 4-6, 14-16
Charlemagne, 28-29, 31, 35-36; Inspector General of, 35
Charles II, King of Spain, 144, 157
Charles IV, Emperor, 92, 98, 102-103, 109, 111
Charles V, Emperor, 122-123, 124, 126
Charles V, King of France, 92
Charles the Bald, 36
Charles the Fearless, Duke of Burgundy, 119
Charolais, 119
Charlotte, Grand Duchess, 16, 236, 237, 238, 257-258, 272
Charlotte Bridge, 146, 291
Charters, Municipal, 76-78, 86
Chiers River, 22, 30
Chimay, Prince of, 141
Chiny, 69, 71, 103, 111, 141, 144; Counts of, 152-153
Christianity, 28-29, 32-33
Christophory, Jul, 326
Church buildings, 8-9
Ciney, 65
Clairefontaine, Abbey of, 79, 80; Rue de, 44
Clares, 118, 173
Claude, André, 327
Clausen, 48, 59
Clermont-en-Argonne, 69
Climate, 302
Clothair II, King of the Franks, 28, 31
Clovis, King of the Franks, 28, 30, 31, 33-34
Coblenz, 22
Colmar-Berg, 286
Cologne, 25, 90, 103; Archbishop of, 50, 66, 70, 73;

Hamm Cemetery, 266
Han-sur-Lesse, 88
Hardships (World War I), 235
Hardt, Mathias, 231
Hauterive, Philip of, 70
Hémecht, 322
Hemmer, Carlo, 323, 327
Herchen, Arthur, 319
Hermessend (see Ermesinde)
Henri, Prince, 16
Henry, Archbishop of Trier, 45
Henry (the Quarrelsome), of
    Bavaria, 50
Henry I, Count, 53, 55, 56, 57
Henry II, Count, 51, 55, 57, 58
Henry II, Count of Champagne,
    67
Henry III, Count, 55, 56, 60
Henry III, Emperor, 56
Henry IV, Count, 63-68
Henry IV, Emperor, 59
Henry V (the Blond or the Fair),
    Count, 71, 73, 82-83, 85
Henry VI, Count, 83-84, 85
Henry VII, Count, 85, 87-88
Henry, Prince Lieutenant, 208,
    209
Himmler, 262
Hirsch, Joseph, 323
Hoeffler, Albert, 325
Hoffmann, Emilie, 327
Hoffmann, Fernand, 325
Hoffmann-Ziger, Louise and
    Camille, 327
Holland, 115, 119, 127, 151
Hollenfels, 7, 155
Hollerich, 217
Holy Ghost Plateau, 150
Hugh Capet, King of France, 50,
    52
Hugh the Great, Duke of
    France, 52

Hugo, Victor, 7, 197
Huncherange, 82
Hungarians, in the Ardennes,
    37; soldiers, 143
Hungary, 274
Huns, 27
Hury, Carol, 326
Huy, 8, 45

Immigration, 204, 242, 244-245,
    252, 294
Independence, 207, 215
Industry, 307-310
Infiltration by Germans (1920-
    1940), 258-259
Inflation, 290
Information and Press Service,
    320, 324, 327
Inquisition, 126-128
International Bank, 223, 277
Invasion, German (1914), 227,
    229, 233
Investitures, War of, 61
Irish soldiers, 143
Iron, deposits, 216-217;
    depletion of, 285; production
    of, 93, 196
Iron foundries, 155, 168, 170
Iron-steel, 3, 4, 198, 199, 209,
    211, 216, 217, 218, 219, 226-
    227, 250-252, 286-287, 306,
    308-310
Isabella, Archduchess of Austria,
    134-137, 228
Isolation, 171-172
Italian soldiers, 143
Italians, 4, 231
Italy, Sigefroid in, 49
Itzig, 40

DESIGN AND GRAPHIC ART ARE BY
JUDITH OELFKE SMITH
OF TEXAS CHRISTIAN UNIVERSITY,
FORT WORTH, TEXAS.
THE BOOK WAS SET IN GOUDY OLD STYLE BY
FORT WORTH LINOTYPING COMPANY.